"PBS has struck gold!"
— *New York* magazine

"This stellar literacy tool can claim pride of place with the best of the best: PBS, *Mister Rogers' Neighborhood,* and *Sesame Street.*"
—*Los Angeles Times*

"Animated librarians Theo and Cleo Lion and their cubs from the PBS television series *Between the Lions* form the centerpiece of this resourceful parents' guide to teaching children how to read and fostering a lifelong enjoyment of reading…. Parents and teachers will enjoy this imaginative resource with tie-ins to the award-winning show."
—ALA *Booklist*

"Especially appealing….This is a helpful resource for parents who want to enrich their child's reading experiences."
—*Publishers Weekly*

"An extraordinary achievement. *The Between the Lions Book for Parents* magically clarifies the often murky waters of early reading. Mothers and fathers will not only be able to guide their children's emerging minds through the initial reading process, they will also be formed and enriched as they share in the experience."
— Mel Levine, M.D., author of *A Mind at a Time*

"A wonderful resource for moms and dads who want to understand how kids learn to read. Reading opens up new worlds for our children and brings a lifetime of joy and wonder. But for many youngsters, learning to read is not an easy task, and *The Between the Lions Book for Parents* helps parents understand why. Providing scientifically based information in a clear and compelling manner, this book is a gift to children and their parents."
—G. Reid Lyon, Ph.D., Chief of Child Development and Behavior, National Institutes of Health

"Every so often, human hearts, minds, and mission come together to create something far better than seems humanly possible. *The Between the Lions Book for Parents* is one of those miracles—it is as exuberant as it is powerful. As one so deeply immersed in our country's literacy challenge, my greatest wish is that this treasure would find its way into every beginning reader's day, whether in the home or through afterschool, or summer school programs. And here, thanks to Rath and Kennedy, this is a truly wonderful book that will help parents and teachers to use it still better."
—Marilyn Jager Adams, author of *Beginning to Read: Thinking and Learning about Print* and Visiting Scholar, Harvard Graduate School of Education

"This book helps to dispel the dangerous myth that only teachers can teach children to read. It contains dozens of effective and fun ideas on how parents can help in this all-important process."
—Nancy Faust Sizer and Theodore R. Sizer, authors of *The Students Are Watching: Schools and the Moral Contract*

HarperResource
An Imprint of HarperCollinsPublishers

The Between the Lions Book for Parents

Everything You Need to Know to Help Your Child Learn to Read

Linda K. Rath, Ed.D., and Louise Kennedy

With a Foreword by Christopher Cerf

BETWEEN THE LIONS is produced by WGBH Boston and Sirius
Thinking, Ltd. BETWEEN THE LIONS is funded in part by a
Ready to Learn Television Cooperative Agreement from the
U.S. Department of Education through the Public Broadcast-
ing Service, and by the Corporation for Public Broadcasting.

First HarperResource paperback edition published 2005

Designed by Ellen Cipriano

Library of Congress Cataloging-in-Publication Data has been
applied for.

ISBN 0-06-051027-7
ISBN 0-06-051028-5 (pbk.)

04 05 06 07 08 WBC/RRD 10 9 8 7 6 5 4 3 2 1

To the memory of my beloved parents,
Max and Tibie Klinger
—*L.K.R.*

To the future of my beloved son,
Christian James Kennedy Corrigan
—*L.K.*

Contents

Part III

Foreword

My colleague Michael Frith has always said that every great project begins with a bad pun. If Michael's right, he may have stumbled upon the reason for the success of the PBS KIDS television series the two of us helped create, because it's hard to imagine a worse pun than BETWEEN THE LIONS. The title refers, of course, not only to Theo and Cleo, the lion husband-and-wife team that guards the doors of (and runs) the library featured on our program; but also to the process of reading, which is the centerpiece of everything that goes on in the hallowed—if more-than-slightly-unorthodox—halls one enters by walking between our leonine hosts.

Why the focus on reading? Well, for one thing, literacy is by far the most important skill children must master if they are to perform well in school, and later in life. Clearly, if kids don't learn to read in a timely fashion, it will become increasingly hard for them to acquire knowledge about virtually anything else.

Secondly, it should hardly come as a surprise to anyone who's bought this book that there is a full-fledged reading crisis in the United States. *The National Literacy Survey*, a comprehensive survey conducted by the U.S. Department of Education during the 1990s, showed that fewer than one-third of our nation's third-graders could read proficiently. Worse still, more than 20 percent of America's adult population—over 40 million people—are "functionally illiterate," which means they don't read and write well enough to understand the instructions on a bottle of medicine, or to follow a recipe, or to fill out a job application. And almost half our adults—nearly 90 million of us!—cannot read at a high school level. In other words, as former U.S. Secretary of Education Richard Riley phrased it, they "do not have the literacy skills they need to function in our increasingly complex economic system."

Clearly, a country with the unmatched resources of the United States ought to be able to do better. And so it was that, back in 1995, a few of us who had worked on television projects such as *Sesame Street* and *The Electric Company*—including the aforementioned Michael Frith, for 25 years a key creative executive with the Muppets; and Norman Stiles, the longtime head writer of *Sesame Street*—decided it was time to make whatever contribution we could to help turn the tide.

We had always admired the model that Joan Ganz Cooney, the visionary founder of the Children's Television Workshop, and the Workshop's original chief educational adviser, Dr. Gerald Lesser, instituted when they were creating *Sesame Street* back in the late 1960s. Their goal for the series was to help young children, especially those who were not receiving adequate preparation at home, to get ready for school by helping them learn things—letters, numbers, simple "sight words," how to recognize likenesses and differences, the value of cooperation, etc.—that would give them a reasonable chance to succeed once they entered kindergarten. Joan and Gerry realized that they couldn't get educational specialists alone to create their show—it was highly unlikely that, on their own, they'd be able to dream up a program that could successfully compete for ratings in what noted publisher Jason Epstein called the "bunny-eat-bunny"

world of children's entertainment. On the other hand, without early and continuing guidance from educators and researchers, writers and performers weren't likely to have a clue what early learners needed to be taught, what techniques had proven most successful in teaching them, and whether the material was truly helping children learn. Joan and Gerry's solution: recruiting the very best educators, researchers, producers, writers, animators, puppeteers, and musicians they could find and persuading them to work together as a team.

The results speak for themselves (at the time of this writing, *Sesame Street* is preparing for its 35th consecutive year of production), and we felt confident that the same approach that had made Big Bird, Elmo, and Bert and Ernie so helpful in delivering a preschool curriculum could be applied to early reading instruction. (Indeed, *The Electric Company*, a literacy show created by the Children's Television Workshop using the "*Sesame Street* model," showed great educational promise but has not been produced since the mid-1970s.) With the invaluable help and support of two friends—John Sculley, the former CEO of Apple Computer; and Ray Chambers, the visionary New Jersey businessman and philanthropist—Michael, Norman, and I founded our own company, Sirius Thinking, Ltd., and set about the task of developing the program that was to become BETWEEN THE LIONS.

"But literacy and TV—aren't they supposed to be inimical?" you might ask. "Isn't the easy availability of television programming a principal reason why kids have lost their desire to pick up a book or—worse—to master the skills required to read it?"

Well, when someone presents me with such questions (and, indeed, several people did when we were talking to them about our fledgling project), I invariably tell them an anecdote I call "The Verb Story." After I graduated from college, I had the good fortune to land a job at Random House, working with the great Ted Geisel—Dr. Seuss—on Beginner Books. (You know Beginner Books: *The Cat in the Hat* was the first one, and an incredible array of other easy-to-read children's classics soon followed: *Green Eggs and Ham, Hop on Pop, Are You My Mother?*, and many more.) My dad, Bennett Cerf, who founded Random House, was Dr. Seuss's publisher, and my mother, Phyllis Cerf, was responsible for figuring out that *The Cat in the Hat*—which combined the inspired lunacy only Seuss can provide with the simple, word-list-driven vocabulary of venerable elementary school primers such as Scott Foresman's *Dick and Jane* books—was not merely a one-book wonder, but the basis for an entire series. Nonetheless, I still fiercely dispute the idea that more than coincidence was involved in my being hired.

Coincidence or not, I happened to be present one morning when Ted Geisel walked into the Beginner Books offices with what he thought was an inspired idea. "Every alphabet book I've seen features nouns," he announced. "You know, *c* is for *cat*, *d* is for *dog*, etc. Why don't we do an alphabet book featuring verbs?" Well, everybody got incredibly excited by this breakthrough concept—for about two minutes, until we realized that the limitations of the medium we were working in made the idea virtually impossible to pull off. The problem, of course, was that if one tries to

draw a picture illustrating, say, *r* is for *run*, one has to picture somebody or something—say, a little girl or a pony—doing the running. And children looking at the book will invariably decide—if indeed they recognize the letter *r* at all—that *r* stands for *girl* or *pony*.

As *Sesame Street* proved the moment it came on the air in 1969, television had the power to solve the "alphabet book–verb" problem. First and foremost, verbs such as "run" could be illustrated by *animated* images, making it clearer than any static picture could that what was relevant was an *action*, not the person or animal performing it. In addition, thanks to TV's accompanying sound track, it was suddenly possible to *tell* kids as well as show them that *r* is for *run* (and to help them learn the /r/ sound of the letter *r* in the bargain).

The point here, of course, is not that television can or should *replace* books as a tool for teaching literacy—much less as a continuing source of pleasure and knowledge in our children's lives. Rather, what I want to make clear is that different media have different strengths and advantages that can be called upon as needed in the service of literacy education. (Of course, each medium has its weaknesses, too. It's hard to carry on a meaningful dialogue while watching TV, as you can when you and your children are enjoying a story together. Television doesn't stop conveniently for you when you want to ask a question. And, the last time I checked, I found it a bit more satisfying to curl up with a good book than with my home entertainment center.)

The fact is that television can do *many* things to advance literacy instruction that can't be done in a book alone. A few examples:

❖ We can highlight text as it's read, demonstrating as we do so not only that your eyes should move from left to right, and from top to bottom, as they scan a printed page, but that there's a one-to-one correspondence between spoken and printed words.

❖ We can light up all the *b*'s in a sentence or paragraph and show that, in every word in which they appear, they stand for the /b/ sound.

❖ We can change one item at a time in a word or sentence while leaving everything else the same, thereby demonstrating the exact role each letter (or letter combination) plays in the word, or that each word plays in the sentence. (Educators call this technique "slotting," indicating that at least some of them might have been spending too much time watching bananas change to oranges on the one-armed bandits in Las Vegas!)

❖ We can add humor, animation, music, and world-class production values to lessons that, until now, could only be presented with flash cards or on a blackboard. (Consider, for example, the Motown-style singing group, the Vowelles, who impart vowel sounds on BETWEEN THE LIONS; or the Monty Python-inspired knights who charge together on our show to "blend" phonic elements into words.)

❖ And, of course, television can reach virtually every family in the United States, and—when it's broadcast over the airwaves, as is PBS—it's absolutely free to the end user.

Luckily for us, some of the top reading experts saw value in our idea (including the legendary Gerry Lesser himself, who, as I've already noted, put together the *Sesame Street* and *Electric Company* advisory boards, and agreed to head ours). You can read more about our educational advisory team, and the innovative early reading curriculum they helped design for our show, in Part I, Chapter 2, of this book.

Brigid Sullivan, Kate Taylor, and Judy Stoia, of WGBH in Boston, arguably the most prestigious public broadcasting station in the country, were also enthusiastic about our concept, and WGBH's decision to become our production partner opened the door to a major development grant from the Corporation for Public Broadcasting and PBS—and, eventually, to PBS's decision to broadcast BETWEEN THE LIONS every day as part of its Ready to Learn service.

Next, some of the most talented writers, musicians, and puppeteers we've had the pleasure of working with in all our years in educational television signed on—folks who, like us, take immense pleasure in working with like-minded educators to create characters, stories, skits, and songs that, while entertaining kids, can deliver vitally needed instructional material. Over the weeks and months that followed, BETWEEN THE LIONS—and the magical library that serves as its home base—began to take shape. In April 2000, all our work paid off, and BETWEEN THE LIONS made its debut on PBS.

We've been on the air now for over three years, and all of us involved with the program have much to celebrate. A few highlights:

❖ BETWEEN THE LIONS is broadcast daily—in many cases, twice a day—on over 300 PBS stations nationwide, and we reach an average of 5.5 million viewers every week.

- The Television Critics Association has chosen our show twice as the "Outstanding Children's Program" on television, and we've won four Emmy Awards. (As I'm writing this, we've just learned that our third season of shows has been nominated for seven more Emmys!)
- The National Education Association, the country's largest teachers' organization, has endorsed us. It's the first time they've recommended a TV show in over a decade. ("The BETWEEN THE LIONS program, as well as the Web site, offer first-class lessons that playfully demonstrate the joys of reading," said NEA President Reg Weaver. "We encourage teachers, parents, and other caregivers to take advantage of the many resources from BETWEEN THE LIONS as a way to extend teaching and learning reading for young children.")
- Many of the nation's leading literacy organizations—the American Library Association, Reading Is Fundamental, the International Reading Association, First Book, and the National Center for Learning Disabilities, to name just a few—have agreed to join forces with us to increase our program's effectiveness at the grassroots level.
- Our Web site (www.pbskids.org/lions), with a section connected to every one of our BETWEEN THE LIONS episodes, logs an average of more than 15,000 visitors per day and has won several prizes of its own, including the New Media Invision Award and the American Library Association's Notable Children's Web Site Award.

- Perhaps most exciting of all, research is demonstrating that BETWEEN THE LIONS is really helping kids learn to read. A study conducted at the University of Kansas showed very significant gains in the reading scores of kindergartners who watched our program for just a few weeks. Research performed by Mississippi State University showed that children on Mississippi's Choctaw Indian Reservation and in the Delta community of Indianola who viewed episodes of BETWEEN THE LIONS regularly, and whose teachers carried out related activities, outperformed control groups in several key reading-related skill areas.

And now, much to our delight, our colleague Linda Rath, who, right from the beginning, has supervised our program's curriculum content, has teamed up with Boston journalist Louise Kennedy to create this book—a guide to using BETWEEN THE LIONS to help your child (as Linda and Louise put it) to "find the path into a rich and rewarding lifetime of reading."

If there's one thing Linda and Louise stress throughout these pages, it's the importance of reading to your child every day. ("If your schedule is packed," they advise, "find someone who can share this task with you.") "A parent, a child, and a book—that's a whole world, and one that's full of literacy and love."

I couldn't agree more. And I'd like to add one further suggestion. We intentionally designed BETWEEN THE LIONS to appeal to parents as well as kids—in large part because research has shown that when parents and children watch together, and talk later about what they saw, the kids will learn more. So, in addition to reading with your children, and having fun sharing with them the wonderfully creative literacy activities that Linda and Louise have assembled in this book, we hope you'll take the opportunity to enjoy watching our show with them.

Or, to phrase it the way our theme song does, every weekday on PBS . . .

Come on
Come in
Begin
Come and read . . .
BETWEEN THE LIONS.

Christopher Cerf
Creative Producer, BETWEEN THE LIONS
March 30, 2003

Acknowledgments

We are grateful to our friends at WGBH Enterprises who initiated this project: vice president and general manager David Bernstein, managing director Betsy Groban, and publishing manager Caroline Chauncey. Betsy's common sense and good humor and Caroline's gracious, serene, and careful attention turned this endeavor into a delightful collaborative experience. Doe Coover, our literary agent, brought us together for this project and eagerly shared her wisdom and confidence with us. Gail Winston, our editor at HarperCollins, encouraged us and offered valuable assistance at critical moments. Our thanks extend to Gail's able assistant Christine Walsh, copy editor Judy Eda, and designer Ellen Cipriano.

We are also grateful to the BETWEEN THE LIONS team from Sirius Thinking, Ltd., who have inspired us by creating such a wacky and wonderful show. We continue to be amazed by Christopher Cerf's irrepressible creativity and touched by the combination of heart, comedy, and vision that Norman Stiles brings to his role as head writer. Other writers on the team also deserve recognition: Louise Gikow, Sharon Lerner, and Fred Newman for creating wonderful stories, characters, and concepts. The music is the special pride of BETWEEN THE LIONS, and Chris Cerf is ably assisted here by the talented team of Paul Jacobs and Sarah Durkee. Michael Frith created the look of the show during the early years of production, and Kathy Mullen's warm influence is still felt in many ways. The Lions themselves—Theo, Cleo, and the cubs—are all one could hope for in a model family, and the extraordinary dedication of puppet performers Peter Linz, Jennifer Barnhart, Tim Lagasse, and Heather Asch are deeply appreciated.

The Boston BTL team, led by vice president Brigid Sullivan and executive producer Judy Stoia, also receives our heartfelt thanks. Judy read a preliminary draft of this book and offered her usual brand of high-quality analysis and encouragement. Project director Beth Kirsch and outreach manager Mary Haggerty also reviewed the manuscript and lent their steady support throughout. They have a strong group of colleagues to back them up, of whom Tia Kaul and Jill Mackay deserve special mention.

Our thanks, too, to the BTL advisers for their guidance along the way: Alma Flor Ada, Marilyn Adams, Kyra Gaunt, Elsa Cardenas Hagan, Pat Kelly, Ed Kame'enui, Gerry Lesser, Reid Lyon, Susan Neuman, Jim St. Clair, Dorothy Strickland, and Junko Yokota. Each has contributed in his or her own way. Marilyn and Dorothy have been especially generous with their time and knowledge, and Jim and Pat, our local practitioners, have helped enormously with outreach as well as ideas. Jim Wendorf and Sheldon Horowitz at the National Center for Learning Disabilities provided invaluable and expert assistance by reviewing sections of the manuscript.

On a personal level, each of us has our special support network to thank.

LKR: My ability to tackle this project grew from my contact with several world-class teachers: Jeanne Chall and Caleb Gattegno stand out for their insight and powerful influence. My late colleague Sara Brody coached enthusiastically from the sidelines until her strength was gone. Kate Taylor and Kathy Waugh of WGBH were my original contacts at BETWEEN THE LIONS; I am grateful for their confidence in me. My coauthor, Louise Kennedy, read my knotty, academic explanations and turned them into parent-friendly conversation, and I am honored to have my name associated with her graceful prose. Finally, it is the loving presence of my husband, Jerry, that has made everything possible.

LK: I am grateful to all the teachers, from Mrs. Barnes in the first grade to Kelly Wise and beyond, who taught me to love reading and writing and to see that I could make a life out of doing both. I am also deeply grateful to Fiona Luis, Scott Heller, and Mark Morrow for giving me the opportunity to write for *The Boston Globe*—and for having the grace and patience to let me write this book at the same time. Paula Dolan, Lyn Schmucker, and Diane Wear of the Auburndale Community Nursery School generously shared their expertise and ideas. And, of course, my coauthor, Linda K. Rath, is the true force behind this book; I have been privileged to gather her vast knowledge and wisdom about literacy and to shape it into this form. I have also been privileged over the past year to watch as my son, Christian, learned how to read, even as Mommy was busy upstairs writing. For that, and for the daily blessing of his presence in my life, I thank my husband, Jim.

Introduction

How to Use This Book

Once upon a time, in a comfortable old brick building that was covered with vines, there lived a most unusual family of lions. The parents, Cleo and Theo, and their cubs, Lionel and Leona, weren't just any lions. They were librarians—and they were experts at helping children explore the world of reading.

As you know if you've seen BETWEEN THE LIONS, this is no fairy tale. It's an award-winning television series that really does help children learn to read. Because so many parents have found the series a useful—and fun!—way to share reading with their children, we believe that parents can also use a practical, engaging book about reading that, like the series, presents information in a clear but lively format. That's the book you're holding in your hands.

The BETWEEN THE LIONS Book for Parents, like the series, is based on the latest and most reliable research into the vital question of how children learn to read. Researchers now generally agree that a two-pronged approach to reading instruction works best. That is, children learn to read most easily when they receive both instruction in reading skills and an introduction to the value of understanding what they read. Throughout this book, we'll give you lots of ideas about how to share both skills and understanding with your children, to build their ability to decipher text at the same time that you're helping them fall in love with books—in short, to give them both the "how" and the "why."

The approach we take in this book, as in the TV series, is practical, comprehensive, and fun. We think you'll find that it's helpful both for children who are struggling a bit and for those who are moving along just fine. For the strugglers, we offer lots of practical, easy-to-use advice on precisely which skills they need and how to help develop them. And the wealth of suggested activities, ways to incorporate reading into your life, and recommended books will enrich the life of any young reader. No matter where your child is on the spectrum, you'll also find plenty of support for your role as a parent, encouragement for your efforts, and realistic, workable advice on what you can do to help your child learn to read.

Because we want this to be a book you can use, we've organized it as simply as possible. In Part I, the first chapter gives an overview of how reading works and what children need in order to learn to do it. Chapter 2 provides background on BETWEEN THE LIONS and explains the format, philosophy, and components of the series—it's a terrific introduction if you're not familiar with the program, and an entertaining refresher if you are.

In Part II, we walk grade-by-grade through the development of children's reading skills and the instruction and guidance they need at each stage, from the preschool years through third grade. Here you'll find tons of specific information about what children should learn every year, how to help them learn it, and how to tell if they're running into difficulties. Each chapter also includes a set of "milestones" that makes it easy to see at a glance how your child is progressing, lots of practical tips for reinforcing what's being taught at school, a list of 30 books that are just right for that age, and a set of fun activities to

try with your child. Think of all this, by the way, as a menu, not a checklist—don't feel you have to do everything we suggest. Instead, pick and choose the activities that seem most enjoyable and useful for you and your child, and forget the rest.

Some of the activities we suggest are particularly useful if you're worried that your child isn't getting a comprehensive program of instruction at school. If a child doesn't seem to be getting much help with phonics, for example, you can play some phonics-based games together. On the other hand, if all that seems to go on at school is "skill and drill," you can emphasize the joy of reading at home by focusing on activities that stimulate an interest in books and literacy.

This section also contains a chapter on learning difficulties, which offers an overview of dyslexia and other common problems, along with lots of straightforward advice about how to tell if your child may have a problem and what to do if you're concerned. Here you'll also find a concise summary of the federal law that covers learning disabilities and an explanation of how to use the law to help your child.

Part III features a list of ten activity kits for kids of all ages to foster literacy-related play. This section also includes a list of Resources—books, Web sites, organizations, and more—that can help with reading, and a Glossary of terms you may come across in reading about reading.

As you read, you may note that we use some unfamiliar conventions in writing about phonics—for example, displaying a letter between slashes to represent a sound, as in /s/

for the "sss" sound, while writing letter names in italic. So, for example, /m/ means "the sound *mmm*"; /ee/ represents the long *e* sound, as in *sleep*; and /f/ means "the sound made by the letters *f*, *ph*, or *gh* as in *rough*." And, speaking of conventions, we've worked around the outmoded gender conventions of English by using "he" to refer to your child in one chapter, and "she" in the next; in each case, we use the opposite gender for adults.

Here's a bit of advice about how to read it all: Don't. This book is designed to help you help your child, not to make you feel as if you're back in school yourself, and there will not be a quiz. Use the parts of the book you find helpful, and skip the rest. The chapter on learning difficulties, for example, contains information about special education that you may never even need—but it's there if you do. What might make sense is to start with Part I to get the context and basic information, then go straight to the chapter in Part II that covers your child's current age. Then, if you want, you can look ahead to see what's coming next or look back to see what's already passed. But—big "but"—you shouldn't use that backward glance to beat yourself up if you didn't do some of the things we suggest. No one does everything we recommend, and you probably won't have, either. That's fine.

Besides, the most important things you can do to help your child learn to read are the ones you're probably already doing: cheer his efforts when he succeeds, encourage him when he struggles, and let him know you love him and want to help him master this important skill. You can also support your child by surrounding him with books and giving him a cozy place to read them. This need not cost a lot: a stack of library books next to a comfortable chair, with a bright light to read by, is really all that's required. That, and a loving and interested parent who will read some of those books to him and listen happily as he reads some more.

Reading is a joy and a powerful tool—but you already know that. What we hope *The BETWEEN THE LIONS Book For Parents* will do is to help you figure out how to share that joy and power with your child. And so, as you prepare to dip into the smorgasbord of information we've gathered, we'd like to leave you with the one tip we came across, over and over again, in just about every erudite summary of the latest reading research. If you want your child to read, read to your child. Read fairy tales, read nature guides, read picture books, read poems, read biographies, read novels, read comic books—heck, read the phone book, if the two of you get some pleasure out of it. Just read together, every day, and welcome your child into the reader's world.

Part I

Chapter 1

What Is Reading?

As parents, we come face-to-face every day with mystery. How does that tiny baby figure out, without being told, how to roll over, sit up, crawl, and walk? Where did your preschooler learn all those words and how to put them together? How can your third-grader program the VCR when you can't? And who left those cookie crumbs all over the floor?

We can't help you with the cookie crumbs—although, let's face it, you probably don't need Sherlock Holmes to figure that one out—but we can offer some useful information, guidance, and encouragement about one of the great mysteries of childhood: what is reading, and how is my kid ever going to learn to do it? Especially in our society, where so much of a person's success seems to depend on his ability to do well in school, parents can feel anxious about whether their children have what it takes to learn to read. So here's the first thing you need to know: just about every child, given the right support and instruction, will learn to read. And, for struggling readers, there's a lot you can do to help.

Just by picking up this book, you've already demonstrated that you're doing the thing that matters most. You care about your child's reading, and you want to help him learn. Your loving support and guidance, more than anything else, will motivate your child and help him find his way toward being a reader. And because you're a reader yourself— you're reading right now, aren't you?—you're probably also already doing the one thing that researchers universally emphasize as a key to children's reading: you're reading to your child. That one simple act, more than anything else you do, builds your child's understanding of books, his grasp of language, and his desire to read for himself. Give him those building blocks, and you've already given him much of what he needs to become a reader.

Of course, he'll still have plenty to learn about the details of the process: how letters represent sounds, how sounds go together to make words, how words combine to form sentences, and how sentences add up to a meaningful whole. But those details are just that: details. They're also small, specific skills that build on and reinforce each other, and that your child will put together one by one to solve the larger puzzle: discovering meaning. That's the point, always, of reading: to make a connection between the words on the page and what they mean—and, by doing so, to make a deeper connection between the reader and the world.

Reading accurately is important, but what's really important is making that connection. And by setting your child in your lap with a book, you're helping him learn how to connect. You're giving him the big picture—a warm and welcoming context into which he can fit all the bits of knowledge about books and reading that he'll assemble in his years at school.

WHAT HAPPENS WHEN YOU READ?

If you're the kind of person who likes to know the fine points of how things work, check out the box "Reading: The Fine Print," which details the current thinking about how our brains decipher print. But, just as you don't need to be able to explain how an engine works in order to drive a car, you don't need to know everything about the visual, neurological, and psychological elements of the act of reading in order to help your child learn to read. What can help (to extend that driving metaphor for just a moment) is to know enough to be able to tell when you might be having engine trouble. So, very briefly, let's look under the hood.

This is trickier than it might seem. Researchers have learned a lot in the past few decades about how reading works, but they're still figuring out some of the details. That's because reading is something a skilled reader does swiftly, silently, and internally. Even if you try to observe the process in yourself, it's almost impossible to see just how you do it. For this reason, many people assumed for a long time that skilled readers don't sound words out as they read and that they probably skip words, just focusing on the important ones.

In fact, all of those assumptions have now been proved to be more or less wrong. Believe it or not, skilled readers look at almost every letter of every word, and their brains attend to the sound as well as the appearance of what they read. We think we read with our eyes, and of course our eyes are part of the process. But what's even more important is the language-processing ability of our brains. Reading is a language skill more than a visual one—an important point to keep in mind as you read in the chapters to come about what instruction your child should receive and which skills it's most valuable to help him develop at home.

Reading, just like learning to read, is a process that starts with small building blocks and gradually assembles them to form a larger whole. Your eye begins with a collection of lines and curves that it assembles into a letter; your brain takes that bit of data and assembles it with others to form syllables, then words, then sentences, then paragraphs, then books. In the same way, when your child is learning to read, he assembles what he learns about letters to build his ability to read words, then puts his knowledge of words together to figure out how to comprehend sentences and the text as a whole. In both processes, knowledge is the goal, but it cannot exist without the smooth assembly of its tiniest parts.

By the same token, you would never have the patience to assemble those parts if you did not know that they were going to add up to something worth having. That's why the most successful reading instruction teaches children not just the individual skills they will need, but also the larger context—the many ways that reading will make a difference in their lives. In a well-designed program, your child will be immersed in the world of print and will be given many enticing reasons to "join the club" of readers, from the fun of stories to the value of acquiring new information. He will also receive instruction in each skill, step by step, so that he can put them together in a useful and meaningful way. Once that happens for your child, as it already has for you, all the steps will become automatic, fluent, and almost invisible. But it's little wonder, given all the parts of the process, that learning to read can be a struggle for so many children. In fact, the more you delve into the details of research on the visual, neurological, psychological, and cognitive aspects of reading, the more remarkable it seems that any of us ever learns to read at all. But you did it, and, by working one by one on the skills that go together to make the process work, your child will do it, too.

GETTING STARTED: WHAT YOUR CHILD NEEDS

There's another body of research that you may find it useful to know something about, and that's the study of which skills and capacities a child needs to have in order to become a reader. The details of each of these areas will come up as they are appropriate in the grade-by-grade chapters of this book, but we'd like to provide an overview here of the areas of competence that every reader needs, along with some ways to nurture them in your child from the very start.

Our grade-by-grade discussions will take us through the generally recognized stages of literacy development, which were set forth by the late Dr. Jeanne Chall—who, by the way,

READING: THE FINE PRINT

With the help of advanced technology that permits close, precise observation of eye movements and brain patterns in the laboratory, researchers have learned much about how skilled readers read. If you'd like to know more, a terrific place to start is with BETWEEN THE LIONS adviser Marilyn Jager Adams's book *Beginning to Read: Thinking and Learning about Print,* a comprehensive but readable discussion of the research into how reading works. Our explanation here is based on that book.

First of all, research has upended some common assumptions about skilled readers—that they don't look at every word, say, or attend to the sounds of words as they read. It turns out that even skilled readers do "subvocalize," or sound out, unfamiliar words or complex texts, and that if an experimenter blocks them from doing this, their comprehension drops precipitously. In addition, a good reader looks at every letter of almost every word. He skips only a few small words such as *a* or *the*, and even those aren't skipped every time they appear.

The eyes also "fixate," or pause, as they move across a line of text, and the pattern of this fixation helps the brain to process the words as they appear. The eye can register not only the letter on which it has paused but also about three letters before it and about six after it. This range permits the brain to process letters in clumps, and it now appears that this clumping is essential to successful word recognition. What happens is that the eye, as it pauses on a letter for about one-quarter of a second, sends a signal to the brain, which compares the letter form, line by line and curve by curve, to its memory of the way each letter of the alphabet is composed. It then "recognizes" the letter.

What's interesting is that the brain will recognize letters more quickly when they are surrounded by letters with which they are more commonly associated in the reader's language. It takes a fraction of a second longer, for example, to process the letters *tqe* than the letters *the* because the brain "expects" to see an *h* and does not expect to see a *q* after an initial *t.* So part of what makes it possible for skilled readers to read quickly and accurately is that they have a vast store of memory regarding the patterns of word formation; they see each letter separately, but they see it in the context of its surrounding patterns and compare those patterns to the ones that are familiar from other reading.

Once the eyes have registered the letters and the brain has assembled a few of them into a syllable or word part, other processes kick in to help the reader figure out the whole word and its meaning in context. (It's worth noting, by the way, that most of this is happening on the left side of the brain, where the sounds and meanings of language are processed, rather than in the visual areas on the right.) The reader has a memory of the sounds of many words, and he uses the letters in front of him to construct the sounds of the word they form. Then—and remember that all of this is happening so fast that we usually don't realize it consciously—he compares these sounds to his store of known words. At the same time, he is comparing the word to his memory bank of words whose meaning he knows.

These processes act together to help him recognize the word by both sound and sight and to understand what it means. He then places it in the larger context of what he's reading to make sense of the text. As if that weren't complicated enough, note that all of these processes are interacting with each other to clarify or correct any confusion in the system. If the text is physically hard to read, for example, the parts of the brain that handle meaning will search for possible words that would make sense in context, while the sounding-out section will offer suggestions based on whatever letters may be legible.

You may have experienced this phenomenon when trying to read someone's handwriting—you squint at a word, then scan ahead a bit, trying to puzzle out the sentence, then go back and notice that it could start with an r, then suddenly realize that it must say "rose." Meanwhile, you're also using your knowledge of the context to decide quickly whether that "rose" refers to the flower or to getting up in the morning—though, interestingly, every possible meaning of a word comes fleetingly to mind as you read it, even though you may be consciously aware only of the appropriate one.

This goes on, word by word, until you come to the end of a sentence—or, in a longer sentence, until you come to a natural break, such as that comma you just passed or the dash a few phrases back. At these natural boundaries of meaning, you pause for an instant to process the latest batch of words you have just read and to assemble them into a meaningful phrase. Then you dump that batch from your short-term memory and move on to the next batch. Gradually, as you progress through the text, you combine these batches to cobble together a larger meaning.

If you are reading especially complex or unfamiliar text, you may have to go back and reread a passage one or more times before you can grasp the larger meaning, or you may simply slow down and process each phrase more thoroughly before moving on. But, in everything you read, the basic steps of the process will remain the same.

SIX STAGES OF READING DEVELOPMENT

The late Dr. Jeanne Chall, who laid the groundwork for much of today's understanding of how young children learn to read, developed the theory that learning about literacy occurs in stages that begin in infancy and continue throughout life. Here are the stages she identified.

Pre-reading (six months to six years): The pre-reading child has some phonological awareness, or sensitivity to speech sounds, rhyming, and alliteration; recognizes some letters and may link some to the sounds they make; and has some understanding of books and print.

Initial reading or decoding (first and second grade): The child who is just beginning to read independently can sound out words one at a time and decode them slowly, carefully, and accurately. He looks "glued to print," meaning that most of his attention is devoted to decoding, with few mental resources left over for deeper comprehension.

Confirmation and fluency (second and third grade): Gradually, as the child becomes more confident in his decoding skills, he starts to come "unglued" from print. He reads more swiftly and fluently, freeing his energies for greater comprehension of the text.

Reading to learn new information (fourth through eighth grade): Once fluency is well established, the reader can make the shift from "learning to read" to "reading to learn." He can acquire information from a text and compare it to his own ideas, but he is generally limited to one viewpoint at a time. His vocabulary now increases more through reading than through conversation.

Coordinating multiple viewpoints (high school): The reader can compare and analyze texts with multiple viewpoints and can put them into the context of his earlier learning. He can read on several levels at once, considering, for example, facts, underlying assumptions, and larger context.

Construction and reconstruction (college and beyond): The mature reader constructs his own system of knowledge from the texts he reads, analyzing, synthesizing, and making judgments about all of them to create his own understanding of the world. His mind is flexible and self-critical, and his knowledge is both the cause and the result of constant reflection, exploration, and curiosity.

was an early and invaluable BETWEEN THE LIONS adviser. (See the box "Six Stages of Reading Development.") In this model, literacy begins in infancy, with a child's first exposure to language, and then progresses in predictable ways through language learning, early exposure to books and stories and to the sounds and symbols of language, experimental play with reading, accurate decoding, and fluent reading, all the way to the most advanced forms of reading to learn and constructing meaning from multiple texts.

As you can see, this way of thinking about reading places a child's level of development on a continuum. We no longer talk about a magic moment of "reading readiness," but rather see children gradually gathering and assembling knowledge about language and print, both casually and systematically, until they know how to read. That's not to say that they shouldn't get specific instruction along the way—they absolutely should—but just to note that there's a whole world of development and play, in addition to formal lessons, that goes into the process of becoming a reader. (To read more about how educators' thinking on this process has evolved over time, see the box "Phonics, Whole Language, and the Combined Approach.")

So what does a child need in order to move smoothly through this process? First of all, even the youngest children need plenty of conversation and stories. All the talking you've done with your child, even before he could talk himself, has done wonders for building his language abilities. Storytelling is important, too—not just the stories you read, but the stories you make up, from the simplest to the most fanciful. Your stories help your

child see how we use language to make sense of the world and our place in it. The more stories he hears, the richer your child's sense becomes of how stories work, why they matter, and what he can get from paying attention to them—all valuable lessons for a young learner.

As children move toward kindergarten, they start developing a more complete and sophisticated understanding of how language works. Their sentences grow longer and more complex, and they can understand more of what adults say to them; they can listen to longer and more complicated stories, remember short stories and poems, and make up stories of their own. All of this is an important foundation for the learning they'll do in school. In addition, there are five key areas of understanding that will be essential as they move into the process of learning to read.

The five areas are: *phonemic awareness*, or the ability to focus on the speech sounds that make up words; *phonics*, or the knowledge of connections between letters and sounds; *fluency*, or the ability to connect the words we read in a smooth, flowing way; *vocabulary*, or the knowledge of both spoken and written words; and *comprehension*, or the understanding of text. These five areas of skill build on each other and develop gradually, and growth in one area tends to spur growth in another. But they're all so important to reading success that they were designated the five key areas of instruction in *Put Reading First*, the 2001 report of the Partnership for Reading (a collaborative effort of three federal agencies: the National Institute for Literacy, the National Institute of Child Health and Human Development, and the Department of Education).

PHONICS, WHOLE LANGUAGE, AND THE COMBINED APPROACH

Over the years, there have been many different theories about how best to teach reading, and the pendulum has swung back and forth between focusing on skills and emphasizing meaning. Here's a flashback:

❖ The ancient Greeks, among others, emphasized the alphabet, drilling students letter by letter and having them recite aloud.

❖ In colonial America, teachers followed much the same approach. The famous *Horn Book* featured a "syllabarium" of letter combinations like "ba, be, bi, bo, bu."

❖ In 1850, Horace Mann brought back a new idea from Germany: the so-called "whole-word" method, focusing from the start on meaningful words rather than the alphabet.

❖ Meanwhile, more phonetic methods like McGuffey's *Eclectic Reader* also remained popular.

❖ By the 1950s, Mann's school of thought had led to the so-called "look–say" method—hello, Dick and Jane.

❖ In 1955, Rudolf Flesch's *Why Johnny Can't Read* assailed look–say and called for intensive phonics instruction. Flesch's relentless insistence on phonics launched a sometimes heated debate, as well as a new era of research.

❖ In the 1960s, Jeanne Chall synthesized decades of that research. Programs that stressed explicit phonics, she found, led to greater gains than those that stressed "whole-word" reading.

❖ Incorporating these findings through the 1970s, publishers created programs that delivered more systematic phonics lessons and stories based on "decodable" words.

❖ In the 1980s, however, educators began to tire of the lifeless, unnatural-sounding practice texts. They began to embrace the so-called "whole-language" approach, which stresses the importance of imbuing children with a feel for language and a love of literature.

❖ Today, most researchers favor a combined approach that teaches phonics systematically, sequentially, and explicitly, while engaging students in reading literature that anchors skills to meaning.

PHONICS

Characteristics
Systematically and sequentially teaches the correspondence between letters and sounds, beginning with the simplest, most obvious aspects of the code and building cumulatively from the most predictably spelled and simplest words to the most complex and unusual ones

Emphasizes accurate decoding

Pros
Promotes accuracy and independence

Reveals the structure of words by mapping the connections between sounds and symbols, demonstrating a general principle of how words work

Appeals to the human aptitude for seeking patterns and relationships

In its step-by-step instruction, has proven helpful to students who are struggling to learn to read

Helps build spelling skills

Cons
Is sometimes delivered as a series of drills and exercises, where word and sentence meanings are overlooked

Does not in itself help students understand why reading matters and so can seem pointless to students who have not experienced the power and pleasures of reading

WHOLE LANGUAGE

Characteristics
Immerses children in books and literature and encourages them to explore reading and writing on their own

Emphasizes motivation, communication, and social engagement

Pros
Promotes interest in books

Encourages students to follow their own interests

Provides lively, diverse activities for students

Emphasizes the delights of reading

Appeals to students' social and communicative instincts

Helps build interest in writing and composition

Cons
Does not present skills in a step-by-step manner

Can be overwhelming to students with limited book experience and students who have language-processing difficulties

Does not always help students hear the sound structure of words and see how that directly relates to written language, information that is particularly important for struggling students

Does not do enough to build knowledge of spelling rules and generalizations

A so-called comprehensive program is one that embraces all five of these areas.

Because the five key areas are so important, we've organized the grade-by-grade chapters of this book around them—with the addition of writing, because current research underscores the important links between reading and writing. We'll be looking at the development of these skills in detail in those chapters, but it's also helpful to keep them in mind in a general way when thinking about how your child moves along the path toward reading. (See the box "Five Words to Remember.")

By the time they enter kindergarten, many children are beginning to develop phonemic awareness. As we've seen from looking at how the brain processes text, it's essential for a reader to be able to connect letters with sounds—and you can't do that unless you can pay attention to the sounds themselves. There are plenty of playful ways to call attention to the sounds and rhythms of speech—nursery rhymes, word games, and songs are great ways to help your child develop this ability.

A kindergartner also needs to understand some basic things about what print is and what it does: that letters represent speech sounds, that letters go together to make words, and that changing the letters changes the sounds and the words. (This is what's known as "the alphabetic principle.") Reading to your child, early and often, is the best way to start; you can also sing the alphabet song and point to the letters. And you can help him write his name, play with books, and see all kinds of print all around him, so that he's surrounded from the first by a wealth of written language. This also makes it easy to introduce him to the "concepts of print"—the basic conventions about how to hold a book, where to start reading, and reading from top to bottom and left to right—that he'll need to know before he can learn to read.

As your child starts to move into formal reading instruction, he'll start learning the specific correspondences between letters and sounds—in a word, phonics. Research shows that the most helpful phonics instruction is systematic and direct, so you may want to talk with your child's teachers to find out what kind of program they use. You'll find plenty of detailed information on phonics in the grade-by-grade chapters to come, particularly those on the first and second grades. You can help at home by playing phonics games and by gently encouraging your child to pay attention to accurate decoding as he reads to you.

Once your child starts to make the connections between letters and sounds, he can begin to read some very simple texts. Now he'll need time to polish and refine his skills at "decoding," or figuring out unfamiliar words. He'll also learn how to move from identifying or sounding out words one at a time to recognizing them instantly and connecting them into smooth, flowing, meaningful phrases and sentences. This ability is called fluency, and it's what lets a skilled reader stop focusing on the actual process of reading and start thinking instead about the meaning of what he reads. Reading aloud is a great way to show your child what fluent reading sounds like, so that he can imitate it as he practices on his own.

Reading aloud to your child—even if he has already learned to read—can also help develop his vocabulary. This is important

FIVE WORDS TO REMEMBER

The most important words to bear in mind throughout this book refer to the *five key areas of reading instruction,* as set forth by the federal Partnership for Reading. Making sure that children receive instruction in each of these areas is the best way to help them learn to read; these areas are so important that we've used them as the organizing principle for our grade-by-grade discussions of what a good program teaches each year.

The five keys are:

Phonemic awareness: The ability to focus on the individual speech sounds in words and to break words into their sounds, play with the sounds, and blend them back together again. (Breaking words into sounds is called *segmenting*; playing with sounds is called *manipulating*; putting sounds together into words is called *blending*.) Paying attention to individual sounds makes it possible to learn how letters represent sounds, which is the foundation of written English.

Phonics: The study and use of letter-sound relationships to help identify written words. Systematic, direct instruction in the relationships between letters and sounds gives children a solid foundation for reading and spelling.

Fluency: The ability to read in a smooth, flowing, connected way. Reading fluently makes it possible to link words together into meaningful phrases.

Vocabulary: Knowledge of word meanings, in both spoken and written language. A large vocabulary makes it easier to understand what you read, both because you know the meanings of more of the words and because the known words provide clues to the unknown ones.

Comprehension: Understanding of text, both its individual words and its whole meaning. This is the goal of reading, the point toward which all the component skills are directed.

because it won't do him any good to sound out words if he doesn't know what they mean. Vocabulary is an important building block for comprehension. Just about any fun experience, from a picnic to a trip to the zoo, offers opportunities to build vocabulary.

The final goal, and in some ways the most

BETWEEN THE LIONS tries to help young readers become more fluent by "chunking" words on-screen into meaningful phrases. Sometimes, animation will highlight several words at a time; sometimes a "bouncing ball" will lead the reader's eye from one word to the next in a rhythmic and fluent way.

---

obvious one, is comprehension—putting all these different skills together so that he can read with understanding. You can help your child improve his comprehension by reading a variety of books with him, because the structure and nature of written language is different from speech, and the more he reads, the more he'll be able to understand that special language. You'll also find that the more deeply your child understands what he reads, the more pleasure he'll take from reading and the more eager he'll be to work on improving his reading skills.

In addition to these five key areas, current research underscores the value of linking reading with writing. Connecting reading and writing is important because each skill reinforces the other—in fact, it may be more accurate to think of them as two aspects of the same skill. You can help your child write stories, notes, and letters, and this will help him with reading, too. BETWEEN THE LIONS does a

lot to emphasize the value of writing, from Chicken Jane's scratched-out messages to the cubs' stories and fan letters, and we've also made it an element of each grade-by-grade chapter in this book.

WHAT YOU CAN DO

As your child moves through the stages of learning to read, you may sometimes wonder how best to help him. The specific answers will depend on your child and what he needs at the moment, and no one is better situated to know those things than you. But, in general, it may be helpful to think of yourself not as a backup teacher or at-home tester, but as a loving and supportive coach and guide. In other words, your intuitive sense of when to step in and offer advice or information, and when to stand back and let him try for himself, will serve you better than any set of rules about what to do when.

Remember, too, that learning to read is a long process—in fact, it's a process that begins in infancy and continues throughout the rest of life. Of course, the early primary grades, when your child is learning to "crack the code" of print, stand as the most intensive period of instruction in reading, but these important years really are part of a continuum, and it can take some of the pressure off to remember that. Think of it as a long process of development, like learning to crawl, walk, jump, and run, rather than simply mastering a discrete skill, like learning to throw a ball, and you'll be on the right track.

You may notice, as you read through this book, that we introduce some skills in an ear-

THE PARENT–TEACHER PARTNERSHIP

Throughout your child's education, your relationship with his teachers will be an important part of his success. It's worth thinking about how you can best collaborate to be sure he gets the support he needs.

It may be helpful to start with a few basic assumptions:

❖ You share a common goal: you both want your child to learn effectively and be happy in school.

❖ The teacher is a professional who works hard on behalf of all the children in the class.

❖ The two of you see your child from complementary perspectives that are both valuable. You see your child "longitudinally"—as a person who has grown and changed dramatically. His teacher sees him for just one year, and she sees him in relation to other children his age.

With these assumptions in mind, here are some suggestions for maintaining a healthy and helpful relationship with your child's teacher.

❖ Do show an interest in and support for the classroom program.

❖ Do send in a nice note if it's warranted, every now and then.

❖ Do ask the teacher if you can set up an appointment to discuss a question or concern you might have. Don't try to grab time at drop-off or dismissal.

❖ Do arrange a conference to bring any worries or troublesome observations about your child to the teacher's attention. Don't send in a note with a negative message.

❖ Do arrange to meet with the teacher to discuss any classroom practices that make you uncomfortable. Don't speak with the principal about these issues until you have spoken directly with the teacher.

❖ Do volunteer to chaperone field trips or be a classroom helper, if your work and family schedules permit.

lier chapter, then go into them in greater detail later on. That's because it's helpful to your child to be exposed to a variety of reading-related skills even before he's ready to try them himself. It doesn't mean that anyone expects a child to master a skill the moment it's introduced. You'll probably find that some skills come quickly, but others may take years to understand and acquire.

It's kind of like riding a bike: we show children the bike, let them touch the handlebars, maybe even take them for a ride, long before we expect them to start learning how to ride it themselves. But their earlier experience with bikes gives them a base to work from once they are ready to learn. In fact, this is a useful model for helping your child that you may already use without even thinking about it. First, you just do something yourself as your child watches. Next, you invite him to do it with you. Finally, you encourage him to give it a try on his own. You can follow these steps for anything from teaching a baby how to hold a book to helping a high-schooler organize a research project—or, for that matter, teaching your child how to shoot a basket or sew a hem. Model, share, and let go, and watch your child soar.

Finally, there are a couple of ways in which you, as a parent, can be especially helpful to your child. For one thing, starting in kindergarten, you can develop a strong partnership with his teachers. (See the box "The Parent–Teacher Partnership.") More generally, by your enthusiasm and example, you can give your child a deep understanding of why reading matters. Being motivated to learn is essential for your child, and you can do more than anyone else to whet this appetite. By showing him the many ways in which you use literacy in your own life, by sharing your love of books, by helping him find something to read at home or on regular visits to the library, and by cheering his efforts to learn, you make it clear to your child that his reading matters to you and will make you proud of him. And, as you already know from being a parent, your approval and support are powerful motivators for your child.

But the single most important thing you can do to help your child read is simple, and, as we said at the start, it's something you probably already do. Read to him, every day. Repeated studies have shown that children who are read to daily learn to read more easily than those who are not. If your schedule is packed, find someone who can share this task with you. But do also find time to do it yourself as often as you can, not only for your child's sake but also for your own. A parent, a child, and a book—that's a whole world, and one that's full of literacy and love. By entering into that world with your child, you are helping him find the path into a rich and rewarding lifetime of reading.

Chapter 2

The BETWEEN THE LIONS Curriculum

When you and your child watch BETWEEN THE LIONS together, you may think it's just an entertaining series about a family of lions who run a library. And, on one level, it is. Theo and Cleo Lion and their cubs, Lionel and Leona, do indeed live in a library, along with a rare dinosaur called a Thesaurus, a computer-savvy mouse named Click, and a pigeon or two. Let's face it: the place is a zoo.

Well, no, it really is a library. And that's no accident. The series' creators chose this setting because it's a wonderfully rich, welcoming, and appropriate environment in which to carry out the real purpose of all the Lions' carryings-on: helping children learn to read. Brought to the air by many of the same people who created *Sesame Street*—and developed with the same collaboration between education specialists and television artists that has made that series an enduring classic— BETWEEN THE LIONS is much more than just good fun. It is serious education, backed by sound research and a carefully constructed curriculum, that has been shown to help children learn to read.

The series got its start when the creative teams at Sirius Thinking, Ltd., and WGBH Boston got together to develop a series about reading. They wanted a series that could do for early readers what *Sesame Street* did for preschoolers learning numbers and letters. The creative team brought in some of the most respected researchers in the field—Gerald Lesser of *Sesame Street* fame, Marilyn Jager Adams, Robert Slavin, Catherine Snow, Dorothy Strickland, and the late Jeanne Chall, to name just a few. Together, they worked to figure out which skills it was most important to reinforce and how to incorporate those elements into a format that would appeal to kids—and their parents. (The parent-friendly part is no accident, because it encourages parents and children to watch together, and that helps children learn better.) Out of those discussions came the basic structure of the series, which uses a "whole-part-whole" format to place the various "parts" of reading instruction into a "whole" context of a larger story that anchors the specific bits of information, making them easier to remember—and more fun to watch, too.

By the fall of 1995, Sirius and WGBH had created their "mane" characters: parents Theo and Cleo, and cubs Lionel and Leona. At seven, Lionel is an avid reader; Leona, four, is just starting to put the pieces of the reading

puzzle together. (See the box "Meet the Lions" for a complete introduction to the cast.) They had also come up with the setting and the title BETWEEN THE LIONS, calling to mind the statues that often guard the entrance to public buildings.

You'll find plenty of other silly puns in the Lions' library, along with songs, cartoons, tongue twisters, puppets, skits, visiting stars— and books, of course. Lots of books. It all comes together in a lively stew that's been proven to appeal to its target audience, four- to seven-year-olds—and to help them learn to read. It's so effective, in fact, that it has been endorsed by an organization that hardly ever encourages children to watch TV: the National Education Association.

The way it all works is easiest to see when you look at a single episode in detail, and we'll do that in a moment. But it may also be helpful to have an understanding of the philosophy behind the program and its "whole-part-whole" structure. Underlying everything that happens on BETWEEN THE LIONS are four key goals:

❖ To serve as a model for reading, writing, speaking, and listening skills—all vital elements of literacy;
❖ To motivate children to read and write, by demonstrating that reading and writing provide deep pleasure and serve as stepping-stones to every other kind of learning experience;
❖ To provide an explicit introduction to the vitally important listening skills that children must master in order to learn to read: being able to hear the separate sounds that make up words and knowing the connections between letters and sounds;

❖ To acquaint children with a wide variety of texts, including stories, letters, newspaper and magazine articles, poems, plays, songs, and reference materials and other forms of nonfiction.

The series works toward these goals within the context of its "whole-part-whole" structure. Each episode opens in the library, with the lions interacting with each other and with a text—a story, an article, or perhaps the operating instructions for a robot. Reading the text is an important part of this opening "whole" segment. Then, a key word is plucked out of the text and highlighted on-screen. A series of segments focuses the viewer's attention on this word and on the vowel sound it contains— usually a short vowel, because a systematic understanding of short vowel sounds is key to beginning to read and spell in English, and because they're the hardest sounds for young readers to match to letters. One series adviser called short vowels the "sink-or-swim" elements for beginning readers; a child just has to learn these sounds and spellings in order to read and spell with any accuracy. So the "parts" sequences zero in on these and other important elements. Finally, the story line returns to the "whole" text the lions have been reading and connects it to their lives.

You may notice that the "parts" segments of each episode focus on just one or two key words and their component sounds. This narrowing of focus allows children to concentrate on a particular sound, the letter or letters that represent it, and the many words that have that sound in common. For example, when the "Bug Beard" episode introduces the key word *bug*, the segments play with a variety of words from the -*ug* family and the neighboring -*un* and -*unk* families (*sun, sunk*), both in and out of story context. Being able to link knowledge in this fashion makes it easier for a young learner to build her understanding of how words work.

Because of its structure, rather than just providing assorted tidbits of phonics instruction, BETWEEN THE LIONS anchors its mini-lessons in the context of meaningful text. There is the overall story and "whole" of an episode, but in each of the "parts" segments, as well, animations or gestures illustrate the meanings of the words in the spotlight. Knights hug after blending together *h* and *ug* in one segment. Simple animated drawings illustrate each word in the -*ug* word family in the catchy song "If You Can Read *ug*." Books and workbooks can't offer this kind of appealing and immediate presentation. Television can: it's uniquely capable of using action to bring the words in phonics lessons to life. Such lively (and often wacky) demonstrations help children acquire and retain the phonics information they will need in order to read. And, of course, having a story to follow, featuring beloved characters, makes the series more engaging for young viewers.

Beyond the details of each episode, the Lion family displays a lot of the behavior that makes for happy young readers. The Lion parents read to their cubs every day, and they respond with enthusiasm and encouragement to the cubs' own efforts to read. Older brother Lionel works hard to improve his reading and writing skills; he also frequently demonstrates to his little sister how useful reading can be and assists her as she makes her first forays into reading, writing, and storytelling. For her

MEET THE LIONS (AND FRIENDS)

The stars of BETWEEN THE LIONS are, of course, the lions. So let's start our cast list with them.

Theo is the dad and, with his wife, Cleo, chief librarian. He's one voracious reader—and, with his deep, leonine voice, he's a born storyteller.

Cleo is the mother, chief librarian with Theo, and executive huntress. As befits the head female of the pride, she's an expert at tracking information, pouncing on facts, and carrying books back to share with her cubs.

Lionel is seven years old and, like his parents, a ravenous reader. He's especially fond of series books—in his case, the "Cliff Hanger" novels by one Livingston Dangerously. Lionel reads just about everything, though, and takes particular pride in reading aloud to his younger sister.

Leona, at age four, isn't reading yet, but she still can't wait to get her paws on a good book. She loves being read to and especially enjoys making up stories of her own. She and Lionel both love to act out stories, to imagine new endings or sequels for books, and sometimes even to enter into a book with the magical intercession of Click the Mouse.

That brings us to some of the non-lion residents of the library.

Click the Mouse is a cyberrodent—a mouse in both senses of the term. She is always happy to help library users with technology. If a character from the library wants to enter a book, Click simply "drags and drops" the character onto the page.

Barnaby B. Busterfield III is the stuffy, irascible founder of the library—or, actually, he's the stuffy, irascible stone bust of the founder of the library. He sticks around to lend the place tone and, from time to time, to chat with his nearest companions, the dim but eager pair of rock doves known as **Walter** and **Clay Pigeon**.

Heath the Thesaurus is a paleontological oddity who lives in the basement and runs the library's reference department (with the occasional but able assistance of the **Information Hen**, who finds answers in her dictionary and is never too chicken to sing about it). Heath is always happy, delighted, ecstatic, and thrilled to supply a synonym for any word, which is sometimes useful, handy, and efficacious but can also grow tedious, tiresome, and a bit much.

Dr. Nitwhite, founder and director of Dunderhead Labs—and that's pronounced Dunder*heed*, thank you very much—bursts on the scene periodically with his astounding discoveries. Unfortunately, every time he comes up with a brilliant insight, his assistant **Watson** offers a response that happens to prove him wrong. "I have just found the only three-letter word in the English language that reads the same forward and backward," Dr. Nitwhite declares. "Mom!" But Watson answers, "Wow!" and back Dr. Nitwhite goes to the lab.

Gus, a rabbit friend of Lionel's, is a champion jumper but has not had much success at learning to read. He tries to hide his difficulties in one episode ("Humph! Humph! Humph!"), but the Lion family discovers his secret and begins to offer help.

part, Leona is eager to enter the world of readers, and her enthusiastic experiments with print can point the way for non-leonine viewers who are about her age. Most important of all, the Lion family loves to tell stories and share books with each other, and their heartfelt enthusiasm for the pleasures of literacy is just about irresistible.

"RED HAT, GREEN HAT": A SAMPLE EPISODE

To get a clearer sense of how all this works in practice, let's look in detail at one episode, "Red Hat, Green Hat." We've chosen this one because it's available on videotape and also because it features many, though not all, of the elements of a typical episode. (To learn more about other segments that appear frequently in the series, check out the box "The Parts Department.")

"Red Hat, Green Hat" begins, as every episode does, with the BETWEEN THE LIONS theme song. Notice how the words on the screen change as the lyrics do: the *n* of *now* gives way to the *w* of *wow*, which in turn is replaced by the *h* of *how*. This playful but meaningful animation reminds the viewer that letters and sounds are connected, and that when one changes, the other does, too.

The story opens with Leona going up to the patio on the roof of the library and begging her big brother, Lionel, to look at her beautiful new hat. Lionel is too engrossed in reading the sports page to pay her much attention, but he finally glances at the hat, which is red on one side and green on the other, "just like the one in this book!" Leona exclaims. Unable to

engage Lionel in conversation, Leona runs off to parade her hat through the library. Lionel, curious, picks up the book and begins to read.

The featured book, *Red Hat, Green Hat*, is an adaptation of an African folktale called "A Quarrel Between Friends." As Lionel begins to read, the scene shifts to the story itself, brought to life with stick puppets and paper cutouts. Two farmers are great friends until the day when another farmer walks between them wearing a hat. One farmer sees a red hat, the other a green one, and the two friends argue with increasing heat over which is right. "Red!" shouts one. "Green!" shouts the other. With each shout, the word appears on the screen—in the appropriate color, of course.

After a few rounds of this, we cut back to Lionel, who closes the book in distress. "Why would Leona want a troublemaking hat like that?" he wonders. Maybe she didn't read the book, he thinks, so she doesn't know what could happen. Suddenly, he realizes: "She can't read! She's too young! *Leona!*" Lionel runs to warn his sister. Leona, however, thinks Lionel is jealous of her hat and won't listen to him. She marches through the library's main reading room and, soon enough, a disagreement breaks out.

Let's pause for a moment here to note all that's happening as the cubs interact with this story. Leona has learned that, even if you can't read yet, you can use a book to get good ideas, and you can try out those ideas in your own life—you can even make a hat you love. Lionel has been amusing himself with the baseball scores, and he also has started reading an engaging story. And he has been forcibly reminded of the power of reading, because he now knows something that Leona doesn't:

that the hat will stir up trouble. Ah, the power of text comprehension! More subtly, the background scene in the library before Leona walks in gives young viewers an enticing view of the riches that libraries hold. People (and puppets) are consulting reference books, reading for pleasure, looking at picture books, and quietly sharing their discoveries with each other as they explore the treasures on the shelves.

Meanwhile, the scene shifts back to the last page Lionel had read before closing the book: one of the farmers shouting, "Red!" "Red," the narrator's voice repeats, and the key word is highlighted. Then the word ending -ed is highlighted and pulled out of the word. We are leaving the "whole" section of the episode and moving into the "parts."

What follows is a fast-paced sequence of segments that work, individually and together, to reinforce the word ending -ed and its component parts. We get Martha Reader and the Vowelles, "singing the short e sound from their sensational hit word, *bed*," as the announcer intones. We get Cliff Hanger, rescuing himself (temporarily, alas) by leaping from his cliff to a bed. We get a few "word morphs," with robots combining *b*, *e*, and *d* to get *bed*, then morphing it to *bet*, *pet*, *pen*, and *hen* (and saying the individual sounds and the words each time). And so on—on through the Information Hen, Fred and his blended sounds, an animated limerick about a boy named Ben, and a sleight-of-pants performance by Arty Smartypants, the Great Smartini. It's all quick, lively, and fun, and it's also carefully focused on that short e sound.

Then we're off to the library again, where the fight is growing really heated. Leona hopes

her parents will resolve it—but, instead, they end up on opposite sides, shouting "Red!" and "Green!" as loudly as everyone else. In desperation, she begs Lionel to tell her what people did in the book to resolve the conflict. "Did they fix it? Was there a happy ending?"

"I don't know," Lionel replies. "I didn't finish it."

"Could we finish it now?" Leona pleads.

"I think we'd better," Lionel says, and they set off in search of the book.

We, meanwhile, dip back into a few more segments for some work on the "parts." We'll see other short e words and even a glimpse of some words with double e, to pay some attention to the vowel sound in the word *green*, which is a vital part of this story. Finally, we'll return to single e in a wild festival of short e words that begins with the tongue twister "Sven said, 'Ted, send ten tents.'" Then, no doubt exhausted from this celebration, the -ed family slips back onto the page of *Red Hat, Green Hat* from which it came—just in time for Lionel and Leona to finish reading the tale. They learn that the farmers' dispute ended as soon as the hat-wearing farmer walked by again, this time in the other direction—so each could see the hat from the other's point of view.

"Now I know what I have to do," Leona says, underscoring the idea of learning something from a book. Bravely, she marches back into the library and shows everyone both sides of her hat. "Oops!" they all exclaim, with many apologies and hugs all around. Everyone is content—except for Barnaby B. Busterfield III, who provides a grumblingly comic last line just before the credits roll. But then he's always a grouch.

THE PARTS DEPARTMENT

In addition to the "whole" story that takes place in the library, every episode of BETWEEN THE LIONS includes an assortment of "parts." These quick segments reinforce a number of key concepts.

Dr. Ruth Wordheimer helps anxious readers overcome the dreaded Long Word Freakout. By talking them through the steps of "taking one part of the word at a time" and then blending the parts to say the whole, Dr. Wordheimer (yes, she really is played by Dr. Ruth Westheimer) demonstrates the benefits of careful persistence. And her encouraging demeanor bolsters young readers' confidence in their ability to identify any word if they just look closely and decode it systematically.

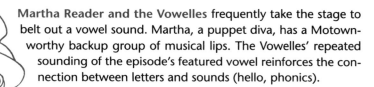

Martha Reader and the Vowelles frequently take the stage to belt out a vowel sound. Martha, a puppet diva, has a Motown-worthy backup group of musical lips. The Vowelles' repeated sounding of the episode's featured vowel reinforces the connection between letters and sounds (hello, phonics).

Fred, known to many young viewers as "the white-haired guy," likes to play around with sounds. A word appears before him on the screen and he points to each letter in turn, saying its sound. He repeats the sounds, a little closer together. Then he puts them so close together that they form a word. He always has props to help him act out the word, reinforcing vocabulary knowledge by connecting sound to meaning.

In **Gawain's Word**, the important skill of blending takes center stage. Two knights in full armor gallop toward each other (no live horses in the budget, just the broomstick kind), each brandishing a sign with his letters. **Sir st**, for example, might joust with **Sir op**, or on another day he might meet **Sir uck**. In any case, the knights rush together, each saying his part, until they crash. Then they proclaim their combined sounds—*stuck*, say—and act out the word.

Arty Smartypants and Smarmy Marmy have a mother–son vaudeville act that demonstrates the power of words. As the Great Smartini, Arty drops words into his giant "smarty pants," does his "dance in Smarty Pants," and pulls out a series of objects. He drops in the words *fish* and *star*, for example, and pulls out a starfish! Arty also pleases the crowd simply by reading a series of related words: *art, smart, smarter, smartest!*

Chicken Jane is an affectionate homage to the old "basal readers" that many of today's parents may remember, the ones featuring Dick and Jane. In each episode, the cartoon children, Scot and Dot, and their protective friend Chicken Jane interact in a simple story. Each word is highlighted on-screen as the narrator pronounces it. The repetitive story lines—boy and girl play, peril threatens, chicken rescues boy and girl at her own expense—help young readers read the high-frequency sight words, since they already know what will most likely happen.

Cliff Hanger also uses repetitive text, though it's aimed at slightly older readers. Time after time, we find our hero, Cliff Hanger, hanging on a cliff. He sees some chance of escape and refers to his trusty Survival Manual for guidance, but his efforts are always for naught. Cliff's antics show that phonics skills help you identify words in exciting stories that keep you hanging on for more.

An animated feature about the un and re People helps young readers see the power of prefixes. The nasty un People might undo something, but the helpful re People always redo it.

Another animated character, the spunky young Punctuator, comes to the rescue with her powerful marks. Just by judiciously applying commas and periods, she can recast a few sentences to rescue a character or right a wrong.

The Lone Rearranger appears in a cloud of eraser dust when a sign just doesn't make sense. He snaps his rope to change the word order and clear up the confusion, reminding viewers to question what they read; it may be an error! Then the Lone Rearranger and his sidekick, Russell Upsome Grub, challenge on to the next move. See? Make that "move on to the next challenge"—and thanks, Lone.

MAMA, WATCH WITH ME!

Television is most helpful and educational for children when their parents watch with them at least part of the time, and when parents take the opportunity to teach critical thinking skills. Here are a few pointers:

❖ Use what you watch together as a starting point for conversation, just as you would with a shared book.

❖ Ask questions that encourage your child to analyze the program and link it to other forms of storytelling. "What do you think will happen next? Why? Who's your favorite character?"

❖ After the episode is over, discuss what you saw and what your child liked and didn't like about it. "What might have happened differently?"

❖ Feel free to weigh in with your own opinions. If you thought a character was sterotypical, say so. This shows your child how to engage actively with a medium, just as you do with books.

❖ Encourage your child to join in with the activities in an educational program like BETWEEN THE LIONS. When there's text on-screen, read it aloud with her. If there's a silly song, get up and dance.

❖ You can go to the BETWEEN THE LIONS Web site, www.pbskids.org/lions, to read the text of any featured story. And visit that site with your child to explore a wealth of games, songs, and printable activities.

That's a lot to fit into a half-hour episode, but the series' fast pace and varied elements are a key part of its charm for young viewers. And, again, it's important that these aren't just random bits; they're a series of connected segments all focusing on the letter *e*—and all taking place within the larger context of an engaging story. The idea is that the young viewer comes away with a stronger grasp of the letter-sound correspondences presented in the episode, anchored in her memory of a lively, interesting narrative brought to life by familiar characters.

In addition to presenting key words and demonstrating the correspondences between letters and sounds, Between the Lions also seeks to show its viewers some other important facts about the world of print. For one thing, the series consistently underscores the benefits of being able to read. That's one reason for featuring such a wide range of texts—so that young learners will see that reading is useful for much more than just the books they may encounter in the classroom. The series also shows that writing serves many purposes, both practical and creative. It demonstrates, as well, that learning to read and spell can be a struggle, but it's worth it. And the series makes a point of introducing new vocabulary words, as well as showcasing the high-frequency sight words that readers need to recognize automatically if they are to read fluently.

In fact, as you've probably realized, the curriculum content of Between the Lions regularly addresses the five key areas of reading instruction we mentioned in Chapter 1. Every episode includes segments that demonstrate comprehension strategies and define new words, in addition to serving up the phonics fun that's easy to recognize. What the content of Between the Lions is designed to provide is nothing less than a model of a comprehensive instructional program.

Most important, Between the Lions does all of this in the context of a warm, busy family, in which the parents love language and can't wait to share it with their children, and the cubs respond with an enthusiasm about learning that the parents gladly encourage. The Lions and their cubs read together, talk together, and learn together in an atmosphere of joyous excitement and affectionately shared discovery. That's what Between the Lions is all about, and that's what we're hoping to help you do at home.

Part II

Preschool Milestones

By the time a child is ready to head off to kindergarten, you can expect to see these signs of emergent literacy. A preschooler who is progressing smoothly through this phase:

* Speaks and understands spoken language well, with an increasingly expressive vocabulary
* Enjoys looking at books and being read to
* Participates in storytelling, playacting, simple word games, and conversation
* Understands that print carries a message
* Can sing the alphabet song or recite the alphabet
* Can write his name and name the letters in it
* Recognizes about half the letters of the alphabet and knows some of their sounds (mostly consonants)
* Experiments with "writing" to create signs, notes, and other messages.

Warning Signs
You should look for help if your four-year-old:

* Had persistent difficulties learning to talk or, by age four, still struggles with spoken language
* Seems unable to follow simple directions
* Cannot speak clearly enough to be understood by people outside the family
* Shows little interest in the names of letters and in reading as a pleasurable activity
* Appears to have any problem with vision or hearing (both of which should be tested annually, starting at age four)

Remember that children follow different paths to literacy. If you are concerned about your child's hearing, speech, or development, consult his pediatrician, who will be able to refer you to other sources of help. If your child is in preschool or day care, the teachers and caregivers there can also offer valuable insight.

In addition, your school district is required by federal law to identify and assist children who need help—even before they start school. The principal's office of your local elementary school can help you arrange screening (and remediation, if necessary) by specialists, at no cost to you. See Chapter 8 for more information on these services.

Chapter 3

Emergent Literacy: Reading and Writing for Preschoolers

Our age-by-age exploration of your child's journey into literacy begins in his last year before entering school, when he's about four. In reality, your child has been moving toward his future as a reader from his earliest days of life, and we'll look back on those first steps in this chapter, too. For the moment, though, let's start with how a typical four-year-old approaches language and books—a phase that's often called "emergent literacy."

As the term implies, emergent literacy is the stage of a young learner's development when he's just beginning to discover that the world is full of print, that print means something, that the adults he cares about use it to communicate with each other, and that someday he will be able to use it, too. Just as babies

turn their heads and smile in response to spoken words long before they begin to babble on their own, so do preschoolers love to point to pictures, turn (and tear) pages, and even chew on books as they are read to, long before they can decipher the printed word. A lot of what young children do with books looks like play, and it *is* play—but play, after all, is how children learn about the world. Playing with books, words, and writing is one way children start to learn about reading, and it's something you'll see your child do a lot this year.

Emergent literacy, though, isn't just about printed texts. It's also about speech—both talking and listening. Everything your child has been learning over the last few years about words, meaning, and how they go together will come into play as he begins to learn about print. That's because spoken language is the foundation of written language: without language, print is a meaningless code. Children who have trouble putting their thoughts into words or comprehending what others are saying will find it hard to figure out how the little black squiggles sprinkled across the page actually convey meaning. That's why hearing difficulties contribute to difficulties in reading—and it's one reason why, if you have any concerns about your child's hearing, you should consult your pediatrician right away.

Most children, however, are well prepared for reading by the simple fact that their parents have cooed, babbled, talked—and listened!—to them as they grew from infancy through toddlerhood. Helping your child become a confident, eager speaker and responsive listener is one of the most valuable things you can do as a parent to lay the groundwork for literacy, and it's something you have probably been doing since the day your child was born.

In this chapter, we'll look at a variety of ways you can reinforce your preschooler's natural interest in language and print. After recapping the development of spoken language, we'll look at the specific skills and interests that help a young child prepare for learning to read, and what you can do to nurture them. We'll discuss why preschoolers love storytelling and how you can build on that enthusiasm to foster a lifelong love of narrative. Then we'll look at ways to help your child grasp "concepts of print," those basic—but not necessarily obvious—facts about written text that every child needs to know, and suggest ideas for creating a "print-rich environment." Finally, we'll discuss a few ways to help your child begin to establish the correspondence between letters and their sounds. Naming letters, singing the alphabet song, and understanding that different letters stand for different sounds are all essential steps in learning to read.

Do remember that children move at different speeds along the road to reading. Your four-year-old may already feel comfortable with many of the skills and concepts of emergent reading. If your child has already reached the milestones listed at the start of this chapter, you may want to skip ahead to the kindergarten chapter to prepare for what comes next. On the other hand, if these milestones seem far out of reach for your child, reading through the suggestions in this chapter may help you find ways to encourage his progress. No matter where your child falls in the range of young learners, this chapter may help you get a better sense of how the process works, how it is likely to proceed from here—and how it all began.

THE DAWN OF LANGUAGE

Every child's path to reading begins at birth. Your child began learning about language the first time you gazed into his eyes and said his name. What's more, as you held him close and whispered to him, you showed him that language is associated with love. All the things we parents do without being told—talking to our infants, playing with them, smiling when they coo—convey the message that communication is meaningful, loving, and fun. Through you, your child discovered that he is a creature of language. And that discovery continues to unfold as children approach the task of reading.

Whole books have been written on the development of language in infants and young children. For our purposes, it may be helpful to provide just a quick overview of the process. (See the box "Stages of Language Development.") From birth, your child started attending to language: listening to your voice, distinguishing it from others', and soon looking at you in response. But he was also finding ways to communicate through sounds of his own.

The first sound that babies make, of course, is crying. But with remarkable speed—usually at only about one month of age—they start to coo, making "aah" and "ooh" sounds. A few months later, they begin to babble, forming both vowel and consonant sounds. Soon, they combine these sounds into syllable-like sequences: "mamama, bababa, dadada." You may not have noticed at the time, but babies are more likely to do this in the company of parents or other caregivers. Already, it seems, they've noticed that people use sound to communicate, and they're trying to do it, too. The more we respond to their efforts, the more they continue to reach out through language.

Even more interesting, they start to mimic the kinds of sounds they hear from us. Long before they say their first real word, for instance, the babies of Spanish-speaking parents are choosing to produce the kinds of sounds that occur in Spanish, and the babies of English-speaking parents are experimenting with the sounds more typical of English. That's one reason it's hard for older students to produce the special sounds of a language that isn't their own, like the trilled *r* of Spanish or the *th* of English—they haven't practiced those sounds since earliest infancy.

Around the first birthday, most babies say their first recognizable words (though they may be pronounced very differently from the way adults say them). These early words are usually labels for objects, people, or events. Often a single word may convey the meaning of a whole sentence—"Book!" for example, may mean "Give me the book," or "That's a new book," or "Read to me." Young speakers also may use the same sound to refer to a person, to label something that they associate with that person, or to ask for something from that person. "Ma," say, could mean, "Mama's here!" or "This is Mama's book," or "Mama, pick me up." No wonder parents and other close caregivers tend to understand young children better than outsiders do—because they share the child's experience, it's easier for them to fill in the blanks.

By the second birthday, most children have begun to combine words into simple sentences. They usually start by combining just two words, then gradually form longer strings. This early speech is often called "telegraphic"

STAGES OF LANGUAGE DEVELOPMENT

Children progress toward mature language in a predictable way. The ages given here for each step are approximate and can vary greatly from child to child, but the order of the steps is generally the same for most children. Talk with your pediatrician if you have any concerns about your child's progress along this path—particularly if he seems to progress steadily for a while, then falls back to a less complex stage, or if he starts talking and then stops.

Prebirth
Sensory stimulation—like hearing a parent's voice or music—promotes brain development.

Infancy
From his first days, your child is already learning about nonverbal dialogue and turn-taking. He will also make sounds that progress predictably from unintentional to intentional ones and from simple to more complex.

Birth
cries, burps, sneezes, coughs

2 months
goo, aah, ooh, and other vowel-like sounds

4–6 months
babbling (consonants and vowels: *mamama, kakaka*)

9–12 months
advanced babbling, with sentence-like phrasing and rhythm

12 months
Around his first birthday, your child will say his first real word. He will start with single syllables, then may double some syllables, as in *wawa* or *mama.* He will continue for a few months to say only one word at a time.

18–24 months

At around one and a half, your child will start putting two words together in order to use a telegraphic style of speech, as in "Want cookie" or "Give milk." This telegraphic speech, which is used for making requests, commenting, or asking questions, continues until about the second birthday. It includes no suffixes for person, number, or tense—that is, "want" can be both singular and plural, as can "cookie," and "give" can mean "you will give" or "you gave."

Preschool years (two to five)

Around the second birthday comes a veritable explosion of language. Your child, seemingly almost overnight, will start using new vocabulary, speaking in expanded sentences, and combining words with greater fluency. Other features of this stage include:

- ❖ Sustained turn-taking
- ❖ Advanced sentence structure and grammar, developing in stages from simple to more complex
- ❖ Formation of negatives and questions
- ❖ Use of prepositions and suffixes
- ❖ Overgeneralized language patterns and rules (*teached, mouses*)
- ❖ Growing social awareness, with some knowledge of language etiquette and of what's appropriate in different situations

School age (five and up)

As he moves through the primary grades, your child gradually fills in the remaining pieces of knowledge about how language works. The areas that develop during these years include:

- ❖ Understanding of the passive construction ("I was told by you," rather than "You told me")
- ❖ Mastery of all parts of speech and suffixes
- ❖ More language etiquette and subtlety
- ❖ Awareness of and control over different aspects of language
- ❖ Code switching, or adapting the style and dialect of speech to match the language and the context of the people he's speaking with—for example, using slang with friends and more formal language with teachers

because a typical sentence ("Want cookie!") sounds like a telegram: the essential words, such as nouns and verbs, are there, but articles, prepositions, and pronouns are missing. Though sentences like these do not follow the conventional rules of grammar, they have a consistent inner logic, and they do just what language is supposed to do: they convey meaning.

Over the next year or two, children continue to learn new words and to develop a more sophisticated understanding of how language works. Their sentences grow longer and more complex, and they become easier to understand, even for those outside the immediate family. Conversation with adults plays a vital role in helping children develop and refine their ability to speak: by hearing adult speakers, children learn the patterns and structures of speech, expand their vocabularies, and learn to find their way through the give-and-take of conversation (see the box "Let's Stretch").

All these oral-language skills are essential to prepare a child for reading. Yet, for the most part, they don't have to be formally taught. Children learn so much from conversations with adults that, for every word you carefully define for your child ("That's an aardvark!"), there are dozens more he will pick up by hearing you use them in context and trying to use them on his own. For this reason, you may occasionally want to include sophisticated words in your conversations, with explanations if needed. Simply put, the more words you use, the more words your child will know. And the more words your child knows when he starts kindergarten, the more likely he is to become a skillful reader. That's why taking

your child to the firehouse, zoo, or aquarium is such a valuable pre-reading activity—it's a great way to build vocabulary, and chatting about the trip on the way home is a natural way to strengthen his language skills.

That doesn't mean that your child will speak English flawlessly on his first day of school. He will probably continue to make grammatical mistakes for several years, particularly in such tricky areas as irregular verb forms and plurals: "choosed," "mouses," and "goed" are all typical errors at this age. But these kinds of mistakes show you just how much he's already learned. A child who says "teached" has learned how most verbs in English form the past tense. He will soon learn the exceptions, but for now it is enough that—thanks to the hours you've spent talking together—he has learned the rule.

STORYTELLING AND WHY IT MATTERS

Along with encouraging your child to talk, you have also been helping him learn to listen. One of the things children learn most from listening to is stories. Stories aren't found only in books, though some of the best ones may be. Stories are the way you reflect back on your day at bedtime, the memories you share from your childhood, the anecdotes you tell about funny moments, pets, or people. You may not think of yourself as much of a storyteller, but you're probably wrong: stories are among the most basic ways that people share experiences with one another.

Stories are important for early reading because they use language to impose a structure on experience. In telling each other about

LET'S STRETCH: EXTENDING YOUR CHILD'S LANGUAGE

Here's a step-by-step guide for using ordinary conversation to help stretch your child's language ability and vocabulary in a natural way:

❖ Encourage your child to talk to you
❖ Let his comments guide the conversation
❖ Accept what he says and show that you understand what he means
❖ Respond by modeling correct grammar—just using it yourself, not pointing out his errors—and expanding on his statements
❖ Introduce a new word or concept into the conversation
❖ Encourage your child to use the new word or concept
❖ Refer later to this new word or concept
❖ Note whether your child adopts the expanded descriptions or corrections in future conversations

Here's how this kind of conversation might go:

Child: My truck got breaked.
Parent: Yes, I see—it's broken. What happened to it?
Child: I want a new truck.
Parent: But this is such a sturdy yellow dump truck. It's just missing something. What's missing?
Child: The wheel.
Parent: Yes, the left rear wheel is missing. Let's see if we can find it. What kind of wheel are we looking for?
Child: A black wheel.
Parent: Right, it has a black tire on it. How big is the wheel?
Child: About this big. And it's fat and bumpy.
Parent: You're right, it has a thick rubber tire on it, with deep treads for traction. Let's go hunt for a wheel with a thick black tire about that big.
Child: Okay.
Parent: Okay. Up to your room to find a missing wheel! What kind of wheel are we looking for?
Child: A fat, black, tired one, about this big.
Parent: Right! The rubber on the tire is thick and bumpy.
Child: But I want a new truck . . .

events and our reactions to them, we intuitively establish a beginning, middle, and end to the story. We decide what information to include and what to leave out. We use detail to set a mood or reveal a character. We use turns of phrase ("Lo and behold . . .") that might not occur in ordinary conversation. We instinctively choose a tempo for our narrative and look for ways to hold our listeners' attention. All these devices distinguish the reality of the story from the reality of life as we live it, full of messy and undigested information. Listening to stories, children learn that language offers a way to step back from experience, frame it, and reflect on it.

Through stories, children also learn that language can forge connections across time and place. Stories deepen our own sense of what we have lived through, how it affects us, and who we are. By telling the shared stories of our cultures, we keep those cultures alive. By exploring the stories of other cultures, or other people's experience, we help children discover what is universal about themselves, as well as what is individual. And when we tell stories drawn from our own imaginations, we show our children how to tap into their own creative powers.

In all these ways, stories help tune a young child's ear to language and its possibilities. The world of stories is the gateway to the world of the written word. A child attuned to stories has developed habits of listening that will ease the transition to literature—and whet his appetite for the work of learning to read.

You can harness the power of stories without being a master storyteller (see the box "Cleo's Storytelling Secrets"). All that really matters is that you introduce your child to the

pleasures of narrative—to hearing what happened first, and then what, and how it all came out in the end. And you don't even have to make things up. You can retell a fairy tale or a familiar book in your own words; pass on the legends of your cultural heritage; reminisce about a childhood adventure, or tell the stories you heard from your grandmother about her own childhood. Try telling part of the story in dialogue, using different voices for different characters, or adorning the narrative with sound effects.

Encourage your child, too, to tell you stories. You can start by telling stories together. "Remember what happened at the park today?" you might ask, then take turns describing what happened. Or try starting with a "what-if?" You can have fun together inventing things that could have happened, or that might happen tomorrow, or that you hope never happen. Or give him some pictures and ask him to make up a story that goes with them.

When you're reading a book together, invite your child to reimagine the story by introducing a new character or coming up with a different ending. What if Snow White ended up at the Three Bears' house instead of the Seven Dwarves'? Did the Trickster Coyote ever meet the Big Bad Wolf? What if Abiyoyo took a bath? These kinds of questions help your child start thinking like a storyteller, paying attention to character and incident and how they intersect.

As children get older, they may start making up stories on their own. That's great, too. If your child gets stuck, ask a question like "Then what?" to get things moving again. Learning to tell a story in his own words—

CLEO'S STORYTELLING SECRETS

❖ If you don't have much practice at telling stories, don't worry. Remember that almost any story you tell your child will interest him, just because you're the one telling it.

❖ Can't think where to start? Tell a story from your childhood. Tell your child about the day he was born. Make up a story about the squirrel outside the window. Imagine what his favorite toys do when he's not in the room. If he's fascinated with spaceships, tell him what happened the day he rode a rocket. When imagination fails, start telling a fairy tale you already know and let it change if something funny or interesting occurs to you.

❖ Try using a few simple props: finger puppets, hand puppets, a stuffed animal or two. Or put on a silly hat to go with a silly voice.

❖ Find a photograph that appeals to you—a family snapshot, a scene from a travel magazine—and use it as the launching point for a story. Encourage your child, too, to find pictures he wants to hear stories about, and then engage him in making one up together.

even retelling a well-known story—helps him practice and eventually master the most basic techniques of literature. To help your child along, ask him to tell you "the beginning, middle, and end." This encourages him to distill the story down to its essence.

Beyond the sheer enjoyment it offers, telling stories is a way to imbue your child with a bone-deep sense of narrative structure and language. Literacy is not just about decoding the letters on the page. It's also about grasping the rich and various ways in which language distills and conveys meaning. Exposing your child to a range of storytelling styles and forms will deepen his grasp of this complex process.

READING ALOUD: GETTING INTO THE HABIT

In addition to telling stories, you will also want to make time for reading stories to your child. The single most important thing parents can do to prepare a preschooler for reading is to read to him. Just thirty minutes a day is enough to make a real difference. And it's never too soon to start! Reading to babies helps to forge connections in the brain that stimulate the development of language abilities. Children who have been read to since their earliest months do better in reading than do those who weren't—an advantage that persists all the way to high school. That's not to say that kids who start later don't do fine later on; most, of course, do. But the younger children are when they start seeing, touching (and even tasting!) books, the easier their transition to literacy is likely to be.

Beyond that, getting into the reading habit early is fun for parents, even those who initially feel self-conscious about reading aloud. As you may already have discovered, most young children love the sound of your voice and the coziness of cuddling in your lap with a book. Many parents find that the time they spend curled up together with a book is one of the calmest, most pleasant interactions they'll have with a busy preschooler all day. Reading time can become something both of you look forward to. You can also enlist older siblings, other relatives, or friends to take turns reading to your child.

Whoever is reading, don't be afraid to ham it up with silly voices, funny faces, and dramatic sound effects. Emphasizing reading as a source of pleasure, rather than as a skill, makes children more eager to read. Parents who are enthusiastic about books, and who share that love with their children, will help their children become more successful readers. It's worth finding books that you enjoy reading (again and again and again), so that your reading sessions will be not a chore, but a chance to have fun with your child.

If you're looking for suggestions of books that you and your child might enjoy at this stage, check out the list at the end of this chapter. But remember that you know your child best—some "classics" may not appeal to him at all, and some books no one else has ever heard of may become favorites in your house. Many preschoolers love nonfiction books about animals—dinosaurs, of course!—outer space, trains and trucks, or any other subject that captivates them. It's likely to be the pictures, not the words, that first draw them in, so feel free to dip in wherever your child shows an interest. In nonfiction books, unlike storybooks, you don't have to read the text in order from beginning to end.

Whatever kind of book you choose, go ahead and read books that you and your child enjoy, rather than feeling you have to force-feed him a diet of the "right" books. The right book is any book that gets read—and enjoyed. (See "Thirty Really Good Books for Pre-schoolers" at the end of this chapter.)

LETTERS, LETTERS EVERYWHERE: CREATING A "PRINT-RICH ENVIRONMENT"

If you've read about preschool development, you may have come across the phrase "print-rich environment." This is simply a way of describing a home or classroom that is full of print—not just books but signs, newspapers, magazines, cereal boxes, labels, maps, lists, charts, really anything you can think of that has words on it.

You don't have to spend a fortune on books to create a print-rich environment in your home. You can visit the library often, borrowing books and magazines for yourself as well as your child. For books you want to keep, library sales and used bookstores may offer some great bargains. If there's a particular magazine your child loves, try pooling a sub-scription with a friend—the kids won't notice if they're reading an issue a few weeks late.

But print isn't only found in books. Try putting up a few hand-printed labels in your child's room: *crayons*, *puzzles*, or *books* on shelves, perhaps, or *shirts* and *pants* on different drawers. Some parents even label the room: *door*, *window*, *bed*, etc.

Write your child's name in as many places

as you can think of, and tell him the names of the letters. Sew a label inside his jacket; paint a plate or mug with his name; put a nameplate on his bedroom door. The more he sees his name, the sooner he'll learn to recognize it. That's another good predictor of future read-ing success for preschoolers (see the box "Hey, Hey, Hey, What's Your Name?").

On BETWEEN THE LIONS, a series of music videos featuring hip-hop artist Makeba Mooncycle uses children's names to teach short vowel sounds. Is there a short vowel sound in your child's name? Can he think of other names that have the same sound in it, or that start with the same letter as his?

You can also use the world around you to get your child looking at and thinking about print. You might point out a stop sign when you're in a car, name the letters, and help your child guess what they say. On a bus or subway, you could show him a route map and explain how to use it. In the grocery store, look at labels with him. Read aloud signs that send a message you need to know: Wet Paint, Watch Your Step, or Closed on Mondays. Try pointing out license plates on the street, billboards, the print on your TV—anywhere you notice letters, point them out to your child. If he knows the first letter of his name, he might enjoy looking for words that start with that letter. Once he knows a few more letters, try playing "I Spy" to have him spot a familiar one. A little of this can go a long way toward sensitizing your child to the world of print and stimulating his curiosity about what all those letters are for.

Another important component of creating a

HEY, HEY, HEY, WHAT'S YOUR NAME?

Here are some tips and ideas for helping your child recognize and write his name.

❖ Write your child's name on his belongings, from his lunchbox to his boots, as well as books. Label the hook for his jacket, his chair at the table, and the door to his room. Write his name as you would in a sentence, with the first letter capitalized and the rest lowercase.

❖ Play a "name game" to reinforce the sounds and rhythms of your child's name. Say your child's name slowly, and clap the syllables: *Mi-a, Jon-a-than, Twy-la.* Then try some playful variations: *Mi-a My-a, Ti-a Ty-a; Jonathan, Jon-Jon, J-J-J; Twy-la, Sky-la, Smy-la, Smile.* See if your child can come up with a name variation he especially likes. Play similar games with the names of others in your family and in the books you read.

❖ Show your child how you print all the letters in his name, saying the letter names as you go. Explain how the letters you print stand for the sounds in the name: "*J* is the /j/ at the beginning, then *O* makes the /ah/ sound. Next comes *N* with the /nnn/ sound, and. . . ."

❖ Print his name on two 3 × 5 cards, then cut apart the letters on the second card. Help him arrange the letters to match the uncut card.

❖ Help him trace the letters with his finger in the sandbox or on a foggy window. It's fun to form them out of play dough or pipe cleaners or cooked spaghetti. Once he can form the letters nice and big, he can try practicing on paper with crayons, markers, or pencils.

print-rich environment is to give your child opportunities to see you reading. When children see their parents reading books for pleasure, they learn about one of the powers of print. But you can also demonstrate the many other ways we use print in our daily lives. It's all stuff you'd be doing anyway: look up a movie time in the newspaper; read a recipe as you bake cookies together; note a play date on the calendar; write grocery lists and phone messages and reminders to yourself. What makes a difference is to show your child, from time to time, what you're doing as you do it. Don't just scribble the grocery list, for example, but make your mental process visible: "Let's see, we need milk [write that down], orange juice [keep writing], bananas—*B, A.* . . ." You don't have to do this all the time, as that way lies madness, but just let it happen naturally once in a while. Of course, asking for additions to the list will make it even more interesting to him!

You may find, as your child gets a little older, that he asks to make a list of his own. That's great. Give him a piece of paper and a crayon or a marker, whatever he likes using—thicker implements are easiest for preschoolers' hands—and ask him to tell you what he's "writing" on his list. He may just be scribbling, but this activity is valuable nonetheless: it's the dawn of understanding that print carries meaning and that he can use writing to make meanings of his own.

GRASPING THE CONCEPT: CONCEPTS OF PRINT AND THE CONCEPT OF WORD

Reading aloud to your child also helps him grasp "concepts of print"—assumptions about books and reading that are often so obvious to adults that we forget to point them out to a child. For instance, most children are pretty quick to grasp that we hold books a certain way, that they have a front and a back, that in English we read from left to right and from top to bottom, and that the black marks on the page represent the words we're saying. But

On BETWEEN THE LIONS, parents Theo and Cleo host a "What's Cooking" show in which they read a recipe with almost as much gusto as they devour the results. They especially savor tasty vowel sounds and rare vocabulary words (the closer to raw the better). But when it comes to thorough cooking—well, lions will be lions.

occasionally a child—particularly one who hasn't been read to—may find all this confusing. The more often you read to your child, perhaps pointing to some of the words as you read and letting him turn the pages, the more easily he will grasp these concepts. By age four, most children who have been exposed to books will already have absorbed these concepts. If you wonder whether your child needs instruction, try asking him to show you how to read a book, to see if he needs any additional help. (See the box "Which Way Is Up?") You may be surprised at his answers!

Another simple—but not always obvious—concept that children need to grasp is the "concept of word," or the understanding that language is composed of individual words. Adults know without thinking that language is made up of words and that we combine words into sentences to convey what we're trying to say, and so do most children. But some chil-

WHICH WAY IS UP?

If you're wondering whether your child has mastered the concepts of print, you can ask him to show you how to read a book. Or you can play "Silly Reader" by deliberately doing everything wrong. Like this:

❖ Hold the book upside down. "Is this the right way? No? Show me!"

❖ Read a line from right to left, pointing with your finger. "Oh, that's backward? OK. Then which way do I go?"

❖ Look at the illustrations and say, "Red jacket, yellow sun, green grass—what? I'm reading the pictures—isn't that right? Oh, I'm supposed to read the *words*, not the pictures. What word would you like me to read?"

❖ Read backward, bottom to top, back to front— whatever it takes to make your child laugh and show you how to do it right.

The ucky Duck

by Ernestine Darling

dren, as they move from oral language to written language, have trouble making this leap. They may hear "Iwannaplay" as a single chunk of meaning, one steady stream of speech, and so the printed word *want* may be quite incomprehensible to them.

Clapping and chanting games can reinforce the idea of words. Challenge your child to clap in between the words of a nursery rhyme, or to take a step after each word in a sentence: "Let's . . . walk . . . to . . . the . . . corner." And point out interesting words, as individual words, when you hear them.

You can further underscore the concept of word by pointing out the white spaces between printed words—on street signs, magazine covers, or the pages of a book. Explain that the spaces separate the words from each other, and that each word carries its own meaning. Ask your child if he can think of some words, and offer a few suggestions—familiar nouns generally work best at first, but then you can expand the game to words that describe things we do, and introduce verbs. Try reading a sentence slowly and help him point to each word as you say it. Or count how many words a sentence contains. You can also try pointing to each word as you read, although some children find this annoying. If yours is one of them, you may want to drop it for the moment and try again next week or next month.

THE REASON FOR RHYMES: BUILDING PHONOLOGICAL AWARENESS

If you've ever recited a nursery rhyme, played "Pat-a-Cake," or sung a children's song, you've been preparing your child for reading—even if you didn't realize it at the time. Activities like these help strengthen your child's grasp of oral language, which goes hand in hand with learning to read. In particular, playing with rhyme and rhythm helps your child develop "phonological awareness," or the ability to hear and pay attention to the sounds and rhythms of speech (see the box "Into the Words: Phonological Awareness for Preschoolers"). This kind of play reinforces the concept of word and tunes your child's ear to differences and similarities in how words sound. (See the box "Two Kinds of Awareness.")

Nursery rhymes are an especially powerful tool. Children who are familiar with nursery rhymes when they enter kindergarten often have an easier time learning to read. This may be simply because children who know nursery rhymes have been read to more often than those who don't, but it is probably also because the rhymes themselves help children discover many common word patterns and notice how their sounds vary at the beginning (*down, crown; quick, stick*). The more familiar those patterns are to the ear, the more easily a child will recognize them when he encounters them in print.

Being able to hear rhymes—to know that *pat* rhymes with *cat* but not with *pack*—is an essential skill for learning to read, because it means that children are able to distinguish among sounds. This in turn will help them make the association between written letters and their sounds. Children who have trouble with rhyming in the preschool years will have more trouble than others later on in making this kind of association. Songs also use rhymes, so they're another good way to teach your child about the patterns of sound in English. Without turning into a jukebox, try to

INTO THE WORDS: PHONOLOGICAL AWARENESS FOR PRESCHOOLERS

To learn to read and write, children must shift their attention from the meaning of language to the appearance and sounds of words as objects in themselves. For instance, they will need to notice the features of words: their length, their similarities and differences, and their component sounds.

How does this happen? Experts suggest that it happens step by step—but only if children have guides to prompt and direct them. In other words, they must be taught.

Here's the order in which it's most helpful to guide children toward understanding the features of spoken words.

Rhyming   Young children vary greatly in their sensitivity to rhyme; some are "naturals," and others seem to have a tin ear. For all children, it's easier to identify rhyming words than it is to produce them. And children who hear lots of rhymes are more likely to learn the concept, particularly if they are asked to participate by filling in missing words and phrases.

Alliteration   Once children become adept at noting the ends of words (called *rimes,* which is easy to remember because this is the part that rhymes) they begin to get the idea that the beginnings of words (called *onsets)* can sound alike as well. Parents can help them focus on this feature by exaggerating the first sound, as in *sssun, sssandwich,* and *sssilly.*

Sentence segmenting   Next, after children have learned to focus on the structure of individual words, it's possible to help them focus on segmenting words in the stream of spoken sentences. You can show your child how to clap for each word, beginning with short sentences ("It . . . is . . . late") and building up to longer sentences ("We . . . will . . . all . . . have . . . soup . . . for . . . lunch").

Syllable blending and segmenting   The next step is to clap or tap the syllables in familiar words: *pop-corn, kin-der-gar-ten, com-pu-ter.* Then try the game of syllable deletion: "Say *popcorn* without the *corn.* Say *butterfly.* Say it again without the *butter.*" Next comes segmenting and blending the parts of a syllable: *sss-it; j-ump.* This leads into the more advanced area of phonological awareness known as phonemic awareness. For a step-by-step description of phonemic awareness, see the next chapter.

find as many opportunities to sing to your child as you can—and feel free to make up silly rhyming songs of your own, too. (If you really hate to sing, you can get tapes of children's songs, but remember that even the most tone-deaf parents sound great to their own kids. This might be your only chance in a lifetime to sing to a smiling audience!)

Games that combine rhyming with rhythmic clapping or movement, like "Pat-a-Cake" or "One Potato, Two Potato" further help to reinforce patterns of sound. They're especially great for squirmy or active preschoolers—a child who won't sit still through a whole story may happily stay on your lap through many rounds of "Trot, Trot to Boston," and he'll be learning something about language, too. For quieter moments, try fingerplays like "The Itsy-Bitsy Spider" or "Where Is Thumbkin?" that combine words with simple hand gestures. This kind of play gets your child's whole body involved in absorbing the sounds of speech, which may make it easier for very active children to pay attention and to connect the motion with the words that represent it.

By the time your child is four or so, he may start asking about rhymes and other sounds. Encourage him to play with you in exploring these questions. If he asks, "What rhymes with *cat*?" you could say, "Hmm, I can think of *mat* and *fat*. Can you think of any?" He may shout out, "*Rat!*" Then you could work together to tell a little story about a fat cat chasing a rat. (You could even write the story down on paper, one sentence per page, and have him illustrate it. This will show him how print helps you remember your ideas, share them, and enjoy them over and over.)

As your child gets more adept at rhyming, you could try a more advanced riddle game. "I'm thinking of a word that rhymes with *cat*. It's an animal that likes cheese." Or: "I'm thinking of a word that rhymes with *cat*. It starts with /m/." This can be a real puzzle for many preschoolers—if the answers don't

> The BETWEEN THE LIONS Web site (www.pbskids. org/lions) includes lots of songs from the series that preschoolers will particularly enjoy listening to—from short ones, like the Chicken Jane and Cliff Hanger theme songs, to longer ballads like "But Mama. . . ." The lyrics are printed out so that you can read the words and sing along.

come easily, provide them cheerfully and try again another day.

Most preschoolers love books with sound effects and repeated nonsense sounds. Some also enjoy tongue twisters—"She sells seashells by the seashore"—or knock-knock jokes with silly puns. But if your child gets bored or frustrated with a word game, drop it for now. These games may be more fun in the years ahead. And if a game isn't fun, what's the point?

NOW I KNOW MY ABCS

There's one more piece of the reading puzzle that your four-year-old is probably ready for, and that's the alphabet. It's worth noting that "learning the alphabet" actually consists of several distinct tasks. First, a child has to learn the names of all 26 letters. Next, he has to learn

TWO KINDS OF AWARENESS

Two terms that come up in discussing the development of reading-related abilities can sometimes cause confusion. These are "phonological awareness" and "phonemic awareness." Though, unfortunately, they're sometimes used interchangeably, they are two distinct concepts, and it's useful to preserve the distinction between them.

Phonological awareness includes a whole range of abilities that have to do with focusing on oral language. A child who is phonologically aware is able to pay attention to the rhythms and rhymes of spoken words apart from their meaning; he is able to treat a word *as* a word, to think of it as an object that can be played with, in addition to understanding what it means.

Being able to hear normally is an important requirement for this awareness, but the child must also be able to focus on the sounds he hears—for instance, to notice whether words have two syllables or three, whether they rhyme, or whether they start with the same sound. He may also be conscious of rhythmic patterns, such as the "beat" of a limerick or nursery rhyme.

Typically, this ability begins to emerge well before a child is ready to start exploring written language. Compared with phonemic awareness, this is a more general kind of awareness of the sounds of language.

Phonemic awareness is one important aspect of phonological awareness. A child who is phonemically aware understands that spoken words are made up of separate sounds, and he can break words into their component sounds, play with those sounds, and put sounds together to form words.

Most children begin to develop this ability spontaneously as they master other, less advanced phonological awareness skills. But the more complex aspects of phonemic awareness, such as segmenting and blending (breaking words into sounds, then combining those sounds back into words) usually require instruction—and this instruction is important, because phonemic awareness is strongly associated with future success in reading and spelling.

which name goes with which letter shape. This can be tricky—he will need to recognize the letter in different print styles (g or g) and, eventually, in cursive script as well as in print, and in its lowercase and uppercase forms (A or a or a). While uppercase letters are easier for very young eyes and hands to navigate, most early childhood educators now agree that lowercase letters should also be taught even in preschool, because that is the way letters look most often in books.

Once your child has all this sorted out, he has to learn what sounds each letter represents. That last task is the one that makes English so tricky, because many letters stand for a number of different sounds, and many sounds can be represented by more than one letter or a combination of letters. In fact, your child will need to spend much of the first few years of school mastering that information. (See the box "The Alphabet in Steps.")

For now, though, he's certainly ready to learn letter names. The easiest way to do that is to sing the ABC song, and sing it often. He can also start learning to match printed letters with their names. From there, he can probably move toward learning some of the sounds connected with letters, particularly the consonants, which are more consistent than vowels.

Alphabet books offer many wonderful opportunities for reviewing the alphabet and savoring its sounds. They come in a host of formats, and many feature the advanced vocabulary words you want your child to hear. From *A, You're Adorable* to *The Z Was Zapped,* there are bound to be some that will capture your child's fancy. (See "Thirty Really Good Books for Preschoolers" at the end of this chapter for details on these and other

alphabet books.) Keep the reading playful and let children enjoy the pictures, letter shapes, and sounds, as well as the discovery of new words.

Parents sometimes wonder whether they should use flash cards or other systematic ways of introducing this information to their

---

If your child is getting tired of the standard ABC song—or if you are!—check out the *Alphabet Song* on the BETWEEN THE LIONS Web site (www.pbskids.org/lions), in which each letter is linked to a familiar character or word.

---

children. It's really up to you. A patient, methodical child like Aliyah may love mastering the rules of all kinds of games. For her, sitting still and playing matching and sorting games with the cards can feel delightfully grown-up. For a lively child like Toni, flash cards can seem dull and repetitive, and insisting on using them may backfire. Try making alphabet pretzels for a more enjoyable—and equally valuable—experience.

In fact, playing with food offers terrific opportunities for learning letters: there's alphabet soup and pasta and cereal, of course, but you can also write letters in mustard on a hot dog, in whipped cream on a dessert, in berries on a plate, in chocolate chips on a cookie. Anything you can garnish, you can garnish with ABCs.

You can also draw letters almost anywhere. Use a stick in the dirt at the playground; spell out words with shells at the beach; use chalk on the sidewalk or a hose on the grass. Go ahead and use your finger on

THE ALPHABET IN STEPS

Learning about the alphabet is more complicated than you might think. Here are the ABCs of the ABCs, taken age by age.

Preschool
- Learn to sing the alphabet song
- Learn that the alphabet song is about the shapes we call letters
- Learn that each letter has a name, and see how many you can identify
- Recognize your name in print
- Learn the names of the letters used in your name
- Begin to write some of the letters in your name

Kindergarten
- Learn the names of all (or most of) the letters
- Learn to match uppercase and lowercase forms
- Learn to identify every letter, in different cases and styles
- Learn to write your name, with upper- and lowercase letters
- Learn how the letters in your name stand for the sounds in your name
- Begin to learn the common sounds that each letter represents, beginning with the consonants

First Grade
- Know all the letter names and their shapes, and be able to identify them quickly and fluently
- Learn the different sounds each letter can make, especially the short–long options for vowels
- Learn how to arrange words in alphabetical order
- Learn how to form upper- and lowercase letters correctly
- Distinguish easily between similar letters: *d* and *b*, *p* and *q*

Second Grade
- Learn when to use uppercase vs. lowercase letters
- Learn to write all letters quickly, consistently, and correctly
- Master correct letter formation so that handwriting is automatic and fast
- Learn the whole array of possible letter-sound matches

Third Grade
- Obtain fluent, fast knowledge of all letter-sound matches
- Learn the correct formation of upper- and lower-case letters in cursive
- Master correct cursive-letter formation so that handwriting is automatic and fast

that dusty windshield (especially if it's your own). Play with shaving cream or soap foam in the bathtub: draw letters on the tiles, or trace a letter in soap on your child's back, then have him guess which one it is. You can buy foam or plastic letters for the bathtub and use them as you would the magnetic ones on the fridge—to spell things, but also just to play around. And soap "crayons" are fun for writing letters, as well as for drawing pictures.

The simplest toys, too, can be more valuable than pricey electronic gadgets. Alphabet blocks and wooden puzzles are great, of course, but also think about alphabet cookie cutters for modeling clay or play dough, alphabet stencils for construction paper, alphabet beads for craft projects. You can also form letters out of ropes of play dough, cut them freehand out of paper, or cut printed letters out of newspaper headlines or junk mail, and then play with them with your child. Let him hold them, twist them around, look at them upside down and sideways and backwards, so that their shapes become as familiar as his own hands.

You can also begin to help your child play with writing. He'll probably be delighted to learn how to write his own name. Start by printing it for him in large letters. Let him trace over your letters to get a better feel for them, then let him practice copying the whole word. He can do the same thing with the names of other family members or simple words that interest him. You could encourage him to "write" a letter to Grandma, or Santa, or Little Red Riding Hood (though you may want to enclose a translation of the scribbles if you think any of the recipients will be confused). Keep washable markers, crayons, pencils, and paper in a spot where he can reach them, then encourage him to play with them at moments when he's looking for something to do. You can put up a small chalkboard in the kitchen for dinner menus and family reminders; your child can help "write" these.

If your child expresses an interest, show him the correct way to form the letters. (See the box "The Write Moves.") But don't push this if he resists—for a preschooler, what's more important than perfect form is to develop curiosity and enthusiasm about the special tools of reading and writing. Ideally, your preschooler will see writing, like reading, as one more way to play: something fun, interesting, and unpressured.

In fact, that's the key to the learning your child will do in this last year before he enters the more formal world of school. By offering him plenty of opportunities to explore the world of language and print, responding with enthusiasm to his questions and ideas, and accompanying him as far as he wants to go down the path toward literacy, you will have done more for him than all the flash cards in the world could ever do. And you will know, as you send him off to his first day of kindergarten, that you have done a great job.

THE WRITE MOVES

For some young children, it helps to chant these directional moves as they practice the strokes to form lowercase letters.

a around, up, and down
b down, up, and around
c around and stop
d around, way up, and down
e across, around, and stop
f curve, down, lift and cross
g around, way down and hook
h down, hump
i down, with a dot
j way down, hook, and a dot
k down, slant in, slant out
l down
m down, hump, hump
n down, hump
o around and close
p way down, up, and around
q around, way down, hook right
r down, up and over
s curve, slant, and curve
t down, lift and cross
u down, curve up, and down
v slant down, slant up
w slant down, slant up, slant down, slant up
x slant right, lift, slant across the other way
y slant right, lift and slant way down
z across, slant, and across

BUILDING BLOCKS: WHAT YOUR PRESCHOOLER NEEDS

Language and conversation
- ❖ Rich vocabulary
- ❖ "Let's pretend" play

Lots of experience with books and storytelling

Attention to the forms and functions of print all around

Attention to speech sounds
- ❖ Rhymes and alliteration
- ❖ Other word features: length, rhythm, syllables

Focus on alphabet letters and their sounds; the alphabet song

1 PRINT'S CHARMING   Use the flood of magazines and junk mail that comes into your house to help your child find letters, words, and pictures that can go together in his own creations. Cut out pictures from magazines and catalogs; glue them to cardboard if you want them to last longer. Help your child use them to make pictorial grocery lists, decorate a poster of his name with objects that start with the correct letters, or play matching and sorting games. ("This is a picture of a banana. Can you find another fruit?" "Can you find all the things that start with /b/?" "Can you put all the food pictures in one pile and the animal pictures in another?") Your child can put a few pictures into a sequence and then tell a story about them: "The boy walked out of the house and got on his bike. Then he rode to the beach." You can take dictation if he wants to save his story. Your child can also look through all kinds of printed material to find words and letters, cut them out, and play with them. He can match the letters to some of his pictures. You can also paste a large picture—a full-page ad, with words, is especially good—onto cardboard, then cut it into a simple jigsaw puzzle.

2 SCRIBBLE, SCRIBBLE   Help your child experiment in scribbling with lots of different inks, pencils, crayons, paints, and chalk on different kinds of paper, cardboard, and even cloth. You can encourage him to make scribbly patterns that use the strokes he'll later need for forming letters: straight lines, curves, and circles. When he's drawing, ask if he'd like to draw a story—as simple as three pictures, one for the beginning, middle, and end—and dictate it to a grown-up, who can write it down and help him create captions for the pictures. Ask him to draw a beautiful scene full of things he loves, and help him label it.

3 THE SIGHT OF MUSIC   Help your child come up with simple hand motions to accompany his favorite songs—and check out all the songs on the BETWEEN THE LIONS Web site (www.pbskids.org/lions) to learn a few more. Make a family songbook to help you remember your favorites—or keep an easy-to-read list of song titles near the bathtub, in the car, on the refrigerator. Practice the alphabet song while finding letters to match—you can clap when you sing a letter to signal that that's the one to find in a pile of letters cut out from magazines, or among the letter magnets on the fridge. Learn the sign language alphabet with your child and sign the letters as you sing them.

4 SIGNS OF THE TIMES   Take your child on a "word hunt" around your neighborhood. Look together for street signs, billboards, and other examples of print in your environment. Help your child find the letters of his name or other letters he knows; ask if he can find a single word on a sign. (Remind him that the white spaces separate one word from the next.) To reinforce his understanding of what words are, take turns looking for the shortest or the longest word you can find. Explain the purposes of different signs, and show him how some signs combine words, pictures, and symbols to make their point. Talk about what signs you'd like to have around your home: a stop sign at the bathroom door, perhaps, or SLOW at the kitchen counter where everyone comes running in? Go home and make some simple signs together—including, if you'd like, a few labels for each room and some of the objects in it.

5 NAME GAMES Find as many ways as you can think of to play with the sounds and letters of your child's name, because this is an important word to him and one he'll soon learn to recognize by sight. Help your child find the letters of his name in his collection of cutouts or letter magnets. Help him write each letter and hear the sound it makes in his name. Make up a short rhyming poem or song that includes your child's name, then sing it together. Spell out his name in a simple tune, a rhythmic chant, or a cheerleader's rallying cry: "Gimme a *K!* Gimme an *I!* Gimme an *M!* Whaddaya got? Kim!" (It's up to you whether to invest in pompoms and a mega-phone.)

6 RHYME TIME Incorporate rhymes and other simple forms of wordplay into your child's daily life. In addition to reading poems, reciting nursery rhymes, and singing songs together, make up rhymes of your own: think of a rhyme for the name of each family member, for the street you live on, for the name of your town. See how many versions of "Roses are red . . ." the two of you can come up with, or supply other simple opening lines and have your child complete the rhyme. Play with the beginning sounds of words, too: find words that begin with the same sounds, play around with a few simple tongue twisters (Peter Piper and his friends), or try a simple guessing game. "I see a pable . . . mable . . . fable . . . do you know what it is?" Stick to objects that are in your child's view for this one, and ask if he'd like to try making you guess, too.

7 TRY TO REMEMBER Memory games help your child focus on details, categorize information, and learn to think more systematically—all important prereading skills. Try Lotto, Bingo, or Concentration to help your child focus on finding, matching, and sorting similar items. Here's another simple memory game: Have your child look closely at you, then leave the room or have him close his eyes while you change one thing—put on a hat, take off glasses, button the top button of your shirt. Then have him tell you what's different. (Adjust the subtlety of the change according to your child's abilities.) Or play a game that hones listening-memory skills. "I'm going on a trip and taking a sweater," the first person says. "I'm going on a trip and taking a sweater and a teddy bear," says the next. Keep taking turns, repeating all the items and adding another, until one of you misses one. If this is too hard, try an alphabet version: "A is for alligator," says the first. "A is for alligator, B is for bear," says the next—all the way to zebra, if you can all get that far.

8 CRACKER STACKER   Get a pile of crackers, chips (poker or potato!), checkers, pennies, or other counters to use for a variety of games. Have your child add a counter to his stack every time he hears a word that rhymes with one you've chosen together, or a word that starts with a chosen sound. Or add a counter to the stack for each word in a sentence—a great way to help your preschooler start to grasp the concept of word. (Don't be surprised if it's hard for him at first.) You can also use your counters to play a home version of "Chicken Stacker," the sound game on the BETWEEN THE LIONS Web site (www.pbskids.org/lions). You pick a short-vowel sound with your child—"the /a/ in *pan*," say—then you say a series of short words that do or don't contain that sound. "Pan, fan, man, hot, cat, pen . . ." Your child puts a counter on the stack each time he hears the sound. He wins when he gets to five—or has to start over if he picks a word that doesn't have the sound.

9 TAKE A LETTER, MAMMA MIA   Cut letters out of sandpaper—make them nice and big, about three inches tall, so your child can play with them and feel their contours—and use them for a variety of activities, including the ones we suggest for letters cut out from magazines. Sandpaper letters are a classic tool from the Montessori method, and they're a wonderful way to help your child use his sense of touch to reinforce his visual learning about letter forms. You can also make touch-friendly letters out of foam sheets from the craft store, felt, play dough, or corrugated cardboard. Encourage your child to touch them, play with them, spell simple words like *cat* or *sun*, or sort them—put all the curvy letters in one pile, or separate upper- and lower-case letters. Letter stamps are a great tactile way to explore the alphabet, too.

10 JACK BE NIMBLE   A lot of activities that preschoolers enjoy are terrific for developing the fine motor skills and eye-hand coordination that they'll need for writing. Encourage your child to cut paper or thin cloth with child-friendly scissors, place beads on a string (or pasta shapes on a shoelace), play with blocks, and do simple jigsaw puzzles. Beginner's sewing is also great; you can buy "lacing" cards with holes punched in a simple design through which your child threads a string. Or make your own by punching a basic design—a letter, a boat, a flower—and giving your child a shoelace. Even pinching clothespins, if you have a few of the spring-loaded kind around, helps build the muscles your child will use for writing.

Thirty Really Good Books for Preschoolers

Five Rhyming Books

Janet and Allen Ahlberg, *Each Peach Pear Plum* (Penguin)

Nelly Palacio Jaramillo, *Grandmother's Nursery Rhymes* (Henry Holt)

Dr. Seuss, *Green Eggs and Ham* (Random House)

Dr. Seuss, *Hop on Pop* (Random House)

Shel Silverstein, *A Giraffe and a Half* (HarperCollins)

Five Books with Sound Effects

Wendy Cheyette Lewison, *Buzz Said the Bee* (Scholastic Hello Reader! series)

Bernard Most, *The Cow That Went Oink* (Red Wagon)

Phyllis Root, *One Duck Stuck* (Candlewick Press)

Linda Williams, *The Little Old Lady Who Was Not Afraid of Anything* (HarperTrophy)

Harriet Ziefert, *Who Said Moo* (Handprint Books)

Five Predictable or Pattern Books

David Ellwand, *Ten in the Bed* (Handprint Books)

Paul Galdone, *The Little Red Hen* (Houghton Mifflin)

Eric A. Kimmel, *The Gingerbread Man* (Holiday House)

Bill Martin, Jr., and Eric Carle, *Brown Bear, Brown Bear, What Do You See?* (Henry Holt)

Sue Williams, *I Went Walking* (Voyager Books)

Five Alphabet Books

Graeme Base, *Animalia* (Abrams Books for Young Readers)

Buddy Kaye, Fred Wise, Sidney Lippman, and Martha Alexander, *A, You're Adorable* (Candlewick Press)

Bill Martin, Jr., and John Archambault, *Chicka Chicka Boom Boom* (Aladdin Library)

Dr. Seuss, *Dr. Seuss's ABC* (Random House)

Chris Van Allsburg, *The Z Was Zapped* (Houghton Mifflin: Walter Lorraine Books)

Five Nonfiction, Informational, and Vocabulary-Building Books

Gail Gibbons, *Trains* (Holiday House), and others

Tana Hoban, *Is It Red? Is It Yellow? Is It Blue?* (Greenwillow)

Ann Morris, *Hats, Hats, Hats* (Mulberry Books), and others

Jerry Pallotta, *The Icky Bug Alphabet Book* (Charlesbridge Publishing), and others

Karen Wallace, *Duckling Days* (Dorling Kindersley: DK Readers), and other DK Reader books

Five Storybooks Featured on BETWEEN THE LIONS

Gail Herman, *The Lion and the Mouse* (Random House)

Ruth Krauss, *The Carrot Seed* (HarperFestival)

Lisa McCourt, *I Miss You, Stinky Face* (Troll Associates)

Rosetta Stone, *Because a Little Bug Went Ka-Choo!* (Random House)

Simms Taback, *Joseph Had a Little Overcoat* (Viking Children's Books)

Kindergarten Milestones

By the end of kindergarten, you can expect to see these signs of experimental literacy. A child who is progressing smoothly through this phase:

* Enjoys being read to
* Can retell simple stories, learning and using new words
* Knows the proper way to hold a book and understands how to follow the print on the page
* Recognizes that print contains a constant message—for instance, that the words of a written story do not change
* Can identify words that rhyme and suggest rhymes of her own
* Recognizes all 26 letters, in both upper- and lowercase forms, and can match most letters, especially consonants, to their sounds
* Can recognize some written words, particularly short or familiar ones (*cat*, STOP, *milk*, or EXIT)
* Prints letters and attempts to write some familiar words and messages, often with invented spelling

Warning Signs
By the middle of the year or so, you should look for help if your child:

* Cannot grasp the concept of rhyming
* Has trouble naming letters or identifying the beginning sounds of words
* Cannot consistently follow simple directions
* Appears to have any problems with seeing or hearing, which in any case should continue to be tested annually

Remember that children follow different paths to literacy. If you are concerned about your child's progress, consult his or her teacher. You can also ask your pediatrician for advice or referrals if you have concerns about your child's hearing, speech, or other developmental issues. In addition, your school district is required by federal law to identify and assist children who need help. At your request, your school will conduct an academic, psychological, and language assessment, at no cost to you. Consult the principal's office of your school, or see Chapter 8 for more information.

Chapter 4

Experimental Literacy: Reading and Writing for Kindergartners

The kindergarten year is an important transition for your child—and for you! And it's about a lot more than reading. As your child moves from the more relaxed setting of home or preschool into the more structured learning environment of school, she faces the challenge of learning how to learn in a classroom. Behaviors like raising her hand, participating in group activities, and paying attention become not just desirable but required. Some children have a much easier time making this adjustment than others. As she works her way through this transition, your child's feelings of enjoyment and accomplishment—learning to love learning—will lay the groundwork for her academic success.

For parents, too, this transition can be dif-

ficult. The mixture of relief and regret at leaving one's child at the classroom door varies from parent to parent. What is universal is the realization that from now on, much of our children's learning—both academic and experiential—will take place outside our own jurisdiction. On the plus side, this means that, as a parent, you can enlist the support of teachers who have experience with all kinds of five-year-olds, and who have a solid base of understanding how children learn. But it can also feel like a loss. By learning to work in partnership with your child's teacher, you can make sure that home and school reinforce each other, so that your new kindergartner feels confident in both environments. (For more on working with your child's teacher, see Chapter 1.)

This year is a time of transition in literacy skills, too. Your child is probably not yet reading—although a few children do begin to do so, even without formal instruction, as early as age three—but she is moving along the path toward becoming a reader. The point on the path where most kindergartners find themselves is sometimes called "experimental literacy." (Other terms used to describe a typical kindergartner's reading level include "early reading," "prereading," and "emergent reading.") We like the term "experimental literacy" because, as it implies, children at this stage are experimenting with print. They are starting to think about how to write messages and stories of their own, and they are beginning to understand how spoken sentences separate into words and words into sounds. They are developing ideas about how sounds connect with letters and then testing those ideas. Not all of their experiments will be successful, in the sense of producing accurate results, but one

way or another they tend to generate useful information! In short, experimental readers are starting to understand the mystery of print.

It's an exciting process to watch and be a part of. You might want to think of yourself as a kind of research associate for your kindergarten scientist as she conducts her experiments: available to answer questions about words, gently reinforcing her conclusions when they're on target and helping her rethink them when they're off base, but always letting her feel in control of the process of discovery. Your child will learn more about how reading works—and be more excited about learning it—if she has the support to start figuring it out on her own.

Besides, this is kindergarten, not first grade. Over the next couple of years, your child will be receiving plenty of specific, direct instruction in the mechanics and principles of reading. For now, it's fine for her reading experiments to be inventive and free-form. After all, much of the "work" of kindergarten still looks and feels a lot like play. What's important is that she have a sense that reading is exciting, important, and within her capability. You can extend that notion by viewing your child's experiments with reading and writing as a source of mutual pleasure.

As we mentioned in Chapter 1, a solid reading program will focus on five key areas of instruction: phonemic awareness, phonics, vocabulary, fluency, and comprehension, along with related instruction in writing. We'll look at these areas in greater detail in the chapters to come. Even in kindergarten, however, you may find it helpful to bear these distinct areas in mind as you track your child's progress. Especially important in the kindergarten year is the development of phonemic awareness, the crucial ability to recognize spoken words as a sequence of sounds (see the box "Two Kinds of Awareness" in Chapter 3).

As you'll see, the chapters of this book that deal with the higher grades are organized specifically with these five areas in mind. Things are a little looser in this chapter, because kindergarten is a little looser, too. We also haven't divided this discussion between what's going on at school and what's going on at home, because the kinds of concrete, hands-on learning a kindergartner does are very similar no matter where she is. It's also worth noting that the philosophy of kindergarten education is in transition in this country right now, and there is no single uniform curriculum or approach. Some programs are developmental and play-oriented; they see kindergarten as an extension of preschool, with a lot of play-based learning but little or no systematic, formal instruction. Other programs are more academically oriented and may begin to offer formal instruction like that not seen elsewhere until first grade. Depending on which kind of program your school follows, you may want to look at either the preschool chapter or the first-grade chapter to get a more rounded sense of the kinds of activities your child's kindergarten may be offering. And, as always, you may want to skip ahead or review a previous chapter, depending on where your child is in relation to the milestones here.

In this chapter, we'll look in detail at how children experiment with print, in both reading and writing. We'll take a closer look at the concept of phonemic awareness, and we'll talk about some things you can do to help your child increase her vocabulary (and why that's important). Finally, we'll discuss ways to help your child make connections between the books she reads and the world she lives in—connections that will deepen her motivation to read, hone her interpretive skills, and enrich her life.

EXPERIMENTING WITH READING

When your child picks up a favorite book and "reads" it to you, reciting the text from memory as she turns the pages, that's experimental reading. When she uses the pictures to guess what a nearby word means, that's experimental reading. When she looks at the first letter of a word and jumps to a conclusion about what it is, that's experimental reading. And when she drives you crazy by asking, "What's this word? What's this one? What's that one say?" that's experimental reading, too.

Children love to imitate adult behavior, as any parent who's bought a toy tool kit or tea set can attest. So it's no surprise that children who have seen their parents, siblings, or caregivers reading books often enjoy pretending to read. And, as with any kind of imitative play that kindergartners engage in, playing at reading is more than just pleasure. It's a way of developing mastery. Pretending to read deepens your child's connection to the world of print, and it gets her thinking about how books work. It also familiarizes her with the look of the particular words in the book she's holding. Gradually, she may get the idea that the words on the page always tell the same story.

You may notice, as your child moves through the kindergarten year, that she can recite more and more of her favorite books from memory. If so, it's a wonderful payoff for all the hours you may have spent reading the same book to her over and over again. You may be tempted to dismiss this kind of "reading" as cheating, because she's not really identifying and decoding the words. But this is an

On BETWEEN THE LIONS, you can feel how desperately four-year-old Leona wants to be a reader like her big brother, Lionel. The desire to imitate older siblings may be a particularly strong motivation for children at this age. If your child has older siblings, cousins, or friends who are already reading, you can encourage them to read with her and confidently assure your child that one day she'll be able to read, too.

important part of the learning process for your child, because it helps her feel confident and comfortable with books. It also helps her learn to recognize some words by sight and to make connections between some sounds and their spellings. Think of it as a warm-up exercise and confidence builder—it's like riding a bike with training wheels, which gives a child the feel of the ride and practice with pedaling, steering, and braking. When the training wheels come off, she'll need to integrate those skills and achieve balance at the same time—a new, more difficult and independent stage. In reading, that's the stage most children enter in first grade, when they are likely to do some wobbling and weaving and spill-taking before they glide off happily on their own.

You can give your kindergartner "training wheels" by continuing to surround her with lots of familiar and interesting books. (See "Thirty Really Good Books for Kindergartners" at the end of this chapter.) Stories with repetitive text are especially good at this age; every time a child chimes in, "You can't catch me, I'm the gingerbread man!" or shouts, "I *will not eat* green eggs and ham!" she's recognizing a familiar pattern. And because the same words appear in the same sequence several times on different pages, children are more likely to notice that this sequence of words on the page always accompanies the same sequence of words spoken aloud. Your child may even point to "green eggs and ham" as she says the words with you.

The same kind of story structure is easy to adapt to stories you tell your child. "When I was little, we used to . . ." you might begin each night, and then tell another episode (fancifully embroidered, if you like) from your childhood. Or you could create a character—a boy astronaut, a girl paleontologist, or some other combination of your child's current self and aspirations—who starts off in his spaceship or her Land Rover every night, then lives out a different but predictable adventure. On a rainy afternoon, you and your child could even draw pictures of this character and caption them with simple, repetitive text to reinforce your child's grasp of the words she's heard in the story.

You may also notice your child becoming more attuned to other forms of print, both predictable and otherwise, in the world around her: street signs, billboards, cereal boxes, newspaper headlines. She sees a word that begins with *M* above the door of the supermarket, for example, and shouts, "Market!" You can respond enthusiastically to your child's correct guesses and gently redirect her wrong ones, encouraging her excitement at the discovery that the world is full of messages—and that one day she, too, will be able to decipher them.

What's important at this stage is not that children read every word correctly but that they feel free to guess meanings with eagerness and confidence. If your child gets discouraged, remind her that it takes a while for kids to learn how to read. It's like putting together a puzzle piece by piece: some pieces are easier to put in place than others. If you notice that some letters or letter-sound correspondences are consistently tough for her—many children, for example, stumble over *b* vs. *d* or get confused by the way *c* can sometimes sound like /k/ (as in *cookie*) or /s/ (as in *cent*)—try looking for those letters in signs or books, and help her notice how they look and sound. The more that children are surrounded with different forms of print, the more chances they have to see words in different contexts and to absorb into their very bones the connections between print and sound.

EXPERIMENTING WITH WRITING

Just as your child imitates the adult practice of reading, she will also imitate the writing she sees. Even in the preschool years, she probably began making marks on paper and calling it "writing"—scribbling a grocery list alongside yours, drawing a circle or a few lines and telling you what it "said," marking dots on a napkin and calling it a map. As she moves through kindergarten, though, you are likely to see this behavior become more purposeful,

less random, and more recognizable as writing. She may already be writing her name; by the end of the year, most kindergartners will do so easily, and the result will look smoother and less awkward. By the end of the year, she will probably be able to write most, if not all, of the uppercase and lowercase letters without assistance, as well as the names of family members and friends and a few familiar words.

Encourage your kindergartner to practice handwriting at home, not just at school. (See the box "The Write Moves" in Chapter 3.) If she wants you to buy cookies and grapes, for instance, ask her to add them to your grocery list. If she is laying out a street pattern for her toy trucks, show her how to make a set of traffic signs: STOP, ONE WAY, NO PARKING. When she tells you a story about her day, encourage her to write it in a journal entry or a letter to her grandparents. By incorporating writing naturally into the flow of daily activities, you will help her see that writing is something she can use in every aspect of her life.

Children often begin by writing only the initial letter of the word they have in mind, or by writing a word they know and scribbling the rest. That's okay for now. Just as you responded to your child's early efforts to talk by answering enthusiastically, working to understand her, and only gently redirecting her toward more correct forms, so with these early attempts at writing you'll want to focus more on what she's trying to write than on how she's writing it. The desire to write, not the perfection of writing, is what counts.

Bear in mind that children use a lot of "invented spelling" at this stage—writing *pz*

MAMA HEMINGWAY: NURTURING A WRITER

If you are lucky enough to have a young child with a lively imagination and a story-teller's instincts, you may want to help nurture her writing talent by taking dictation, so she doesn't get frustrated by the task of writing. Here are some tips for taking dictation:

❖ Do try to print legibly, so that your child will be able to read the words as her reading ability develops
❖ Do record the exact words your child offers—no editing!
❖ Do offer prompts and encouragement as needed—but use a light touch and follow your child's lead
❖ Do read the finished creation to your child
❖ Do urge her to provide illustrations and artwork for the text
❖ Do date the composition and have the author sign her name. Add an "as told to" note with your own name
❖ Do express your delight in such creative activity
❖ Don't insist that your child copy over the sentences in her own writing. It will feel like drudgery
❖ Don't expect your child to be able to read the text you recorded. It's typical for children to be able to express far more complex thoughts than they can read at this stage

When your child's writing becomes more fluent, consider offering to serve as a "brainstorm buddy" or "human tape recorder" from time to time. You can help your child stretch her ideas and record them accurately by remembering long sentences and restating them phrase by phrase, as your child captures them on paper.

for *please*, for example, or *cot* for *caught*. Some of their inventions may be particularly hard for you to decipher. For instance, children sometimes write *y* for the /w/ sound or *h* for a long /a/ sound, because the letter names start with the sound they're trying to represent. Parents sometimes worry that if they permit invented spelling, their children will never learn to spell correctly, but this concern is misplaced. Children seem to understand, even from a young age, that there is a difference between the way they spell words and "real" spelling. Given proper instruction in first and second grade, they start to move toward spelling words the "real," or standard, way. And their mistakes in writing provide a valuable window on their learning—just as their earlier mistakes in spoken language revealed their efforts to master the rules of grammar. Even in kindergarten, they don't randomly choose a wrong letter but instead work hard to pick one that makes some kind of sense. (See the box "Invented Spelling: Speling Kownts!")

For now, invented spelling frees kindergartners from having to learn a whole set of individual spellings at the same time that they're learning that letters stand for predictable, specific sounds. That freedom also allows them to relax and to express their thoughts in writing, which means they're likely to write more. And, of course, the more they write and the more enthusiastically you support their efforts, the more fluent, confident, and motivated they become as writers.

Many of today's parents are surprised to learn that writing is a central component of learning to read. Most of us grew up in an era when reading and writing were seen as distinct

activities. We spent part of the school day looking at printed letters in books, and another part practicing our handwriting. To most of us, the two felt separate, no more connected than, say, addition and coloring. Today, reading and writing are seen as two parts of an interconnected whole, reinforcing and supporting each other. You might think of it as decoding and encoding. Children who are encouraged to write down stories that they have made up, for instance, are quicker to grasp the idea that they can use the same system of letters and sounds to read stories that other people have made up.

If handwriting is a struggle for your child, as it is for many whose fine motor skills are still developing, you can try a few different strategies to encourage her to compose her own thoughts without having to fight the pencil. You could suggest that she dictate a story to you, then read it back to her. (See the box "Mama Hemingway: Nurturing a Writer.") You could let her tap out a story on a computer, then print it out and read it together. She'll still need to work on her handwriting, of course, but these other techniques give her the freedom to discover the joys of composition without having to work on a tricky physical task at the same time.

There are lots of ways you can strengthen the connection between writing and reading. You could read your child a story, for example, and then have her write a new ending for it. Or have her draw a picture of her favorite character from a book, and then write a new story or poem about that character. She could even compose a fan letter! You can do the same kinds of things with nonfiction, too—for instance, after reading her a book about

WHY, OH, *W*, *H*, *Y*: THE HARDEST CONSONANTS TO LEARN

Besides those unruly vowels, there are also a few consonants that are known troublemakers. You can begin to see what the trouble is by looking at how young writers sometimes represent these sounds with letters. Here's an example:

I YNT A NU FEH

Now, let's translate—and note just *why* a beginner might make some choices that seem illogical to a skilled speller.

I YNT = I want

The letter *y* is a logical stand-in for *wa-*, because its name starts with that sound. A first-grade writer who includes both consonant sounds at the end of *want* is demonstrating a high level of phonemic awareness.

A NU = a new

The letter *u* is a smart choice to represent the vowel sound /oo/ because, in fact, the letter name contains the /oo/ sound. Again, this error shows good listening and phonemic awareness.

FEH = fish

This writer has tried to find a letter to represent the short *i* sound. The letter *e* is closer than any other alphabet letter, a sensible choice. (Say /ee/ and /ih/ several times and note how similar the mouth positions are for each.) And *h* is nearly correct for that /sh/ sound, because of its name. If you stretch out the ending sound (*aitchhhh*), you can hear the *shhh*.

By first grade, most children know the names of the letters and use them as an aid to spelling. Often this works pretty well, but a few of the names can lead a young speller astray—the sounds in their names are quite different from the sounds they make. That's why *h*, *w*, and *y* are the hardest consonants for beginners to learn.

INVENTED SPELLING: SPELING KOWNTS!

Children's attempts to find logical ways to spell unknown words are a beautiful thing—a window into their growing knowledge of our spelling system. Invented spellings tell us what children have learned so far and what we need to teach them next.

When your kindergartner asks you how to spell a word, you may want to encourage her to "give it a try" on her own. You'll see that spelling development usually progresses in stages:

1. **Preliterate** Makes no connection between symbol and sound
   - Uses scribbles or random symbols to mark the page
   - Arranges random letters or symbols in horizontal lines

2. **Letter Name** Uses the names of letters to represent sounds
   - In the early stages, a letter may stand for a whole word (for example, J = Jack; RUDF = are you deaf?)
   - Eventually the speller represents most sounds in words (KM = came; YT = wet [because *Y* begins with the /w/ sound]; LIK = like)
   - Uses letter names as stand-ins for vowel sounds (FDR = after; REH = reach)
   - Omits some consonant sounds within words, especially those that occur in tandem with other consonants (BOKN = broken; PAT = paint)
   - Usually writes from left to right

3. **Transitional** Represents every sound in a word by a letter or combination of letters
   - Uses plausible letters for consonant and vowel sounds (TRUK = truck; TUCH = touch; BUMPEE = bumpy)
   - Begins to note visual patterns and conventions (e.g., BOTE = boat; MASS = mess)

4. **Standard** Just like in the dictionary!

To guide your child through these stages from invention to convention, start by asking her to "think about which letters have the sounds" she hears in a word. The first sound is usually the easiest to hear. Later, you can encourage her to "listen for all the sounds." At this point, it may be helpful to *sss-t-rrr-ehhh-tch* the word out to help her hear all the sounds. Once your child is able to represent all the sounds in a word, she is ready for a nudge toward standard spelling.

insects, ask your child to draw up a list of her favorite bugs. Any of these tasks underscores the interactions among reading, writing, and meaning.

CONCEPTS OF PRINT AND THE CONCEPT OF WORD

Taken together, experiments with reading and writing generate most of children's learning about literacy during the kindergarten year. But there are also several specific tasks that kindergartners need to master, since these will serve as building blocks for the formal, systematic instruction that they will begin to encounter in first grade.

On BETWEEN THE LIONS, Lionel and Leona often pick up a pen to come to the rescue of their fellow characters. For instance, in "The Lucky Duck," Lionel provides an antidote to the duck's terminal cuteness by changing "Lucky" to "Yucky."

The first building block is one we described in the preschool chapter: mastery of the concepts of print. As we mentioned in that chapter, these principles are ones that adult readers may take for granted—so much so that they may forget to make them explicit to beginning readers. By the end of kindergarten, each child should be clear on the following concepts:

- ❖ We read text from left to right and from top to bottom, starting at the top left corner of each page
- ❖ We read books from front to back

- ❖ We read the text in books, not the pictures
- ❖ The text always carries the same meaning
- ❖ The text consists of letters and special marks used to punctuate the text: they tell us where to pause, stop, or ask a question. Some marks tell us who said what.

(For a fuller discussion of concepts of print, see Chapter 3.)

In addition, by the end of kindergarten, children need to know the names of all the letters and be able to recognize both their uppercase and lowercase forms. That's one reason that singing the alphabet song is particularly important this year. They should also grasp that we use lowercase letters most of the time and use uppercase letters for special reasons (to start a sentence or a name, or to show excitement, for instance).

They should also be starting to make connections between many of these letters and the sounds they make, though most kindergartners will not be able to complete this process for another year or two. That's partly because it takes a long time for them to be able to break the sounds of words apart in their heads (an oral language skill). And it's partly because the system of representing sounds in written English is so complex (see the box "Sound vs. Symbol").

As for the concept of word, or the understanding that language is made up of individual words, looking closely at your child's invented spelling may give you clues about her development of this understanding. If she writes, "We ganu the stor," for instance, you can gently slow it down and say "we are going to," then show her how the phrase is spelled. It may also help if you point to each word as you

SOUND VS. SYMBOL

One reason it's so hard to learn to read English (as opposed to a language like Spanish) is that English has many more sounds (phonemes) than we do letters. As a result, many of our letters represent more than one sound.

❖ The letter *a*, by itself, can stand for eight different sounds in English. Try this sentence: "All was lost as many hares raced around the village swamp."

❖ Because the roots of English come from different languages, we also have many sounds that can be spelled in more than one way—*f* and *ph* for /f/, say—and many words that sound alike but are spelled differently.

❖ Our vowel sounds, in particular, are a thicket of confusion. We have about 19 different vowel sounds (depending on who's counting and where y'all live) and only five letters to spell them with (A, E, I, O, U). So we have to combine the vowels and add some switch-hitting consonants (*y, gh*) to get the job done.

❖ Take a look at the long *a* sound and the many ways to spell it: in *eight, bait, hate, may, obey, ballet,* and *great*. And it gets worse: Every single one of those spellings can also be pronounced a different way, as in *height, chai, paté, cay, key, pallet,* and *read*.

No wonder it takes children two to three years of solid study to match sounds to letters!

say it. This is called "tracking print," and teachers often do it to help children follow along as they read and to reinforce the child's recognition of each word as a separate entity.

None of these concepts should pose any lasting difficulty for your child. If you have the chance to introduce them casually now, it may help your child stay on target when more formal reading instruction begins. If she seems to have trouble following along as you track print with her, you might want to consult with her

teacher. Down the road, it will be important for her to be able to follow along accurately in order to participate in more formal instruction.

PHONEMIC AWARENESS: THE SOUNDS OF SPEECH

The single most important ability for your child to develop this year is phonemic awareness. This is the ability to recognize the spoken word as a sequence of discrete sounds (see the box "Into the Words: What is Phonemic Awareness?"). A "phoneme" is the smallest unit of sound, so these are the units a child should be able to hear in sequence. The word *sun*, for example, contains three phonemes, or sounds: /s/, /u/, and /n/. A child who has developed phonemic awareness will be able to break the word down into these three separate sounds, to blend them again into a word, and to recognize the word as *sun*.

Although phonemic awareness is an oral-language skill, not a written one, it is one of the best and most reliable indicators of whether a child will have difficulty in learning to read. That's because reading is not just a visual system; it's a visible representation of sound. Writers make marks on paper that represent, to them and to their readers, the sounds of the words they have in mind as they write. If a child has trouble breaking words down into sounds or combining sounds into words, she will stumble when she tries to translate those marks into the sounds and meanings of spoken language.

In first and second grade, your child will receive an orderly program of instruction in the system of letter-sound correspondences that makes up written English. But if she goes into first grade without having learned to pay attention to the distinct sounds that make up spoken language, this system will be of little use to her. It would be like having a map of a city she's never seen. The central task of the kindergarten year is to make sure that your child knows her way around the city of sound—that she knows what words sound like, how they can be broken down into their component sounds, and how those parts can be recombined to make new words. That way,

when she gets the map, she'll understand what it's for and where it can help her go.

There are two specific skills, "segmenting" and "blending," that are particularly important aspects of phonemic awareness. Those two processes—of breaking words down into sounds, or segmenting, and of combining sounds into words, or blending—are essential skills for children to develop as they are learning to read. Blending is easier than segmenting, so your kindergartner will probably do a better job of putting sounds together than of taking words apart. But it's not too soon to help your child start developing the ability to stretch words out by saying them slowly enough to hear their component sounds. If she starts now, she'll have plenty of time to develop and practice this skill.

A wonderful way to enhance your child's phonemic awareness is to sing lots of songs with her—something that kindergartners may love more than children of any other age, and something that will really help them learn this year. Songs help children develop a sense of story structure, as well as a feel for rhythm and rhyme—especially when you encourage them to move along with the music. You can also reinforce your child's grasp of the concepts of print by encouraging her to follow along with the printed lyrics as she sings the words. Music

The Between the Lions Web site (www.pbskids.org/lions) features several songs that are particularly fun for kindergartners. Check out "Dance in Smarty Pants," "Grubby Pup," "Rocket-Doodle-Doo," "Sloppy Pop," and "We Choose to Cha Cha Cha."

INTO THE WORDS: WHAT IS PHONEMIC AWARENESS?

Phonemic awareness involves the ability to hear, segment, and manipulate the individual sounds in spoken words. Although it need not involve letters or print, it is the foundation on which reading and spelling are based. A child's level of phonemic awareness is a strong predictor of reading and spelling success.

In kindergarten, your child will gradually be moving beyond the preliminary tasks of phonological awareness (see Chapter 3) to the more sophisticated challenges of phonemic awareness. These fall into two general categories:

❖ **Onset-rime blending**   Once children have experience with rhyme and alliteration, they can start mixing and matching the beginnings and ends of words—just the beginning and ending parts, without stretching each separate sound of the word. Try saying, "Guess what number I'm saying: fff . . . ive; sss . . . ix. Guess what color I'm thinking of: p . . . ink; rrr . . . ed."

❖ **Phoneme segmentation and blending**   Children can begin manipulating the sounds within words by focusing on separate sounds in sequence. For instance, try saying, "Guess my number: thhh . . . rrrr . . . eee; sss . . . eh . . . vvv . . . uh . . . nnn. Now, you try to say a number a little at a time: Say two (t . . . ooo); say ten (t . . . eh . . . nnn)." Some sounds are easier to stretch than others—sounds like /b/ and /t/ are impossible to say without adding "uh" or "ih" ("buh," "tih").

also makes it easier to remember things; that's one reason we teach children to sing the alphabet instead of just reciting it. And it's why so many of the phonics lessons on BETWEEN THE LIONS come wrapped in a tempting package of rhythm and melody.

There are plenty of specific activities to help build phonemic awareness, and you'll find some listed at the end of this chapter. More generally, there are lots of ways to incorporate into everyday life a sensitivity to the sounds of speech. Some of these may feel more natural to you than others. As you write a note to yourself, for instance, you could draw out the sound of the words you are writing. If you sing a song or recite a poem, you could accent the rhyming words more heavily than usual, or pause to point them out. (Words that rhyme begin with different sounds but end with the same ones, so hearing rhymes is a great way to emphasize the phonemes in words.) When your child asks about a word on a passing sign, you might say, "Street, that sounds like feet, or beat . . ." and encourage her to suggest her own rhyme. Presto—you've just given a mini-tutorial on the phonemes /ee/ and /t/.

Experts recommend screening for phonemic awareness in the middle of the kindergarten year to identify children who may be at risk for reading difficulty (see the box "Screening for Phonemic Awareness"). If your child's school does not routinely screen kindergartners for phonemic awareness, you may want to ask your child's teacher or an administrator to consider it. You will certainly want to make sure that your child's teacher understands the importance of this ability and is working to help your child develop it. You can talk with the teacher about your child's development in this important area, and you can also ask for advice in helping your child improve. And, if you have persistent concerns that your child is not making smooth progress, you can ask that the school arrange a formal screening for her.

VOCABULARY BUILDING: WORDS, WORDS, WORDS

There's one other specific area that you can help your child work on this year, and it's something that will make a real difference in how well she reads in later years. Generally speaking, the larger a child's vocabulary, the better a reader she will be. This may be partly because children who know a lot of words have probably been read to more than children who know fewer words. But it's also likely that a large vocabu-

lary has a value of its own. The more words a child knows, the more words she will be able to recognize when she sees them in print. As she sounds out a word, she will try to identify it by reaching into the pool of words she knows, and the more words there are in the pool, the more likely she will be to catch this one.

The BETWEEN THE LIONS Web site (www.pbskids.org/lions) offers vocabulary-building tips under the feature "Literacy Tips for the 10-Minute Parent." Children may enjoy games like "Word Play," where they can click on a word and watch it act out its meaning.

Your child's kindergarten will probably offer lots of opportunities to expand vocabulary: thematic study, hands-on experiences, and role-playing. Exploring a theme like space, animals, or weather leads children to learn specialized words (*rocket*, *polar bear*, *tornado*). Activity centers equipped with manipulatives, water play, art supplies, writing materials, or dress-up costumes and props give rise to expressive language: *squishy*, *soaked*, *sparkling*, *crinkly*, *elegant*. This kind of play not only spurs children to acquire words but also provides memorable experiences that make it easier for them to retain the meaning of the words they hear.

One of the simplest ways to develop your child's vocabulary is just to keep on reading to her. Explore books with a range of styles, formats, and subjects, noting and savoring the juicy words you encounter. Nonfiction books on topics that interest your child can be a particularly rich source of new words; any parent who's

SCREENING FOR PHONEMIC AWARENESS

If you're curious about your child's level of phonemic awareness, you can invite her to play with sounds and see how she responds. For instance, you can segment a word (stretch it out) and see if she can blend the sounds together. Try starting the conversation like this:

"I'm going to say some words to you, a little bit at a time. See if you can tell me what the word will be when you put it all together."

"Here's the first one: *sss . . . eee.*"

"That's right! The word is *see*. Now, try *g . . . o*
    sss . . . it
    h . . . op."

"Watch out, here's a harder one: *sss . . . uh . . . nnn*
    fff . . . ih . . . shhh
    nnn . . . oh . . . zzz
    sss . . . t . . . ih . . . ck
    lll . . . a . . . sss . . . t."

If your child is able to do this blending task, suggest that you change jobs:

"Now I'll say the put-together word, and you try to say it a little bit at a time.
    so   *(s . . . o)*
    fish   *(f . . . ih . . . sh)*
    good *(g . . . oo . . . d)*
    ten   *(t . . . eh . . . n)*
    stop   *(s . . . t . . . ah . . . p).*"

If your child is able to do these blending and segmenting tasks—celebrate! Most children in kindergarten will find them challenging. They will probably say the first sound separately and then the whole rest of the word, without stretching out all the sounds. It may help to move an object (a penny, token, or small square of paper) as you say each sound slowly, then let your child take a turn doing the same. This "say it and move it" routine can help her keep track of each sound, one by one.

If your child is confused by these tasks, she may need more experience with rhyming, alliteration, sentence segmenting, and syllable manipulation before her ears are attuned to this kind of challenge.

heard a young dinosaur fan discuss the finer points of pteranodons and pterodactyls knows that children quickly soak up every detail of a subject they care about, along with the vocabulary to talk about it. Exposure to a wide range of styles and subjects is another reason to make frequent visits to the library, where the shelves hold far more varied books than any home ever could. More variety means more vocabulary, and more vocabulary means better comprehension.

You can also use conversations with your child as a natural way to introduce new words. If the topic is something she's interested in, there's no reason to shy away from using sophisticated or technical words. Try using words she may not know in a context that makes the meaning clear. You can provide a definition if she seems to need one. This sounds forced but comes easily once you start doing it. If your child asks, for example, why some trees lose their leaves and others don't, you could work words like *deciduous* and *coniferous* into your answer, along with more familiar ones like *autumn* and *pine cone*. It's great to encourage your child to ask questions about words, too. Learning new words is a pleasure for both of you: as your child learns to express herself more precisely, you get a better understanding of how her mind works.

CONNECTING PRINT TO LIFE

All these skills are important in laying the foundation for your child's life as a reader. But there's one more thing you can do for your child, and it's something so basic that literate parents sometimes take it for granted. We adults know intuitively that reading is an

important part of our daily lives. But children may not make that connection unless you point it out to them. If their only interaction with print is in a bedtime story, they may not see the many other ways in which reading makes a difference in their lives.

You can make the connections between print and life explicit by pointing out all the ways you use reading:

"Do you want to make cookies? Okay, let's find the cookbook and read the recipe."

"I forget what kind of batteries this toy takes. Let's see what's written on the bottom here."

"Oh, good, Daddy left me a note about the plumber. Now we know when we can go to the park."

On BETWEEN THE LIONS, the Lion parents often choose a book that relates to a current concern of one or both cubs. Theo reads *Earl's Too Cool for Me* to Lionel to help him overcome shyness; Cleo reads *I Miss You, Stinky Face* to help Leona prepare for Cleo's absence.

Beyond such obvious, practical applications of reading, you can also help your child see the ways in which reading enriches her understanding of the world. If you've been reading a book about birds, you can point out the sparrow outside your window and talk about how it is or isn't like the ones in the book. If a story has a castle in it, you can talk about all the different kinds of places where people live, and you can draw pictures together of what your "castle," or perfect home, would include. If your child asks a question that stumps you, you can say, "I don't know. Let's go look it up." The idea in all this is to help your child see that books and reality are connected, and that learning about one will help her learn about the other.

This is true in more than practical terms. Encyclopedias are a great source of wisdom, but so are novels. It's easy to focus exclusively, when you're thinking about helping a child dive into reading, on the details of technique and skill.

But it's important to keep the larger picture in mind, too, and remember not just what reading is, but what it is for. If you encourage your child to turn to books whenever she is curious, and to seek out in the world the things she's read about in books, you will help her discover a source of wisdom, comfort, and stimulation that will serve her well throughout her life.

BUILDING BLOCKS: WHAT YOUR KINDERGARTNER NEEDS

Language and conversation
- ❖ Lots of new words
- ❖ Talk about books and stories and their connection to real life
- ❖ Chances to reimagine or rewrite stories, perhaps dictating them to you

Lots of experience with books and storytelling
- ❖ Chances to hold, examine, and play with books
- ❖ Repetitive or predictable texts
- ❖ Varied genres to build vocabulary

Print everywhere, along with the time and encouragement to figure out its meaning

Attention to speech sounds
- ❖ Rhymes and games to build awareness of sounds
- ❖ Simple practice in segmenting and blending sounds
- ❖ Familiarity with rhyming texts and songbooks
- ❖ Screening for phonemic awareness, and remediation if necessary

Focus on alphabet letters and forms
- ❖ The alphabet song
- ❖ Chances to practice forming letters
- ❖ Encouragement to express thoughts in writing, using invented spelling, and to play with writing in other ways

1 BETWEEN THE COVERS   After reading a book with your child—or even in the middle of a story—go "between the covers," as Cleo does on BETWEEN THE LIONS, and take on the role of an intrepid reporter interviewing a character in the story, played by your child. Ask her to retell the story so far. Pose a few questions about who the other characters are and how your child's character feels about them. Ask why events in the story happened the way they did, and what she thinks will happen next.

2 DEAR DIARY   When you and your child watch BETWEEN THE LIONS, have her create a "view-and-do book" that you can work on together. She can draw pictures and, perhaps, write some of the words presented in an episode; to help with this, you could write down the words for her to copy. She could also dictate a "review" to you, summarize the story and what she thought of it, or tell how she'd have done it differently. You can make this an ongoing viewing log, with each installment dated, illustrated, and labeled. And, of course, you can adapt this idea to other series and to other experiences. Just have your child make observations and then dictate a report to you. As she gets older, she'll move naturally into keeping her journals herself.

3 POETRY WALK   To help your child distinguish individual words, choose a simple nursery rhyme or poem. Ask your child to take a step for each word. Or you can take turns, stepping word by word, and see who's ahead at the end. See if your child notices a pattern that correlates to the rhythm of the poem. For a bigger challenge, see if she can take a step for each syllable in a word. See who can find a word with the most syllables.

4 NAME GAMES REVISITED   Kindergartners love to read their names, and it's a great way to reinforce letter recognition. So help your child create all kinds of posters, banners, and labels that use her name. Draw and paint and write her name; use different fonts on the computer; use stamps and stencils and cutouts. Have her collect pictures of objects that begin with each letter in her name, then make a special "name book" featuring a favorite picture or two for every letter. Help her think of simple words that start with each letter, then print the words and have her see what new words she can make with the letters of each one. You can also make place cards for everyone at a family dinner, or create signs and labels with each person's name to identify his or her belongings and rooms: "Mama's book," "Miguel's room," "Ayesha's coat hook."

5 WORD GATHERING   On outings, pick a category and collect as many words as you can find to fit it. You might try flower names in the florist's booth at the supermarket, fish at the pet store, birds at the park, or vehicles at the garage. When you get home, help your child write the words in a "New Word Book" and draw pictures to accompany each one, to help her remember it.

6 STATES AND PLATES When you're driving—or stuck in traffic—look at license plates together. Talk about the names of the different states, where each state is, how far away it is from where you live, and who might live there that your child knows. Look at the other words on a plate—slogans, county names, and months—and talk about what they mean and why they're there. Look at the license number itself and play word games with the letters: make a sentence that has a word starting with each one, think of words and rhymes, scramble the letters and see if you can make a word. Or have a contest to find every letter of the alphabet, in order. (You may want to include road signs in that one to speed things along.)

7 "I SPY"—NEW AND IMPROVED! This classic children's game is a great way to develop phonemic awareness. And you can play it anywhere. Try playing the game with rhyming clues: "I spy something that rhymes with *cat*." (For an added twist, have children provide the answer in the form of a definition: "Is it a little animal that likes cheese? Or something you wear on your head?") Another way to play is to say the initial sound of a word (not the letter name): "I spy something that starts with /s/" or "/f/." Or challenge your child to put words together: "For dinner we're having something that starts with /s/ and ends with /oop/. What is it?"

8 GAWAIN'S WORD You can make your own version of the BETWEEN THE LIONS game "Gawain's Word" using index cards and Popsicle sticks. With a large marker, write an assortment of beginning sounds for common words on index cards. (Try single consonants—*b, s, m, r*—as well as blends—*bl, qu, sn, st*.) Set aside that pile, and make another pile of index cards with ending sounds. Good examples might be simple endings, like *ing; ick, ack, uck, ock; ap, op,* or *ip.* Glue or tape the cards to the Popsicle sticks. To play, one player chooses a beginning card and the other chooses a card from the endings pile. Be sure the two combine to make a meaningful word. Standing a few feet apart, the players take turns saying the sounds on their cards. Then they move toward each other, each repeating her own sound, until they meet in the middle. (Some crashing sounds add to the fun.) Together they can blend their sounds to say the word they've made. Don't forget to act out its meaning! As an extension of the blending skills used in "Gawain's Word," you can help your child make a "word family" flower. Write the ending part of a word in the center of a large paper circle, then write appropriate word beginnings in paper ovals and attach them all around the edge to make a flower. Here's one to get you started: *op* in the middle of the flower, with *p, t, b, h, st, dr, sh, fl* (and any others you can think of) all around. You can extend this even further by illustrating the words or putting them together into a story.

9 BODY LANGUAGE   To help develop letter recognition, have your child form letter shapes with her body. This is a particularly good game for active children, especially if you have them jump as quickly as possible from one letter to the next. They can either go straight through the alphabet, or wait for you to yell out a letter, then jump into formation. (Play "YMCA" for them if you get tired of supplying the sound track yourself!)

10 MY VERY OWN ABCS   Kindergarten is the perfect time to help your child make her own alphabet book. She can use pictures cut out from magazines to illustrate each letter, or draw her own. Help her jazz things up with glitter pens, fancy paper, feathers and sequins, stencils, stamps—whatever gets her excited about playing with those letters, putting them in order, and making them her own.

Thirty Really Good Books for Kindergartners

Five Good Read-Alouds for Extending Phonemic Awareness

Laura McGee Kvasnosky, *See You Later, Alligator* (Red Wagon)

Alice Lyne, *A, My Name Is . . .* (Charlesbridge Publishing)

Alvin Schwartz, *Busy Buzzing Bumblebees* (HarperCollins)

Dr. Seuss, *There's a Wocket in My Pocket* (Random House)

Nancy Shaw, *Sheep in a Jeep* (Houghton Mifflin)

Five Predictable Books for Repeated Reading

Donald Crews, *Ten Black Dots* (Scott Foresman)

Marc Gave, *Monkey See, Monkey Do* (Cartwheel Books)

Gail Herman, *There Is a Town* (Random House)

Uri Shulevitz, *One Monday Morning* (Farrar, Straus & Giroux)

Brian Wildsmith, *All Fall Down* (HarperCollins)

Five Good Read-Togethers Based on Songs

Mary Ann Hoberman, *Miss Mary Mack* (Little, Brown), and others

Thacher Hurd, *Mama Don't Allow* (HarperTrophy)

Cynthia Jabar, *Shimmy Shake Earthquake: Don't Forget to Dance Poems* (Joy Street Books)

Tom Paxton, *Going to the Zoo* (William Morrow)

Nadine Bernard Wescott, *Down by the Bay* (Crown Publishing), and others

Ten Good Read-Alouds for Building Vocabulary

Alma Flor Ada, *Dear Peter Rabbit* (Aladdin Library)

Joanna Cole, *The Magic School Bus* series (Scholastic)

Ruth Stiles Gannett, *My Father's Dragon* (Random House)

Mary Hoffman, *Amazing Grace* (Scott Foresman)

Peggy Parish, *Amelia Bedelia* (HarperCollins)

Francine Prose, *You Never Know: A Legend of the Lamed-Vavniks* (Greenwillow)

H. A. Rey, *Curious George* (Houghton Mifflin)

William Steig, *Dr. De Soto* (Sunburst)

John Steptoe, *Mufaro's Beautiful Daughters: An African Tale* (Lothrop, Lee & Shepard)

Kay Thompson, *Eloise* (Simon & Schuster)

Five Storybooks Featured on BETWEEN THE LIONS for Reading Aloud

Mary Finch, *The Three Billy Goats Gruff* (Barefoot Books)

Chris Raschka, *Charlie Parker Played Be Bop* (Orchard Books)

Pete Seeger, *Abiyoyo* (Simon & Schuster)

Esphyr Slobodkina, *Caps for Sale* (HarperTrophy)

William Steig, *Sylvester and the Magic Pebble* (Aladdin Library)

First-Grade Milestones

By the end of first grade, you can expect to see these signs of independent literacy. A child who is progressing smoothly through this phase:

❖ Can read grade-level books aloud, with reasonable accuracy and some expression
❖ Recognizes an increasing number of words by sight, without needing to sound them out
❖ Tries to sound out unfamiliar written words, one letter or combination of two or three letters at a time
❖ Can break a spoken word into its sounds and tries to represent all of those sounds in writing, though not always with correct spelling
❖ Knows a variety of strategies for figuring out words and meaning
❖ Can write several sentences about a topic that interests him and may try to use punctuation and capitalization

Warning Signs
You should look for help if your child:

❖ Is not reading at all by the middle of the school year
❖ Has great difficulty making connections between letters and their sounds or is unable to identify rhyming words
❖ Is unable to spell grade-level, predictably spelled words—such as *map, hit, jump*—with reasonable accuracy
❖ Has difficulty writing and forming letters in a conventional way
❖ Often struggles with following directions or paying attention
❖ Seems to have any persistent trouble with seeing or hearing, which in any case should continue to be tested annually

Remember that children follow different paths to literacy. If you are concerned about your child's progress, consult his or her teacher. You can also ask your pediatrician for advice or referrals if you have concerns about your child's hearing, speech, or other developmental issues. In addition, your school district is required by federal law to identify and assist children who need help. At your request, your school will conduct an academic, psychological, and language assessment, at no cost to you. Consult the principal's office of your school, or see Chapter 8 for more information.

Chapter 5

Independent Literacy: Reading and Writing for First-Graders

This is it: the year when your child will, most likely, learn to read on his own. Though the ability to read develops along a continuum, with many small and gradual steps along the way, this is often the time when children really start putting everything together and making sense of written texts. A new reader's breakthroughs come in many different forms. One day, your child may read a newspaper headline over your shoulder or call out the name of your town from a highway sign. He may ask a question that makes you realize he has read something silently. Or he may doggedly, and perhaps a bit unevenly, work his way through his first book on his own. No matter what that moment of reading looks like, it's a thrill for parent and child alike. That's why first grade is exciting: up until now, children have been gathering the building blocks of literacy, laying the foundation for their lives as readers. Now, the foundation is in place, and they can start to frame the "building" itself.

First grade can be a scary time for children and parents, because it's not always clear just how—or when—a child is going to make the leap from experimental reading to accurate reading. It may be reassuring to know that children have many ways of becoming readers. For some children, progress is slow and measured. They gradually master each part of the reading process, methodically putting together their knowledge of how print represents language, until they are ready to tackle a book on their own. For others, learning to read really does look like a sudden and mysterious leap; one day they're just playing around with sounds or saying the words they know by heart, and the next day, somehow, they're reading. For still others, some parts of the reading puzzle may come together without much apparent effort, while other skills or concepts require lots of review and practice.

If you have a tendency to worry, you may find it reassuring to keep this wide range of variation in mind and remember that most kids do fine. You may also find it helpful to know what typical first-grade reading might look and sound like. A child like Joaquin, who did a lot of "pretend" or experimental reading in kindergarten, still shows traces of this practice in first grade. He guesses at many of the words on the page, practically inventing his own story as he "reads" the lines. Joaquin will need gentle guidance to encourage him to pay attention to the details of the written words and to begin to rely on more effective

reading strategies, such as sounding out simple words.

Other beginning readers, especially ones like Mahala who have been receiving intensive phonics instruction, may appear, in reading expert Jeanne Chall's memorable phrase, "glued to print." Mahala sounds out each word slowly and carefully, spending much of her energy on making the correspondences between letters and sounds. Her reading is watchful and plodding, with a lot of effort devoted to the accurate sounding-out of each word. As a result, Mahala often loses sight of the meaning of what she reads; there just isn't any mental room left over to hold on to that information. So she tends to sound a little disjointed, choppy, and emotionally flat. For now, that's fine: she is focusing on how letters combine to represent sounds. As more and more words become familiar, most children will begin to "unglue" themselves from print and focus more on meaning.

A skilled first-grade teacher will notice how your child approaches reading and determine which strategies will work best for him. At home, there are lots of things you can do to help your child move from knowing letters and some sounds to reading age-appropriate books. (It may be particularly useful at this stage to refresh your general understanding of what reading is, with all its component skills and coordinated efforts; see Chapter 1.)

In this chapter, we'll look in some detail at the program of reading instruction that your child is likely to receive in first grade. We'll start by discussing the five key areas of instruction for beginning readers: phonemic awareness, phonics, fluency, vocabulary, and text comprehension. We'll also talk about the importance of writing as an aid to reading, and we'll describe what teachers do to help first-graders with both the mechanical details of handwriting and spelling and the compositional skills of writing. Finally, we'll discuss some of the things you can do at home to help your child become an independent reader.

PHONEMIC AWARENESS: HEARING THE SOUNDS OF SPEECH

As we discussed in the chapter on kindergarten, phonemic awareness is essential for beginning readers. This awareness—the ability to distinguish the individual sounds that make up spoken words—needs to be established before a child can start making sense of the written system of representing those sounds. And because it is so important, your child's first-grade teacher will likely begin the year by assessing each child's level of phonemic awareness. If your child seems to be struggling—for example, he can't hear whether two words rhyme, can't make rhymes of his own, or can't break spoken words apart into their sounds—don't hesitate to get help. And even for those children who have good phonemic awareness, the beginning of first grade will include lots of practice in breaking spoken words into sounds and rearranging sounds to make new words. Your child might be asked, for example, to identify rhyming words and to produce rhymes of his own (*hug, rug, bug*). By the same token, he could be asked to think of words that start with the same sounds but end differently (*bug, bun, bus*). The teacher might then "segment" the words (stretch each sound as she says it: "sss . . . uhhh . . . nnn") in order

to help children hear the separate units of sound. (To help children hear some of the unstretchable consonants, she might bounce them in her mouth: *d-d-dog, p-p-pop*.) Then she'd encourage the children to repeat the sounds in order to hear them as separate units. In still other exercises, the teacher could encourage the class to manipulate the sounds of spoken words: "Change the /s/ in *sun* to /f/, and what's that word?" "Say *smile* without the /s/; what's that?"

If your child seems to be struggling with phonemic awareness, it may help to read lots of poems and rhyming stories together, gently pointing out the rhymes along the way. The BETWEEN THE LIONS song "If You Can Read *at*" (along with its variants, featuring *op, ug,* and more) is a terrific one for showing how simple rhyming words give clues for reading and spelling. You might also want to try some of the activities suggested in the chapter on kindergarten, particularly the variations on "Gawain's Word." If your child is still having difficulty hearing sounds and playing with them by the middle of this year, ask his teacher for advice, and discuss the possibility of having him screened by a reading specialist.

PHONICS: LINKING LETTERS AND SOUNDS

In Part I of this book, we looked at the various theories that have shaped the teaching of reading in the early grades in different eras. Nowadays, it's generally agreed that the best practice provides systematic instruction in phonics, along with exposure to good literature and other aspects of a whole-language approach, such as an emphasis on reading meaningful

THE STANDARD SEQUENCE OF PHONICS INSTRUCTION

Good programs may vary slightly in the exact order in which they teach phonics, but they will probably follow approximately the pattern we lay out here. By the end of first grade, students will be expected to have mastered the following concepts:

- Single consonants that correspond to a single, consistent sound: *b, c* as in *cat, d, f, g* as in *girl, h, j, l, m, n, p, r, s, t, v, w, x, y* as in *yes,* and *z*

- Short vowel sounds: *a* (*cat*), *u* (*sun*), *o* (*hot*), *i* (*sit*), *e* (*red*)

- Consonant-vowel-consonant, or CVC, words: *mat, sip*

- Lots of practice with word families—for example, *mat/sat/cat* or *sip/hip/lip*—and listening for sounds in words (the BETWEEN THE LIONS song "If You Can Read *at*" helps children grasp the idea of word families)

- Consonant digraphs, or two letters that combine to make a new sound—*ch, sh, th, ng*—along with *qu*

- Beginning and ending consonant blends, or two consonants placed together that retain their separate sounds: blends with *s* (*st, sl, sm, sn,* and so forth); blends with *r* (*tr, cr, dr, fr,* and the like); and blends with *l* (*bl, cl, fl,* and so on)

- Simple, one-syllable words with silent *e* (sometimes called *CVCe* words): *name, fine, home*

In addition to these basic skills, first-graders will also be exposed to a more advanced set of phonics skills; they will start to become familiar with these patterns but will not be expected to master them this year:

- Vowel digraphs, or two-letter combinations that stand for a single long-vowel sound: *ai, ay, ee, oa, ea*

- Vowel diphthongs, or two letters that combine to make a blended vowel sound: *oi, oy, ow* as in *cow.*

text that children can connect to their own lives. Research has consistently shown that phonics instruction matters: teaching children the correspondence between letters and sounds definitely helps most of them learn to read. Beyond that, the best phonics instruction programs are direct and systematic. That is, they teach phonics directly—they spell out the connections between letters and sounds, rather than just encouraging children to infer the principles of phonics from reading simple books and attempting to spell when they write. And they teach phonics systematically, beginning with simple, regular letter-sound correspondences and progressing to more complex and irregular ones. (See the box "The Standard Sequence of Phonics Instruction.")

Some of the songs on the BETWEEN THE LIONS Web site (www.pbskids.org/lions) offer a toe-tapping way to reinforce the phonics rules your first-grader is learning in school. Check out "Sometimes y," "When Two Vowels Go Walking (The First One Does the Talking)," "Double o, oo," and "Without an s."

Phonics programs pay a lot of attention to vowels—particularly the short vowels. That's because learning the short vowels and their sounds is fundamental to children's early reading success.

In listening to spoken English, it's often the consonant sounds we perceive most clearly, because consonants usually sound pretty much the same no matter who's saying them. Vowels, on the other hand, are highly variable in spoken language. Vowel sounds tend to get slurred (think of how people usually say "should not have"—more like "shud-

nuv"). Regional accents also affect the way people pronounce vowel sounds.

In written language, the letter-sound connections are also more reliable for consonants. Ten of our twenty-one consonant letters represent just one sound: *b, j, k, l, m, n, p, r, t, v.* By contrast, English uses only five letters to represent more than fifteen vowel sounds. The letters *a, e, i, o,* and *u* have to do double or triple duty—sometimes even quadruple duty—or team up with one another (*ea, ai, ou,* etc.) to cover the sounds.

Many children learn consonant letter-sound matches before they enter kindergarten, often without a great deal of formal instruction. But they need much more systematic help to make their way through the unruly vowels.

Consonant-vowel-consonant words like "fan," which have short-vowel sounds in the middle, are the most reliably spelled words in English, and the ones where it's easiest to match letters to sounds. That makes them good examples for teaching the alphabetic principle. And even in longer, multisyllabic words, it's very common to find at least one syllable that follows this pattern. A good early-reading program will include lots of practice with consonant-vowel-consonant words, and a savvy teacher will help students apply their knowledge to more advanced words, noting the *fan* in *fancy* and *fantastic,* and the *man* in *commander* and *mansion.* Beginners need lots of practice with lists of word families, compare-contrast exercises, and spelling tasks, and they need to see these words in the context of simple stories.

Your child's phonics instruction will probably also include several "word attack" strategies—problem-solving techniques that help children read words that are hard to sound out. For instance, your first-grader will begin to learn about "structural analysis"—the ability to see that words are made up of chunks of meaning ("morphemes") and to use an understanding of those chunks to read faster and with better comprehension.

Structural analysis is what lets the fluent reader see connections between *talk, talking,* and *talkative,* and to read each of those words more quickly because each component is familiar and easily grasped. The more complex details of this skill will continue to be part of your child's study for several years, but for now, he will probably be exposed to just a few beginning principles, such as word endings for plurals and verbs (*-s, -ed, -ing*); the concept of syllables (hearing, counting, and manipulating them); and ways to combine and separate compound words (see the box "Long Word Freakout").

First-graders will also learn to check the context of a word and to combine this information with phonics clues in order to come up with a word that makes sense in a particular sentence. You can help your child use this strategy at home. If he stumbles over an unfamiliar word, encourage him to consider the context in which it occurs—to read the rest of the sentence, to think about what's happening in the story at that moment, to wonder what might happen next—and see if he can think of a word that might fit the situation. "Hmm, they're at the zoo," you could say. "Can you think of an animal whose name starts with *E*?" Other strategies help a child use the whole text to bolster his decoding of each part of it: by predicting what will happen, asking questions about the story or information a text conveys, and rereading a sentence to confirm and check the meaning of a word (see the box "Outlaw Words").

It's worth noting that while your child will most likely spend a good deal of time working on phonics skills by himself, he will also be learning phonics within the context of actual books. The best first-grade programs provide practice texts that match the phonics skills being studied. These simple texts let children see the words they are studying in context and encourage them to try out some of their word-attack strategies. Such practice texts are often derided by parents—they can seem plodding and stiff, with little plot or excitement. But they serve an important purpose. Like the short skis that help young skiers gain balance and confidence, these texts give young readers a chance to practice the basic maneuvers.

FLUENCY: GOING WITH THE FLOW

Another important part of learning to read, though it is not as easily broken down into a series of skills, is fluency. Fluency is the ability to read smoothly, in a connected way, with a natural rhythm and a sensible emphasis on the various parts of a sentence. A fluent reader, when reading aloud, sounds as if he is speaking naturally; a reader who is not yet fluent sounds choppy, disconnected, and flat. As your child struggles to decode new words, he will probably sound like this. The effort of matching letters to sounds takes so much of the beginning reader's attention that he has little left over to devote to expression and pace. This is perfectly natural; over the next several years, he will learn to read in a smoother, more rhythmic, fluent way.

Fluency is important not just because it is more pleasing to the listener, but because it is

LONG WORD FREAKOUT

Here are some strategies for reading long words by breaking them into their component sounds:

❖ First, see if the long word can be broken into two familiar words (*cow-boy, tooth-brush, suit-case*).

❖ Look for common word endings (*est, ing, ful, less, tion*) and beginnings (*re, un, dis, pre*). Say them as separate bits.

❖ When two consonants come between two vowels, divide the word between them (*nap-kin, sig-nal, den-tist*). But here's an exception: Do not split up two consonants that combine to make a single new sound (*fash-ion, duck-ling, sing-er*). Try using the short vowel sound in the first syllable.

❖ When only one consonant comes between two vowels, divide the word after the first vowel (*pi-rate, ti-ger, mu-sic*) and try saying the long sound for that vowel. If the word doesn't sound right, try breaking the word after the consonant and saying the short vowel sound: (*mel-on, rob-in, trav-el*).

❖ A vowel by itself can make a syllable (*ro-de-o, e-ven, Le-o-na*). It usually makes the long vowel sound.

❖ When a word ends in a consonant plus *le*, divide it before that consonant (*han-dle, fa-ble*). If the first syllable ends in a consonant (*hum-ble, gam-ble*), try the short vowel sound. But if the first syllable ends with a vowel (*sta-ble, ti-tle*), try the long vowel sound.

OUTLAW WORDS

For some words and word families, it's easy to see how letters and sounds match up. But some words don't play fair. Just look at these: *any*, *does*, *have*, *of*, *one*, *where*, *were*, *there*, *they*, *only*, *some*, *who*, *enough*, *what*. Simple words once you know them, but if you don't, trying to sound them out won't get you very far. You could think of these as "outlaw words," because they just don't follow the rules—and if you don't learn to say them right, they hold you up!

For dealing with outlaws, you need a good lasso. Here are a few rope tricks you can share with your child:

- ❖ Try sounding out the words, making sure you pronounce each letter or combination of letters. If the word doesn't make sense, think about what the word might be if it sounded a little bit different.

- ❖ Check the illustrations to see if there's a hint about this word.

- ❖ Still stuck? Skip over the word and read the rest of the sentence for clues. Then reread the sentence, trying to say a word that makes sense in context.

Another band of outlaws includes words that look almost alike but have very different meanings: *thought*, *through*, *tough*, and *though*, or *that* and *what*, *then* and *when*, or *there* and *where*.

Try making a "word wall" of outlaw words (see Activities)—you'll be able to round up a lot of critters in this corral!

more useful to the reader. A child who is reading fluently is putting the words together into a meaningful statement, rather than seeing each word as a separate unit. His eyes are taking in clusters of words, and his brain is responding to the meanings of those phrases. Instead of focusing on "letter-sound-letter-

---

The BETWEEN THE LIONS song "Ten Small Words" features the ten most frequent words in English: *a, the, is, that, you, of, in, and, it, to.* You can learn the tune on the BETWEEN THE LIONS Web site (www.pbskids.org/lions), where you'll also find the sequel, "Ten Little Words."

---

sound-letter-sound" or even "word, word, word," a fluent reader is processing, "phrase, phrase, sentence." While the beginner gropes slowly through "T-th-the! c-at isss . . . no, 'iz' . . . on th-e mmm-at," the fluent reader is picturing Fluffy curled up by a crackling fire. Fluency allows a reader to delve beneath the surface of the text to grasp the meaning of what he reads. Your child will not be expected to be a completely fluent reader by the end of this year, but his teacher will work with him to help him move toward that goal.

One key to fluent reading is automatic word recognition. The more words a reader recognizes on sight, the more quickly and smoothly he will read—and the more resources he will be able to devote to comprehension. Some words appear so often in written text that it pays to be able to recognize them immediately. In fact, there are just 100 "high-frequency" words (see the box "One Hundred Greatest Hits") that account for 50

percent of all written text in English. Sometimes called "glue" or "sight" words, these often hard-to-spell words—such as *the, of, is, to, was,* and *are*—may be the focus of many tasks and worksheets in your child's first-grade classroom. The teacher may give him a chance to practice them by using flash cards, taking spelling tests, and participating in "word wall" activities.

The best way to become a more fluent reader is by reading—a lot. So your child will spend plenty of class time this year simply reading aloud. He will sometimes be encouraged to read the same texts repeatedly, so that familiarity allows him to focus less on decoding individual words and more on reading with natural phrasing and expression. He may also participate in choral reading, or reading in unison with his teacher and classmates: by matching their pace and intonation to an experienced reader's, children increase their grasp of the links between written words and the rhythms of meaningful speech. Poems and other rhythmic texts are particularly helpful for this, so you can expect to hear a lot of poems from your child this year—and you might enjoy reading some aloud with him at home, too.

Finally, he will be encouraged to spend some time reading silently and independently. Oral reading will take up most of his reading time this year, because a beginner needs to get lots of practice at hearing the connections between written and spoken language, and because hearing your child read aloud helps his teacher gauge his progress. But doing some silent reading is important, too, because it allows the beginner to turn his attention less toward how words sound and more toward how they flow together. And, of course, even-

ONE HUNDRED GREATEST HITS: THE MOST COMMON WORDS IN ENGLISH

Words 1–25	Words 26–50	Words 51–75	Words 76–100
the	or	will	number
of	one	up	no
and	had	other	way
a	by	about	could
to	word	out	people
in	but	many	my
is	not	then	than
you	what	them	first
that	all	these	water
it	were	so	been
he	we	some	call
was	when	her	who
for	your	would	oil
on	can	make	now
are	said	like	find
as	there	him	long
with	use	into	down
his	an	time	day
they	each	has	did
I	which	look	get
at	she	two	come
be	do	more	made
this	how	write	may
have	their	go	part
from	if	see	over

tually almost all his reading will be silent. For this year, however, it's enough just to do a little, and to make the first small steps along the road toward fluent reading.

VOCABULARY: A WORLD FULL OF WORDS

Another component of successful reading is a steadily increasing vocabulary. As we discussed in the chapter on kindergarten, there's a proven link between vocabulary and reading: young children who know more words tend to become good readers, and better readers know more words. So your child's first-grade teacher will help your child continue to expand the number of words he knows with a variety of strategies, many of which you can also use at home. For example, she'll lead the class in discussing the meanings of unfamiliar words as they appear in books, and she'll help the children link unknown words to ones they have already encountered. She will also introduce your first-grader to the specific vocabulary that he will need to use for talking about reading and writing—such words as *sentence, paragraph, punctuation,* and *syllable.*

On BETWEEN THE LIONS Heath the Thesaurus, the library's huge, enormous, gigantic resident word wizard, is eager, pleased, and delighted to help the cubs learn new words. When Leona gets stumped by the word *drought,* Heath lumbers by to offer alternatives: *aridity? dehydration?* Leona still doesn't get it. Finally he settles for "Long time no rain," and the light dawns. As always, a simple explanation is best!

You can help your child acquire new words by continuing to provide a wide range of experiences and reading materials related to them, both fiction and nonfiction. The books you read to him, as opposed to the ones he reads himself, are particularly likely to yield a wealth of new and more complex words and ideas. You can also deepen his understanding of these words by pausing in your reading to discuss and explain an unfamiliar term or idea, and by making a point of using new words from your reading in your conversations over the next few days. By helping your child develop the habit of inquiring into new words and their meanings, you're fostering an interest that will continue to help him learn in the years ahead. There are also more structured ways to work on vocabulary, and you'll find some of them in the Activities section. You may also want to look back at the section on vocabulary in the kindergarten chapter, where you'll find suggestions for incorporating new words into everyday conversation.

COMPREHENSION:
SEEING THE BIG PICTURE

With all of these separate skills to work on, it can be easy to lose sight of the overall goal of reading, which is comprehension. Everything your first-grader learns about reading this year is really intended to help him learn this one larger thing: how to look at a written text and understand what it says. Comprehension, of course, involves a set of skills and strategies that we continue to refine and deepen throughout our lives, but your child will begin even now to learn and develop the strategies that will help him use text as a bridge between himself and the world.

Several basic strategies can enrich a reader's comprehension of a whole text, and your child will start learning about these in first grade. The most common ones include predicting, questioning, and looking for context clues. For example, your child's teacher may begin a session of reading aloud to the class by holding up the book and asking the children to predict what it's about. She may encourage them to look through a book before reading it to get clues from the pictures about its subject and story. Children enjoy the feeling of control they get from having a sense of what's coming next, and knowing the general outlines of a story helps them find the appropriate words in their vocabulary when they come across something unfamiliar in the text. If they know they're reading about dinosaurs and not trains, they're more likely to say "T. rex" than "tracks."

Your child's teacher will probably also encourage her students to read for meaning by asking them questions about the text as they read, and by urging them to ask questions about anything they don't understand and about the characters or the story. As with all of these strategies, you can adopt this one in your own reading sessions at home (see the box "Starter Questions for Reading Together"). Parents sometimes worry that stopping to ask or answer questions will interrupt the flow of the story, but questions help a child connect more fully with what he's reading and bring new words into his vocabulary. Try to focus especially on open-ended questions (those that don't have a right or wrong answer); they are great for spurring language development and helping children's minds grow.

Some of the questions a teacher asks are designed to help children learn to make connections between a text and themselves, or between one text and another. To help them draw a connection between themselves and the text, the teacher might ask, "What does this remind you of?" "Have you ever been in a situation like this?" "Do you have something like this at home?" To lead them toward connecting one text with another, she could say, "Have we read any other books like this?" "Does this remind you of a different story?" "How is this book about butterflies different from the one we read last week?"

Teachers like to "activate background knowledge" before reading—that is, to find out what children already know about a subject, and what kinds of questions they have. This kind of discussion helps anchor children's learning by connecting new information to the knowledge they already have.

After reading, it's useful to ask children to summarize what they've read. This helps them digest the new material and lodge it in their memories. For instance, a teacher might ask the class to recall the beginning, middle, and end of a story, to retell the story in their own words, or to list the most important things they learned from a nonfiction text. All of these strategies further reinforce the connections between the book and the child, between text and life.

WRITING: THE OTHER SIDE OF READING

In addition to these five basic areas of reading instruction, there are several other elements of your child's first-grade program that are connected to his developing skills as a reader. Most

STARTER QUESTIONS FOR READING TOGETHER

Before you begin to read a book for the first time, introduce it to your child by reading aloud the title and the names of the author and illustrator. Ask:

- ❖ Have we read other books by this author/illustrator? What do you remember about them?
- ❖ What do you think this book might be about? How do you know?

While reading the book, use your finger to point to the words as you read along so your child can follow. Stop once or twice to ask questions like:

- ❖ Why do you think the character said or did that?
- ❖ How do you think she feels?
- ❖ What do you think will happen next?

Or if it's a nonfiction book, you may want to comment on new or surprising information.

At the end of the book, you can help children make connections between this book and other books or their own experiences. Ask:

- ❖ What was your favorite part of this book?
- ❖ We read another book about this, didn't we? What happened in that book?
- ❖ This book reminds me of the time when . . . Do you remember? What else do you remember about it?

During subsequent readings, ask questions like:

- ❖ What happens next, do you remember?
- ❖ Who is this in the picture? What is that? What's going on here?
- ❖ Mmm, I love that word—*whisker*. Can you explain what a whisker is?

Remember, the goal is to provide an opportunity for conversation. Listen carefully to your child's response and see if you can find a way to extend it to build vocabulary and encourage a fuller expression of ideas.

HANDWRITING TIPS FOR LEFTIES

❖ If your child is left-handed, you may want to encourage him to keep his arm relaxed and fairly straight, rather than curving it around the top of the page; left-handers who "push" the pencil across the line in this way, rather than "pulling" it from the top, usually find it easier to write.

❖ Young lefties often have trouble with smears and smudges, because, unlike for righties, their hand drags across the letters they have just printed. Gently encourage your child to keep his hand relaxed but positioned below the line he's writing on, not dragging across it. Your child can also experiment with a variety of pencils (hard or soft lead, mechanical pencils, etc.) to see what's most comfortable and legible.

❖ One more note for right-handed parents of left-handed children: if you're helping your child learn how to form letters correctly, he may find it easier to imitate your motions if you demonstrate with your left hand. Don't worry about printing perfectly shaped letters; it's the sequence of movements you're showing him here, not the result.

❖ And, for all parents of lefties: don't worry about your child's handedness or try to make him switch. He's wired this way, and, with good instruction, motivation, and lots of practice, he'll learn to write just fine.

important of these, perhaps, is writing—both composition and the mechanics of putting letters on paper and following the conventions of print. First-graders should have lots of opportunities to write, both for self-expression in personal narratives, stories, and brief journal entries, and for practical purposes, such as making lists and signs. Becoming a better writer will help your child become a better reader. Writing makes him slow down his thoughts and spell out each word, sound by sound. As he labors to write something by using the phonics and

word-learning skills he has just been taught, he makes these skills his own. Children may also be more likely to pay attention to the shapes of letters and the correct spellings of words as they try to communicate with others in writing.

Children often like to hear you read their writing back to them. And that tends to work better than asking them to read it to you themselves. Oddly enough, it can be difficult for children to read their own writing—they may look at the scraggly marks on the page in utter confusion. Their own letters and words may bear little resemblance to the kinds of print they are used to reading.

To make their own reading easier, you can type up their compositions for them, using proper spelling. Then they may feel more confident about sharing what they've written.

Your child's growing understanding that he can use writing for a variety of purposes, from telling a story to making a list to expressing a feeling, will deepen his sense of why reading matters and what he can do with it. For all these reasons, both the mechanics of writing and the rudiments of spelling are an important part of first-grade instruction, so let's take a look at them.

The Mechanics of Writing

Your child's teacher may help him work on his handwriting. If you're not sure whether this is part of his classroom instruction, you can help him at home. First of all, he needs to know how to sit at a desk when he writes: with a straight back and relaxed shoulders, rather than hunching over the paper. It's helpful if his feet are firmly on the floor—believe it or not, it can help to put a box or stool under his feet if they are dangling, so that he is comfortably braced. Some young children also find writing easier on a slanted surface. And the paper should be placed at a 30- to 45-degree angle,

with the top right corner of the paper pointing toward the top of the desk.

You or your child's teacher can show him how to hold a pencil correctly, pinching the pencil lightly between his thumb and index finger, allowing the pencil to rest on his middle finger, with the rest of the fingers lined up underneath for support. If your child struggles with the correct grip, the teacher may suggest using larger pencils or a rubber grip that can be attached to any pencil and that guides the fingers into the correct position. You can also assist your child by gently helping him reposition his fingers if they are in the wrong spot and—most important—by encouraging him to keep his grip relaxed and natural, rather than clamping down as he struggles to form letters. Those chubby little fingers clenching the pencil with all their might are adorable, but he'll find it easier if he lightens up a bit.

First grade is also the time when your child will be asked to work on forming letters, both upper- and lowercase, in the conventional way. He may be given worksheets with dotted letters to trace; ideally, he'll be given plenty of time to practice forming all the letters, both in isolation and in the short compositions he will be asked to produce. You can also help him at home; check out the box "The Write Moves" in Chapter 3 for an easy guide to forming the lowercase letters correctly.

Your child's teacher will also remind him to leave spaces between words and to follow other conventions of print, although he will not be expected to master these details for some time. So you may see, in your first-grader's writing, some attempts at producing correct punctuation and capitalization. Some children are very curious about punctuation marks, while others

For more practice, you might want to steer your beginning writer to Leona's area of the BETWEEN THE LIONS Web site (www.pbskids.org/lions), where "Writing ABCs" offers an animated demonstration of the standard, first-grade-approved way to form each upper- and lowercase letter.

seem hardly to notice them. Noting the punctuation you see on signs or in the books you read may pique his interest.

Spelling

For spelling, too, this is the year when your child will start being asked to pay attention to conventions. Although invented spelling is still common and acceptable at this age, the teacher will be checking to see that your child's inventions follow some kind of logic. He may not spell words correctly, but the choices he makes should make sense in some way. Children frequently use *H* to represent the /ch/ sound, for example, because that sound occurs in the letter's name ("aitch"). Your child should also clearly understand, as first-graders generally seem to, that there's a difference between "kid spelling" and "real spelling." And your child will be expected to spell some words correctly, especially those he has studied in his phonics lessons—simple words like *cap* and *cape,* for example—and some of the high-frequency sight words, such as *to, the, of, you,* and *they.* Some children enjoy keeping a "personal dictionary" or spelling folder that contains these often used, oddly spelled words. Sorted by first letter, these personal word lists can be a quick and handy resource. (Be sure to leave lots of room for the *w*'s—*who, what, when, where, was, were,* etc.)

It's probably not a good idea, though, to give your first-grader a standard dictionary. Most dictionaries clutter an entry with information about pronunciation, grammar, derivation, and other details. This is way too much material for early readers. Plus, when kids finally do locate the word and wade through the definition, they don't usually understand it! Even a beginners' dictionary can be too much too soon. But your first-grader may enjoy browsing through a colorful, well illustrated beginner's dictionary with you. Playful, parent-led exploration of this sort will introduce him to a tool that will become a tremendous resource in the upper grades.

WHAT YOU CAN DO AT HOME

The best thing you can do to help your child this year is something you've probably been doing for years: read with him. What's exciting now, however, is that not only will you be reading to him; for the first time, he'll be reading to you. But don't let his reading replace your reading—both are important. In this section, we'll talk about reading to your child and having him read to you, and we'll suggest some fun variations on that daily routine. Then we'll look at other activities you can do at home to reinforce what your child is learning at school: visiting the library, selecting appropriate books for your child, playing phonemic awareness and phonics games, using BETWEEN THE LIONS as a springboard for reading activities, writing together, and storytelling.

For your first-grader, reading and being read to are different activities, each of which serves its own important purpose. His own reading at this stage is mostly for practice, for helping him put together all the components of the process more and more smoothly. But the books you read to him will enrich his understanding, his vocabulary, and his love of stories. In addition, the experience of being read to, as opposed to reading himself, allows him to stop devoting all his attention to decoding and focus instead on the flow of the book. You can also read more complex, sophisticated, and engaging texts than he can, which will broaden his knowledge and encourage him to keep working on his basic skills so that he can move up to these wonderful books on his own. Put another way, his own reading of simple texts gives him lots of practice in the "how" of reading; your reading of richer and more complex texts gives him lots of reminders of the "why."

Another reason it's important to keep reading to your child is that listening to a fluent reader helps children become more fluent themselves. When you read him a poem, he hears your fluent expression, rhythm, and pace—and your example helps show him how to connect words into meaningful statements. If you feel that your own reading is not smooth enough, or if you simply want a break, you can check out some of the terrific books on tape that are available at most public libraries. Tapes that come with a copy of the book are particularly valuable, as your child can follow along while the narrator reads. Whether with a tape or with a live reader, giving a child the chance to look at the text while a more proficient reader pronounces it aloud helps to show him how the words on the page can come alive in a fluid, expressive way.

If you'd like some help choosing more books to read to your first-grader, check the lists in "Thirty Really Good Books for First-Graders" at the end of this chapter. Your librarian or your child's teacher may also have some great suggestions. If one book doesn't catch your child's interest—or your own!—feel free to drop it and try another. The goal, as ever, is simply to find a story that will enrich the time you spend reading together. Have fun!

Busy parents sometimes wonder how important it is to have their children read aloud to them. Since the children spend time reading in school, couldn't they just continue to listen to stories at home? In fact, though, it's extremely valuable for your first-grader to get as much practice at reading as he can, and your enthusiastic listening to his efforts is also a powerful motivation to keep reading. Ideally, he'll read to you every day. This may require some adjustments in your long-established reading routines, and it can take a little while to figure out what works best for you and your child.

If you have always read together at bedtime, for instance, you may find that you need to start reading earlier, because it will take longer for your child to finish a book himself. Or you may decide that you will continue to do the bedtime reading, but you will set aside another time every day for your child to read to you. The best setting for this activity may depend on what he's reading at a given moment. If it's a book you already know well, you don't need to be able to see it as he reads; if it's an unfamiliar one, you might want to sit next to him as he reads, so you can check occasionally on how well his reading matches what's on the page (see the box "Spotting Difficulties"). Perhaps he could read a familiar book as you fix dinner, and a new one while you ride the bus together; he could read a well-known story to a sibling in the car or try an unfamiliar one out on you in the waiting room at the dentist's office. Whatever fits your lives is fine. If time is tight, try asking him to read just a page or two, so he doesn't feel pressured to hurry. You can also build in some time for rereading, since that may help him develop a smoother delivery.

Parents sometimes wonder if they should correct their first-grader's errors as he reads

SPOTTING DIFFICULTIES

If your child is struggling, it can be helpful to know what parts of the reading process are giving him trouble. Let's take a typical sample of reading material from the middle of first grade:

> Soon there was a knock at the door.
> A voice called, "It's cold out here. Please let me come in."

A child who is reading for meaning might make these kinds of miscues:

> So then he was kicking the door.
> A voice called, "It is cold outside. Please let me come in."

This student is relying on comprehension and ignoring some of the coding details. He needs to learn to track all the letters in words more accurately.

Parents can respond by asking the child to reread the text. If he doesn't correct himself, you might ask: "Kicking the door? Is that what you do when you want the door opened?" Practice with phonics skills (*kn-* and *-ock*) may help this child.

A child who is "glued to print" and not as focused on meaning might make these kinds of mistakes:

> Soon the wass a k-k-k-ock at the doo . . . er.
> A vo-voice cal-led "It's could out here. Please let me comb in."

This student is using his phonics skills on text that is about 40 percent nonphonetic. To progress at this stage, the child needs to think about what words might make sense in this context.

Parents can respond by encouraging the child to check for meaning—for instance, by stopping to ask, "Does that make sense?" or by looking at the pictures that illustrate the text. The child can then reread the passage more accurately. Rereading can be a very helpful strategy at this stage. Practice with sight words will help this child.

aloud. This can be tricky to judge—you don't want your child to be misreading a lot of words, but you also don't want to interrupt the flow. Try waiting a bit after a child makes a mistake; as he continues to read the sentence, he may realize from the context that the word he chose does not make sense, and he will often go back and correct the error on his own. If he doesn't, and if it's a minor error that doesn't leave a confusing gap in the story, you can let it go. If it's a key word for the story, though, you could stop him at the end of the sentence and ask, "A house? Do you think the cat was chasing a house, or is it something else?" Then you can encourage him to read the sentence again with the correct word. As long as you keep the tone playful, rather than critical, it won't spoil the fun.

On BETWEEN THE LIONS, the character of Sam Spud, Hard-Boiled Potato Detective, often models this behavior for children: He types the wrong word, then stops himself and says, "Humbarger? That's not right. Hamburger!" and reads the sentence again.

If you'd like some variety in your daily sessions, beyond hearing your child read and reading to him, there are a few techniques that teachers sometimes use and that you and your child can try at home. We've already mentioned choral reading, which you can easily adapt to home reading. Just read aloud together, in unison. You will probably need to go more slowly than you usually would. Try starting with familiar and very rhythmic texts, such as nursery rhymes, which are easier to pace yourselves on together. Or get a children's songbook and sing the familiar songs

together as you look at (and even point to) the words.

You can also vary things by taking turns. In addition to taking turns reading a whole book to each other, you can alternate within a book—page by page, or even sentence by sentence. This allows your child to hear the book's particular vocabulary spoken, which may make it easier for him to recognize the words when he encounters them on the next page. It also lets him take little breaks from the hard work of reading, so that he can get through longer or more challenging texts without growing tired or frustrated. First-graders still delight in chiming in on a refrain or reading a book's predictable or repetitive phrases as they crop up along the way. Or you can divide a book by roles: he could play the three little pigs, for example, while you ham it up as the wolf.

A good librarian can help you find books that match your child's interests—books you can read aloud to him, since they may be too difficult for him to read on his own—as well as books targeted to early readers. Your local library may also offer story hours, reading programs, and special summer activities—all great ways to help your child remember that reading is fun and something that lots of other kids like to do, too.

As for other ways of selecting books for your child, you may find that your child's school has a "Book Bag" program, in which teachers send home books at the appropriate level for your child to read at home. If you don't have access to such programs, there are a few guidelines you can use in choosing books that are likely to appeal to your child and meet his current needs. For detailed information on selecting books, check "Help with Finding Books for Children" in the Resources chapter of this book. In general, though, you'll want to consider both the content and the level of difficulty of books that you're considering for your child.

When it comes to content, a natural choice is any topic that your child is particularly interested in, from dinosaurs to dolls. Many first-graders like stories about animals, as well as stories about children who are naughty, brave, or good at solving problems. Informative nonfiction on a topic that interests them— outer space, whales and dolphins, trains and trucks, or insects, for example—is another good choice. Early series books, like *Frog and Toad* or *Amelia Bedelia*, help the beginning reader by presenting familiar characters and vocabulary in a variety of settings. Your first-grader may also enjoy simple collections of jokes and riddles. Often, if you go to a library with a sense of what categories would interest your child, the librarian can help you find great books within that category.

Judging the level of difficulty of a book can be tricky. Classic picture books, for example, are very deceptive. *Where the Wild Things Are* has an estimated difficulty level of fifth grade; *Green Eggs and Ham* has the same level of difficulty as the books an average third-grader can read on his own. These are wonderful books, and ones your child may already love, but they are also books that you'll still need to read to him, rather than expecting him to read them to you just yet. Of course, if he wants to chime in on the familiar parts, that's terrific.

The difficulty level of a book depends on several factors. These include the number of words on a page, the length and familiarity of the words, and the length and structure of the sentences. Most books that are appropriate for readers at the first-grade level have fewer than 40 words on a page and an average of 10 to 12 words in a sentence. The stories tend to be simple, familiar, and repetitive.

There's a simple formula you can use when trying to figure out whether a book is too difficult for your child at any stage. If he can read 95 percent of the words in a book without making a mistake, that's a good choice for reading on his own. If he reads 90 percent of the words correctly, the book is too hard to read independently but is just right for reading with a supportive adult—you can help him puzzle out the unfamiliar words, which will stretch his vocabulary. If he reads less than 90 percent of the words, however—that is, if he stumbles over more than one word out of ten—the book is at his "frustrational" level. It's too hard for him right now, and you should help him find an easier book.

An even simpler way to find a book that's just right for your child is to look at the books he's reading right now, then try to find others that look similar: the same size of type, the same number of words on a page, the same kinds of sentence structure. And don't worry if you pick one that's too hard—you can read part or all of it to him for now, and your child will happily move up to it on his own when he's ready.

To help your first-grader improve his phonemic awareness, you can play games that involve listening to words and playing with their sounds. For more specific phonics practice, try some of the games on the BETWEEN THE LIONS Web site (www.pbskids.org/lions), or check out the activities at the end of this chapter. And, in general, you can continue to look for opportunities in your daily life to enhance your child's awareness of sounds and their connections to letters. You can sing nonsense syllables to each other—Ella Fitzgerald is a great inspiration—or make up rhyming games or talk about how you'd spell the sound of a police siren or a pigeon. There are, of course, a lot of products on the market that promise to teach your child phonics, and some of them can be helpful; in the Resources chapter, we talk about a few that you may find worth trying. But one of the best things you can do to help your first-grader with phonics is simply to keep playing with sounds, drawing his attention to how words sound and how they look, and helping him to connect language and letters.

In addition to the writing your child does in school, you can encourage him to write at home. (He might need or want a little help.) Together, you could send notes to family members, make signs, make lists, copy recipes, send invitations, keep a family journal, label a photo album or scrapbook, send e-mails, or play with words on the computer. It's fine to encourage your first-grader to attempt sensible spellings, but don't worry about perfect spelling at this stage.

Another idea is to write a variety of messages for your child to find and enjoy: on a bulletin board in the kitchen, in his lunchbox, on his pillow, taped to the bathroom mirror or stuck on the fridge. Every time your child finds a note, he not only feels special but also is reminded that writing is a great way to communicate with people.

As you may have been doing for years, you can continue to tell stories to your first-grader—at bedtime, during long car rides, or at other quiet times during the day. Telling stories helps children appreciate the power of language, the delights of creative expression, and the compelling appeal of narrative. For first-graders, stories about animals or naughty children have special appeal. Your child might especially love hearing about mischievous episodes from your own childhood—the time you turned up the thermostat on your father's fish tank, for example, or the time your friend dumped a bottle of ketchup on your head. (Naturally, you'll want to emphasize the horrible consequences that ensued, so you don't set off a rash of copycat crimes.) Or turn the family pet into a superhero and send her off on a chain of adventures. For more ideas, you can look at the storybooks that particularly appeal to your child now and use them as inspiration for similar stories of your own.

In all of the reading and activities you do together at home, you have the opportunity to help your first-grader see that reading is more than a collection of skills—and that, above all, it's fun. This year, he will probably be focused on learning the skills, and that's important. You can help him with basic skills, and you can also help him select from the array of reading strategies that we've discussed. Even if some strategies don't seem to help him the first time out, it's wise to keep them in mind—something that makes no sense to him at one stage may suddenly click as a useful technique a few months down the line. What may be most important is to give your child a sense that, if he can't read a particular word or understand a given sentence, there are many different things he can do to help himself out. Having a variety of reading strategies at his disposal is one more way for your child to develop confidence and competence as a beginning reader.

Even when he's reading simple texts, you can gently direct your child's attention toward comprehension by discussing the events and characters of a story. You can ask him what he thinks about the characters, how he might have acted differently, how he would tell the story if he were writing it. You can ask him how the information in a book connects with what he already knows about the world. Questions like these help a first-grader think more profoundly about the text as he reads, and they also point him toward the important skill of analyzing not just what a text says, but how it says it and why. If you talk with him about what books mean, rather than just what the letters on the page spell, you will be helping him prepare for the deeper and more complex learning that lies ahead.

BUILDING BLOCKS: WHAT YOUR FIRST-GRADER NEEDS

Language and conversation
- ❖ Talking about connections between books, and between books and life
- ❖ Hearing more complex books read aloud and talking about them
- ❖ Learning the meaning of new words in books and conversation
- ❖ Books with varied and interesting themes

Direct, systematic instruction in phonics
- ❖ Introduction to the simpler letter-sound associations
- ❖ Lots of practice with short vowel sounds and silent *e*
- ❖ Help with tricky consonants: *h, w, y*
- ❖ Plenty of exposure to word families, like *mat/sat/cat* or *hit/sit/fit*
- ❖ Practice with segmenting and blending; phonics-based games; rhymes
- ❖ Structural analysis of common word endings (*ing* and *ed*)

Writing and spelling
- ❖ Lots of practice forming letters and writing stories and messages
- ❖ Gentle encouragement to focus on spelling
- ❖ Work with sight words, using word walls, flash cards, and spelling tests

Comprehension strategies: predicting, questioning, and context clues

Lots of practice reading
- ❖ Repetitive texts and simple series books to build confidence and fluency
- ❖ Poems and songs to reinforce sensitivity to sound and rhythm
- ❖ Lots of reading aloud and a little time for silent, independent reading

1 BURIED TREASURE   Leaving notes around the house for your child to find is both skill-building and fun—especially if you make it into a game. Try a treasure hunt, where you write a few simple clues—"What starts with *D* and lets you in the room?" "What do you make every morning that rhymes with Fred?"—and then hide them in order, so that the "door" one leads you to the door, where you find the one that leads you to the bed, and so on. At the end of the trail, reward your treasure hunter with a book to read together. You can also hide notes in the sock drawer or the laundry hamper, with a reminder or, maybe, an invitation to hear a story. (How's that for a reward to the child who puts his laundry where it belongs?) Or you can set up a "we-mail" system: a secret location where you and your child can leave messages for each other. Get him into this habit now, and you could still be communicating when he hits his teens.

2 IT'S A DATE   With your child, create a template for a calendar that you can adapt each month—you can draw it or do it on a computer. (Check the BETWEEN THE LIONS Web site for this and other materials.) Each month, fill in the days and dates, and mark any special events, birthdays, or appointments. Your child can decorate the calendar with stickers, glitter, and drawings, then post it on the refrigerator for everyone to use. Or he could use it as his own calendar, or as a chart to keep track of what books he's reading each day. You can use the same process to make personalized memo pads, grocery lists, and phone-message pads for the family; why not have your child devise a family crest or motto while he's at it? Take the design to the copy shop or a local printer to get the pads made up.

3 EXERSET   Work with your child to come up with a simple list of exercises he can do every day—to get the oxygen flowing in the morning, to relax after school, or to burn off a little energy before he settles down to do homework. Help him write each exercise on an index card. Here's a set to get you started. (1) Hop five times on your right foot. (2) Hop five times on your left foot. (3) Touch your toes ten times without bending your knees. (4) Do ten jumping jacks. (5) Stretch your right hand toward the ceiling and count to ten, then your left hand. The first time through, do the exercises with your child to make sure he can read and understand the instructions. You can also help your child create a simple exercise log to record his workout—which will, no doubt, grow more complex as he gets older.

4 GAWAIN SAYS   This is an advanced variation on "Gawain's Word," combined with "Simon Says." As the lord of "Gawain's Word," you will give the knights a command, using a blended word. If you preface the command by saying "Gawain says," the players should blend the word and act it out. (If you say, "Gawain says *j . . . ump*," the players say, "Jump!" and jump.) But if you omit the "Gawain says," the players should stand still. Some simple commands include *w . . . ave, r . . . un, h . . . op, s . . . it, sm . . . ile, g . . . iggle, r . . . ead, n . . . ap, sl . . . eep, sk . . . ip, d . . . ance, t . . . ickle, y . . . awn, str . . . etch, scr . . . atch, r . . . est, sh . . . ake, r . . . ock, cl . . . ap, sn . . . ap, h . . . ide,* and *s . . . ing.* You can make it more complicated with commands like: "Gawain says touch your *n . . . ose*" or "Gawain says wiggle your *t . . . oes.*" Change roles and see if your child can lead the game as the lord of "Gawain's Word." This kind of game can eas- ily be converted into a "Pig Latin" or "Ubbi-Dubbi" version for first-graders with advanced levels of phonemic awareness: "Simon Pig says *iggle-gay.* Simon Pig says *ile- smay. Ake-shay.*" Or, in Ubbi-Dubbi: "Sub-imon sub-ays *dub-ance.* Sub-imon sub-ays *hub-op.* Nub-ow sub-ing!")

5 SIGHT WORD BINGO Make cards ruled into six squares, and write one of the ten most common sight words in each square: *a, the, is, that, you, of, in, and, it,* or *to.* (Each card should have a different combination of words.) Use pennies or dried beans as markers. Call out the words, one by one, until one of the players fills his card. You can also adapt this idea for more advanced readers by making new cards with harder words, or for younger ones by simply using letters instead of words. (See the box "One Hundred Greatest Hits" for a list of the 100 most common sight words, or check out the BETWEEN THE LIONS songs "Ten Small Words" and "Ten Little Words" for the top 20.) You can also write sight words on separate, smaller cards and use them for Concentration or other matching and sorting games—make six pairs of words, for example, then put them face down and have your child find the matching ones.

6 WORD WALL Using a space on your child's bedroom wall or door, in the bath- room or hallway, or even on the front of the refrigerator, build a "word wall" with your child. You can tape up a large sheet of paper, or use smaller separate sheets for each word. Either way, encourage him to find words to put on the wall: frequently encountered words, lively verbs and juicy adverbs, words for his favorite things, words that illustrate common spelling patterns, sight words he has trouble with, or any new words he'd like to learn. When you have a dozen or more, use the words from your wall to write a story together. If you don't want to devote a whole wall to this activity, you could also create a folder, or make a "word album" out of a blank scrapbook or a lined notebook. Keep the album on your child's nightstand so he can look at it every night. He could also decorate the pages with illustrations of each word.

7 WORD PLAY Make a list of action words (*shake, bounce, jump, sleep*) and write each one on an index card. Have your child choose one from the deck and read it silently, without letting anyone else see it. Then have him act out the word: If it's *bounce,* he bounces, and if it's *shake,* he shakes. It's best to use lively action words, of course. (Check out the version of "Word Play" on the BETWEEN THE LIONS Web site, www.pbskids.org/lions, for some fun examples.) You can also use the cards for story-telling. Place them facedown, then have your child pick three, turn them over, and make up a story together using those three words. If you like the story, you can write it down together and save it in a "Favorite Stories" folder or album.

8 LONG WORD FREAKOUT To help your first-grader hone his expertise at breaking down words into their parts, polish up your "Dr. Ruth Wordheimer" imitation. Write several long words on pieces of paper. Cover a word with a piece of cardboard, and then slide the cardboard over to reveal one part at a time. Let your child read each part in turn, and then help him put the whole word together. Voilà—you, like Dr. Ruth Wordheimer, have cured Long Word Freakout. It may be easiest to start with simple compound words, such as *doghouse* or *baseball*, and move on to words like *dinosaur* or *helicopter*. This activity can also help your child practice identifying prefixes and suffixes, like *un-*, *de-*, and *re-*, or *-tion*, *-ing*, and *-ed*.

9 WORDSMITH For more fun with compound words, you could cut the cards into their separate parts, then shuffle them and get silly. *Jellyfish, football, cupcake*—oh, the possibilities. Jellyball, anyone? A slight variation on this is to play a variety of "sound deletion and manipulation" games. For starters, ask your child to say "cowboy" without the "cow." Then stretch it a little and have some fun. You've heard of a cowboy, but what would a cowtoy be? A horseboy? You've heard of a flashlight, but what would a trashlight be? A mashlight? A splashlight? This kind of silliness delights first-graders—and, by the way, helps them learn.

10 FIND IT When you're out and about, agree on a word to hunt for, then see who can spot the most examples. It's a good idea to pick one of the most frequently used sight words from the "Ten Small Words" list. Look for *it*, for example, on billboards and street signs—or in a magazine ad if you're stuck waiting at the doctor's office. Don't forget to look for *it* hiding in other words: ex*it*, f*it*ness, hosp*it*al, trans*it*, c*it*y, univers*it*y, and so forth. Or look for *on*—even on BETWEEN THE LIONS.

Thirty Really Good Books for First-Graders

Five "Start-Out" Books for Decoding
Nancy Antle, *The Good Bad Cat* (School Zone), and other School Zone books
Bobby Lynn Maslen, *Bob Books First!* (Scholastic), and other "Bob" books
Laura Appleton Smith, *The Sunset Pond* (Flyleaf Publishing)
John Stadler, *Cat at Bat* (Puffin)
Martha Weston, *Jack and Jill and Big Dog Bill* (Random House)

"Next-Step" Books: Five Easy Books . . .
P.D. Eastman, *Go, Dog. Go!* (Random House Beginner Books), and others
Syd Hoff, *Danny and the Dinosaur* (HarperTrophy "I Can Read" series), and other "I Can Read" books
Phyllis Root, *Hey, Tabby Cat* (Candlewick Press Brand New Readers), and others
Cynthia Rylant, *Mr. Putter and Tabby* books (Harcourt)
Harriet Ziefert, *Cat Games* (Puffin), and others

. . . and Ten Harder Books
Paulette Bourgeois, *Franklin* books (Scholastic)
Norman Bridwell, *Clifford* books (Scholastic)
Stephen Krensky, *Lionel* books (Puffin Easy-to-Read)
Arnold Lobel, *Frog and Toad Are Friends* books (HarperCollins)
———, *Mouse Tales* (HarperTrophy)
James Marshall, *Fox* books (Puffin Easy-to-Read)
Laura Joffe Numeroff, *If You Give a Mouse a Cookie* (HarperCollins), and others
Peggy Parish, *Amelia Bedelia* books (HarperCollins)
Cynthia Rylant, *Henry and Mudge* books (Aladdin Library)

Marjorie Weinman Sharmat, *Nate the Great* books (Delacorte Press)

Five Read-Alouds for First-Graders
Beverly Cleary, *Ramona the Brave* (Avon)
Astrid Lindgren, *Pippi Longstocking* (Puffin)
A.A. Milne, *Winnie-the-Pooh* (Dutton Books)
E.B. White, *Charlotte's Web* (HarperTrophy)
Margery Williams, *The Velveteen Rabbit* (Doubleday)

Five Read-Together Books Featured on BETWEEN THE LIONS
Verna Aardema, *Bringing the Rain to Kapiti Plain: A Nandi Tale* (Puffin)
Demi, *The Empty Pot* (Henry Holt and Company)
Leah Komaiko, *Earl's Too Cool for Me* (HarperCollins)
David McPhail, *Pigs Aplenty, Pigs Galore* (Puffin)
Margot Zemach, *It Could Always Be Worse: A Yiddish Folk Tale* (Farrar, Straus & Giroux)

Second-Grade Milestones

By the end of second grade, you can expect to see these signs of skillful literacy. A child who is progressing smoothly through this phase:

- Reads grade-level texts fluently, summarizes clearly, and comments thoughtfully on what she reads
- Can read silently for 10 to 15 minutes at a time
- Uses a variety of strategies, including predicting, rereading, and questioning, to check meaning as she reads
- Recognizes common spelling patterns and can use them (among other strategies) to decipher new words
- Is able to complete assignments and projects that require reading
- Writes on a variety of topics, using correct spelling and punctuation for the most part, and can proofread her own work

Warning Signs
You should look for help if your child:

- Is not reading grade-level books by the middle of the year
- Guesses at many words when reading and tends to skip the long ones
- Does not seem to notice her mistakes or understand much of what she reads
- Holds a pencil awkwardly, forms letters in unconventional ways, or writes illegibly or without attention to size, spacing, and placement of letters
- Avoids reading or writing or complains that either is "too hard"
- Seems to be lagging well behind her peers in reading, writing, or both

Remember that children follow different paths to literacy. If you are concerned about your child's progress, consult his or her teacher. You can also ask your pediatrician for advice or referrals if you have concerns about your child's hearing, speech, or other developmental issues. In addition, your school district is required by federal law to identify and assist children who need help. At your request, your school will conduct an academic, psychological, and language assessment, at no cost to you. Consult the principal's office of your school, or see Chapter 8 for more information.

Chapter 6

Skillful Literacy: Reading and Writing for Second-Graders

Second grade is a time of continuation, consolidation, and connecting the dots. For students who have proceeded smoothly through the challenges of first grade, it is a chance to deepen their knowledge of how reading works, extend their mastery of decoding and understanding the written word, and get plenty of practice in using these new skills. For those who have been struggling a bit, second grade offers an opportunity to catch up. While the reading curriculum still includes new material, there is not as much to cover as there was in first grade, so the students who need more time to master last year's lessons will get it this year. No matter where your child falls on the spectrum, you're likely to see her become a more secure, confident, competent reader this year.

A child like Maria, for example, who has been decoding confidently since the middle of last year, will move on this year to longer chapter books and series books. Her learning will come largely in the areas of vocabulary and comprehension, as she increases the store of words she knows and uses this growing knowledge to deepen her understanding of the texts she reads. She will also work this year on becoming a more fluent and expressive reader. Meanwhile, a child like Joel, who is still struggling with some parts of the alphabetic code, will get more practice in word recognition and phonics skills. As he comes up to speed, he will start moving, like Maria, into longer and more challenging texts, but he may still need extra support in figuring out words when he gets stuck. It's particularly important that you continue to read to a child like this, so that any difficulties he has with reading don't interfere with his acquisition of new knowledge and vocabulary. Reading aloud also offers a model of fluency that helps a listener like Joel internalize the kind of natural, expressive speech he should be hearing as he reads to himself.

As for what your child will probably study this year, it's helpful once again to think of the five key areas of reading instruction: phonemic awareness, phonics, fluency, vocabulary, and comprehension. Bear in mind, though, that as your child's reading becomes more expert, she will be focusing less and less on the component skills that support this complex achievement. That's a good thing: just as a skilled bike rider moves smoothly along without thinking about balance or pedaling, so a skilled reader draws on all her available skills without having to think about each of them in turn.

Still, it can be useful to know what's going on in each of these areas as your child moves through second grade. So we'll take a detailed look at each of them, along with what your child will learn this year about writing. In general, what's going on in second grade is a process of filling in the details and reinforcing the basics. In phonics, for example, your child's teacher will most likely extend the work done in first grade by introducing some of the less obvious letter-sound correspondences, such as *kn* and *eigh*, but he will also spend a good deal of time reviewing the patterns introduced last year. In addressing comprehension, too, he will introduce some new strategies, even as he continues to help your child refine the skills she acquired in first grade.

Fluency is a particularly important focus this year. This is the time when most readers start to move from the "glued-to-print" choppiness of early reading to the smoother, more natural flow of skillful reading. As the year progresses, second-graders make the shift from mostly reading aloud to mostly reading silently—in part because their teacher no longer needs to check their progress as often by hearing them read, and in part because silent reading provides better opportunities for extended practice. You can help your child read more fluently by listening to her read and reread text at home and by helping her choose books to read silently that work well for this task; we'll describe these books in more detail in the section on fluency.

One transition that your child will be expected to begin making this year is from using creative or "invented" spelling to spelling words correctly. Your child's teacher may still allow or even encourage her to spell inventively in rough drafts of written work, but he will increasingly expect her to use standard spellings in finished drafts. As with many of the other goals and processes of second grade, this one is gradual and incremental; no one expects your child to move overnight from the "beginner" status of first grade to the "fluent" level of third grade. She may be eager to tackle the chapter books that others are reading, but these will take some time, and skill, to grow into. As long as your child seems to be progressing, building on the skills she has and moving more or less steadily toward acquiring new ones, she's doing just fine. One item worth mentioning, as it often catches parents by surprise around this time: if your child has been doing well and suddenly slumps, have her eyesight checked. Nearsightedness often develops or becomes apparent in about the second grade. (See the box "The Age of Shortsightedness.")

One area where parents can offer particular help to their children is homework. Second grade is usually the first year in which children receive substantial homework assignments, so it's time to lay the groundwork for good study habits. Time management is a challenge for many children, particularly active children with many interests. It's important that parents help children balance reading with other activities and show how reading fits into all of them. Second grade is also a time when motivation may flag, as children become busy with sports, after-school programs, and friends. It's important to help your child cultivate the habit of reading every day. Even for reluctant readers, there are ways to nurture a taste for reading, and we'll look at some of those techniques.

There may be some stumbling blocks in the path ahead for a child like Joel, whose word recognition and phonics skills have been slow to develop. He may need to put in extra time learning those important word patterns and word attack strategies we described in the previous chapter. He may find, however, that a particular series of books captures his interest, and he may insist on reading every book in that series. Somewhere along the way, he will catch on to the process and will get comfortable with reading on his own.

Another child—Tanya, whose spelling test we see in the box "Spell Check" on page 125—will probably have a tougher struggle. She may have less of a gift for language and its refinements. With her delayed phonemic awareness may come several other weaknesses: limited knowledge of word meanings (it's hard to remember new vocabulary words when you don't hear or note the sounds clearly), persistent difficulties in decoding, and confusion about the complex sentence structure of written language. For instance, she might have trouble with this sentence: "The giant ate the little billy goat after he gobbled down the big billy goat." Which goat did the giant eat first? For Tanya, the path to fluent reading will be longer; she may need extra support and practice for a few more years. And she will need a skillful teacher to provide systematic, step-by-step instruction in each of those areas of language required for reading.

PHONEMIC AWARENESS: PLAYING WITH WORDS

Phonemic awareness, or the ability to hear the individual sounds of words, should be well established by the beginning of second grade. To reinforce this awareness, your child's teacher may lead the class in more complex

THE AGE OF SHORTSIGHTEDNESS

Second grade is often the time when nearsightedness, or *myopia*, is first diagnosed. If your child starts having learning difficulties that are otherwise unexplained, don't forget this possibility. She may be unable to see what's written on the blackboard.

You will want to have her eyes checked if she is:

❖ squinting
❖ complaining of headaches or blurry vision
❖ holding her reading material at a funny angle or moving it around to get a better look.

You may also want to be on the lookout for difficulties with *convergence*, the ability of the eyes to focus together on a single point. It's sometimes hindered by weak or unevenly developed eye muscles, and can be treated with eye exercises or by putting an eye patch over the stronger eye. If your child complains that print looks blurry, this is one diagnosis to consider.

The good news is that a second-grader is more likely than an older child to enjoy wearing glasses—she may be delighted by the air of sophistication and maturity they offer!

hearing and segmenting exercises. Whereas last year your child might have been asked to segment simple words like *cap* or *sun*, this year's words might start with combinations of consonants, as in *strap* or *crunch*.

Some teachers make a point of helping students extend their ability to analyze speech. They regularly ask students to count the number of syllables in long words or the number of sounds in shorter ones. When counting the sounds in one-syllable words, students may be asked to hold up a finger for each sound, a task that provides a useful multisensory clue for careful spelling. It can also help a student focus her attention on each sound in a complex blend like *str* or *thr*, which she will be asked to dissect for the first time this year.

Even more challenging are tasks that require manipulating sounds to make new words. For example, say the word *smile*. Now say it again without the /s/. Say *create*. Now say it again without the /ee/. (Did you get *crate*?) Word reversals can be another engaging challenge. Say the word *step*. Now reverse the order of the sounds, and what's the word? Try it again, reversing the order of the sounds in *ice*. (Did you get *sigh*?) These kinds of tasks both require and build verbal agility. And, interestingly, a child's performance on such tasks strongly predicts her reading achievement test scores in third grade and beyond. (See the box "These Words Like to Play" for a list of words to alter and reverse with your child.)

PHONICS: SUBTLE SOUNDS

As we discussed in the chapter on first grade, it's now generally agreed that the best reading programs include systematic, direct, explicit instruction in phonics. These programs teach the correspondences between letters and sounds by spotlighting them and working with them, rather than just by expecting students to deduce the rules of reading and writing on their own. And these programs teach phonics in a systematic sequence, generally starting with the most regular and easily grasped correspondences and moving gradually and logically toward more complex and irregular ones. Though systems vary slightly among different programs, your child's second-grade phonics instruction will probably include the following odds and ends, more or less in the order we describe here:

❖ Soft *c* and *g*, as in *cent* and *gel*
❖ More consonant digraphs, or two-letter combinations that represent a single sound—*wh, gh, ph, kn, gn,* and *wr*—and the silent letters in *tch, dge, mb, bu* as in *build, gu* as in *guard, gue* as in *league,* and *lk*
❖ More consonant blends and clusters, in which two or three consonants appear together but keep separate sounds—*scr, sch, spr, str, squ,* and *thr*
❖ Vowels as they sound when followed by *r: ar, or, er, ir, ur*
❖ Vowel combinations, both digraphs (two vowels that make one sound—*au, aw, oo, ey, ie, ei, ew, ue, ow* as in *blow*)—and diphthongs (combinations that blend two sounds together: *oi, oy, ow* as in *cow, ou* as in *couch*)
❖ The schwa, which is the name for the sound that all vowels make when they appear in an unaccented syllable (like the *a* in *about*)

THESE WORDS LIKE TO PLAY

Here's a list of fun words to use for playing sound-deletion games with your child. You say the word and have her repeat it, and then tell her the sound you want her to leave out. Ask her to try saying the word without that sound. Remember to say the sound, not the letter name, that you'd like her to delete. (For instance, for /s/ you'd say "sss," not "ess.")

Say *spill.* Say it again without the /s/.
Say *pray.* Say it again without the /r/.
Say *belt.* Say it again without the /t/.
Say *rode.* Say it again without the /d/.
Say *desk.* Say it again without the /s/.
Say *went.* Say it again without the /n/.
Say *glow.* Say it again without the /l/.
Say *stream.* Say it again without the /r/.

And here are some fun words for word-reversal practice: *pat, tub, cat, easy, sick, cuts, teach, boot, stiff, judge.* If she has trouble, suggest that she close her eyes, forget about the letters, and just listen to the sounds.

- *y* as a vowel, as in *sky, friendly,* or *myth*
- Homophones such as *red/read, meat/meet, sun/son,* and *there/their/they're*
- The spelling patterns *ough, alk, eigh, ind, old,* and *ook*

The trickiest part of the second-grade phonics curriculum may be the more advanced vowel sounds. The BETWEEN THE LIONS songs "When Two Vowels Go Walking" (which you'll find on the Web site, www.pbskids.org/lions) and "The a-r Song" may help your child keep them straight.

As you can see, that pretty much rounds out the written system of representing spoken sounds in English. If all goes well, by the end of second grade, your child will have learned all of the elements of our phonetic system—she'll have cracked the code. That means that, in third grade, she'll recognize most printed words instantly, decode new words skillfully, and start turning her full attention to the task of thinking about what she reads.

Meanwhile, your second-grader will also continue to hone the higher-level skill of structural analysis—learning how chunks of meaning (called "morphemes") combine to make up longer words. Recognizing these chunks in words makes it easier to read fluently, because it helps the reader break long words down into small, comprehensible parts and then put the parts together to figure out the meaning of the whole. The line between structure and spelling can sometimes blur, by the way, because certain spelling patterns play a role in structural analysis. For example, knowing the ways that verbs change their spelling when *-ed* is added is

essential to being able to read and understand the past tenses of these verbs. If you don't know that *y* changes to *i* in this instance, the word *buried* may stump you.

This year, the structural patterns your child is likely to study will include:

- Syllable types: open syllables, or syllables that end in a vowel and therefore have a long vowel sound, and closed syllables, or those that end in a consonant and have a short vowel sound
- Compound words: two words, each meaningful on its own, that combine to form a new word: *eggplant, starfish, cupcake, sailboat*
- Verb endings and plurals, and the spelling rules associated with them: doubling the final consonant of single or accented syllables; dropping the final *e* with *-ed* and *-ing*; changing *y* to *ie* in plurals
- Prefixes and suffixes: *dis-, un-, re-; -ful, -fully, -ish, -less, -ly, -ness, -self, -tion, -y*
- Adding *-er* and *-est* to adjectives; the *-en* form of verbs, as in *hidden*
- Contractions: *-'ve, -'m, -'ll, -'re, -'d, -'s, -n't*
- Possessives, both singular and plural

Once your child has learned to recognize prefixes, suffixes, and different types of syllables, she'll find it less daunting to break multisyllabic words into their component parts. It's important that she get plenty of chances to practice working with these words, both by studying them in groups—*painful, hopeful* or *agreeable, reliable,* for example—and by seeing them in unconnected lists. (See the box "Untangling Puzzle-ments.") In addition to playing with words by themselves—taking them apart

UN-TANGLING PUZZLE-MENTS

Learning prefixes and suffixes is one key to unlocking the meaning of new words. Here are the meanings of some common ones:

PREFIXES:

ab-	away from (*ab*sent, *ab*normal)
im-	not (*im*possible, *im*mature)
inter-	among (*inter*act, *inter*national)
tele-	far (*tele*scope, *tele*phone)
trans-	across (*trans*it, *trans*port)

SUFFIXES:

-able	worthy of (lov*able*, memor*able*)
-er, -or, -ant	one who (teach*er*, sail*or*, assist*ant*)
-ness, -tion	state of being (sad*ness*, connec*tion*)
-ology	study of (bi*ology*, music*ology*)
-ous, -ful	full of (wondr*ous*, hope*ful*)

Here are some multisyllable words that might be fun to unpack:

disen*tangle*	*forget*fulness
in*depend*ent	un*forget*table
*help*lessness	re*arrange*ment
inter*continenta*l	un*self*ishness
un*expect*edly	im*perfec*tion

or putting them together—it's also important that children get plenty of chances to see these words in the context of a connected text. A good second-grade program will include lots of texts that feature the targeted words.

FLUENCY: FOCUSING ON MEANING

If there's one reading task that's central to second grade, it's the development of fluency. Although children progress toward the goal of fluent reading at uneven rates, this year they will be expected finally to graduate from the choppy, disconnected sounding-out of the beginning reader to the smooth, flowing, connected phrasing of the mature reader. More and more, your second-grader will be expected to read as if she is simply speaking naturally—to make her reading sound like normal speech.

Fluency is important, because it's what allows the reader to switch her attention from the surface of the printed page—the letters and the sounds they represent—to the levels of meaning below. Developing fluency takes time, and it is a gradual process, but your child's teacher will be looking for steady progress over the course of the year. You, too, can look for the signs of increasing fluency. As your child becomes more fluent, she will read with more expression and with more natural phrasing and inflection; sentences will sound like sentences rather than like lists of words. She will pay more attention to punctuation, so that her voice will rise when she reads a question or grow more emphatic for an exclamation. You'll notice that she's sounding out words less and less, and recognizing more and more words and phrases by sight. To put it metaphorically,

the training wheels are coming off the bike, and she's moving faster and getting rid of the wobbles. Her reading is really taking off.

To help your child become more fluent, you can encourage her to find a time every day to read at home, either by herself or with you—ideally, both. Reading, and lots of it, is the best way to become a more fluent reader. When you're choosing books to reinforce fluency, you might want to aim for ones that seem a little too easy for your child. She can read more difficult books to build her vocabulary, too, but getting the chance to relax with a less challenging book is a good way for her to learn how to let her voice and thoughts flow along with the text. If you have a few books that have been longtime favorites for your child, they can also be great platforms for practicing fluency. Because she already knows them so well, she will find it easier to read and reread them with intonation and expression, and this smooth flow can carry over into her other reading as well.

For variety, you might also want to try some of the reading activities we mentioned in Chapter 5. These include choral reading—reading aloud together in a slow, expressive way, which helps your child model her pace and intonation on yours. You can also take turns reading a book—sentence by sentence or page by page—so that she hears the book's

On BETWEEN THE LIONS, Dr. Ruth Wordheimer works with her worried patients to help them develop the important skill of segmenting complex words, thereby avoiding the dreaded "long word freakout." You can gently reinforce her message—"take one part of the word at a time"—to help your child work through the process of reading a long word.

unfamiliar words spoken aloud and can recognize them more quickly when it's her turn. And it can still be helpful to have your child read along with a taped version of a book, either purchased or checked out from the library. (If you're feeling ambitious, you could even tape a few yourself!)

The tape recorder is also a great tool for helping your child practice reading fluently. Encourage your second-grader to tape herself reading a favorite story, listen, and then try again. Techniques like these help reinforce the connections between the words on the page and the sounds of natural speech. It's a firm grasp of those connections that makes for a fluent reader.

At school, meanwhile, your child's teacher will probably be using these strategies along with several others. He might engage your child in repeated oral reading: he reads a book, then she reads it, as he coaches her with tips on phrasing and expression. He might explain that skillful reading doesn't mean reading a whole long line of words without a pause. Good readers group words into phrases, and they pause between the phrases. This grouping of words into phrases is often called "chunking." It takes practice for most children to get the hang of it, particularly because it requires accuracy and on-the-fly attention to what the words mean.

To provide students with some much-needed practice in fluent, rhythmic reading, some teachers allow time each day for paired reading, in which two children take turns reading aloud to each other. And your child's class may work together to prepare a play or other performance—Thanksgiving pageant, anyone?—to get some terrific practice in delivering written lines with expression. A relatively new technique called Readers' Theater minimizes the theatrical demands of play production and emphasizes expressive reading— with script in hand. Small groups of students practice reading simple scripts, or turn the dialogue in a favorite story into a script of their own. Without needing to memorize their lines, students can focus on expressive reading; their performance is more like a radio drama than a stage production. Readers' Theater is a great activity to try at home, as are many of these classroom techniques. In all of these activities, the goal is to help your child increase her speed, ease, expression, rhythm, and fluency. And, of course, the more enjoyable an activity is, the more it will deepen your child's motivation—which is, in reading as in so much else, the secret of success.

VOCABULARY: LEARNING WORDS IN CONTEXT

Building children's spoken and written vocabulary continues to be an important task in the second grade. Your child's teacher will probably work with her on several vocabulary-building skills. In particular, he will help her learn how to figure out what new words mean by looking at how they are used in context. As the class or small group reads a book together, the teacher may draw the students' attention to new words and lead a discussion about what they might mean. The teacher may also use current reading and curriculum themes as a source of new vocabulary words. Lists organized around ideas and themes work better than random collections of vocabulary words, because the meanings are easier to remember when they're clustered in related groups.

Learning about structural analysis will also help build your child's vocabulary. When she studies prefixes, for example, she will learn that *re-* and *un-* change the meanings of many familiar words. Discerning these patterns of change will add many new words to her vocabulary.

At home, you can continue to help your child extend her vocabulary by reading with her and discussing the unfamiliar words you encounter. When you spot those words together, you may want to reinforce the idea of using what she knows about prefixes and suffixes to puzzle out the roots of even the longest words. By locating the root word within a string of syllables, you can help her unlock the word's meaning. For example, the long word *unfriendliness* may seem daunting at first glance. But it can be unpacked and easily understood once you discover the root word *friend.*

Remind her, too, that many words in English have multiple meanings—a fact that poses an added challenge for English-language learners. A *wave* of the hand looks nothing like a *wave* on the ocean or a *wave* in one's hair. Even simple words with multiple meanings (*ring, box, jam, deck, bat*) can sabotage an early reader's understanding. During read-aloud time and regular conversations, keep an eye out for confusing or interesting words to discuss or look up together. (Your second-grader will probably not yet be able to use a standard dictionary on her own.)

When a new word comes up, see if you can find occasion to use it in conversation over the next few days, so that it becomes firmly embedded in your child's memory. (It takes at least five exposures to a word for its meaning to sink in.) Encouraging your child to post a list of favorite new words may help both of you remember them. Some families find that the refrigerator is a great place to post a "wonderful word" of the day or week. And when you're talking with your second-grader, you are likely to find that you can use an increas-

---

On BETWEEN THE LIONS, the *un* and *re* People help children learn about the power of prefixes by taking action. The *un* People may untie a knot, for example, but then the *re* People come along and retie it. Seeing these prefixes in action helps to reinforce their meaning in the young viewer's mind.

---

ingly rich and complex vocabulary, as long as you take time to make the meaning clear.

For children of all ages, the best way to expand vocabulary is through wide and varied reading. If you mostly read fiction with your child, for example, check out a few elementary science texts from the library; you could learn the names of local trees, the diet and habits of common snakes, or the characteristics of Jupiter's moons. If you're more of a scientist by inclination, look for fairy tales or folklore, and pick up a few "facts" about Loki or Anansi. As you extend your own horizons, you'll be extending your child's, too—and showing her by example that learning never ends.

Even the most mundane family outings can provide the chance to learn a bunch of new words and concepts. On a trip to the supermarket, for example, take time to examine such items as kumquats, parsnips, rhubarb, tangerines, and tenderloin. Trips to a local zoo, aquarium, or historic site also help new words, ideas, and information take root together in your child's mind. Best of all, a vacation trip to Washington, D.C., New York's Ellis Island, or any other national historic site is an investment in your child's education. When the time comes to study American history or geography, that trip to Independence Hall or Yellowstone Park is likely to spark recognition, pride, and a desire to learn more.

COMPREHENSION: A MATURING MIND

As your child becomes a more fluent reader, she is becoming a more mature one as well, as the literal, concrete thinking of the early years starts to blossom into a more abstract and complex way of understanding the world. She's not all the way there yet, of course (a second-grader who can expound on plate tectonics may still believe in the tooth fairy, for instance), but second grade represents a new milestone on the road to mature thought. Sharpening her comprehension skills is an essential part of the learning your child will do this year.

Your child's teacher will help her use a variety of strategies to increase her comprehension of what she reads, and you can encourage her to practice these strategies at home. As you read a story together, for example, you can urge her to visualize the action: to picture the characters in her mind and to see, as vividly as possible, what they're doing as they move through the plot. (Check out the box "Seeing the Story.") You can also ask her, "What do you think will happen next?" Anticipating the twists of the story deepens your

child's engagement with it and helps her learn how stories work.

Because this is the age when children really start being able to think logically and to reason their way through an argument, you'll probably see your child making large leaps in her ability to understand and digest nonfiction. You can encourage this development by helping her to think about what she has read and to connect it with what she already knows of the world; you can also urge her to analyze whether a written argument makes sense to her, whether it fits with what she knows and thinks, and whether there are counterarguments that would be more persuasive to her. Some second-graders really love a debate! You may also want to help your child start noticing the unconscious biases of some texts: is an author making some assumptions about women or people of color, say, and do these assumptions contradict what your child knows from her own experience? The more your child learns to engage her own thinking as she reads, rather than just trying to soak up the author's ideas, the deeper her mastery of new material will become.

When your child reads aloud, you may notice her becoming increasingly adept at self-monitoring. As she works her way through a text, she will sometimes pause to ask herself if the words she is reading make sense. And when she makes an error, she may be more likely to stop and catch it herself, without any prompting from you. She will also continue to refine her strategies for attacking an unfamiliar or complicated word or sentence: examining and analyzing the structure of the word, rereading, or asking questions that help her decipher the meaning.

SEEING THE STORY

Visualizing as you read is a natural way to deepen comprehension. The more detail you imagine, the more you immerse yourself in the world you are reading about and the more memorable the text will be. The best way to encourage your second-grader to visualize is by describing the visual images that come to mind as you read and think about a new story.

For example, try reading the text-only version of the story "The Sad Dad," available on the BETWEEN THE LIONS Web site (www.pbskids.org/lions). Describe what you see in your mind's eye, and have your child describe what she may be seeing. (There is no right or wrong to this exercise; each person's inner picture reflects his or her personal experience.)

- ❖ What do you think the "very small farmhouse" that shelters the "very big family" looks like?
- ❖ What kind of furniture does it have?
- ❖ What sounds do you hear?
- ❖ What odors do you smell?
- ❖ How many family members do you see in the scene?
- ❖ How old are they?
- ❖ What are they wearing?

In addition to reinforcing these skills, second-grade teachers will introduce some more specialized kinds of reading. Most second-graders will learn, for example, how to make, read, and interpret charts, graphs, and diagrams. They will also start learning to recognize patterns in the structure of text: what an introduction looks like, how a conclusion pulls facts together at the end, how authors use repetition to make a point or hold a story together. And they will begin to pay more attention to differences in genres—how a fairy tale and a factual account, or a journal and a story, vary in tone and construction. (See the box "Reading to Learn.")

Some second-grade teachers help students focus on what is known as "story grammar": the predictable elements that can be found in most stories. All stories have settings (time and place), characters, and plots. The action in the plots usually begins with a problem to be solved, builds through a series of conflicts or dramatic incidents to the climactic resolution of the problem, and then wraps up after certain consequences are described. Understanding this story structure helps children know what to expect in a story and how to compare different treatments. It also helps them know how to plan a story they would like to write.

Most important, second-graders will make significant strides this year toward becoming *active* readers. Their teachers will encourage them not just to read a text but also to think and write about the books they read and find ways to extend the story in play. Now that your second-grader is becoming a more fluent reader, she will have the energy and attention to respond more deeply to the text.

At home, you can help your child by showing interest in the books she is reading and referring to some of the elements of story grammar (though you don't have to use that term). When you read storybooks aloud, try commenting on the setting or wondering aloud about how the main character will solve his problem. Show that you, also, are an active reader: you notice words, maybe even stumble over unusual ones, and you question, predict, and make connections as you go. Your child is likely to notice this thoughtful approach to text and may also imitate it. Of course, when you read for your own pleasure and information, whether in novels, newspapers, magazines, recipes, or e-mails, you are setting a great example. Be sure to share with your second-grader some of your thoughts and impressions—a joke you found in the paper, an unusual expression or word choice, an interesting fact. Revealing your thinking process helps show your child that comprehension is not something spooned out in a text; it's something we work with the text to achieve.

WRITING: BETWEEN HAND AND MIND

Writing—both the mechanics, such as printing and spelling, and the more abstract skills of organizing and composing written texts—continues to be an important part of your child's learning this year. So let's look briefly at the mechanics of writing, and then turn our attention to what second-graders are expected to know about composition.

As your child moves through second grade, you will notice that her handwriting is

READING TO LEARN

Nonfiction books pose their own set of challenges, and many children need time to absorb the new features. Here are some suggestions for helping your child learn how to read nonfiction.

❖ Preview the nonfiction book with your child and note how it is organized.

❖ Point out the table of contents, index, chapter headings, glossary, and other organizational features.

❖ Discuss topic headings and captions.

❖ Note any maps, graphs, charts, and technical drawings, and help your child understand how to read them.

❖ Point out introductory and summary paragraphs at the beginning and end of each chapter.

❖ Demonstrate how you can look for specific information. You needn't read from beginning to end; you can skip around as you search for facts.

❖ Show your child how to bookmark a page for easy reference.

❖ Check unfamiliar words in the glossary.

becoming more regular in both size and form. The letters become smaller as she gains proficiency and coordination. Her fine motor skills are improving, and the small muscles of her hand are gaining more control over the pencil. All of these changes signal that cursive writing is on the horizon.

Some schools introduce primary students to a style of printing called D'Nealian, which is designed to help children make the transition to cursive writing. Unlike manuscript, or traditional printing, with its perpendicular lines, separate strokes, and block formation, D'Nealian allows one fluid, slanting motion for each letter. Many second-graders adopt this sort of style on their own; for others, practice with D'Nealian can lead to considerable handwriting improvement.

Second-graders are also expected to start spelling more words correctly in their finished work. (See the box "Spell Check.") For this reason, teachers will probably devote some time to discussing the proper orthography of words: how they look, not just how they sound. One of the biggest challenges for children to master is homophones—words that sound alike but are spelled differently. Unfortunately for beginning spellers, English is unusually rich in homophones. (See the box "Sounds Like a Soundalike.")

Several games on the BETWEEN THE LIONS Web site (www.pbskids.org/lions) give children a chance to try spelling and editing challenges. And they point out incorrect answers, so children can focus on the skills they need to improve. Check out "Look Out Below," "Alphabet Soup," and "Sam Spud."

Your child's teacher will probably also go over the basic punctuation marks and encourage her to use them properly. And he will teach her how to proofread her own work, looking for and correcting errors in spelling, punctuation, and usage.

As for what she'll be writing, you'll find that second-graders are expected to create slightly more complex compositions than they were a year ago. This year, your child's teacher will introduce the basic steps of the writing process: initial planning, writing a first draft, revising, and producing a finished piece of work. Your child will learn that writing for different purposes—say, a book report and a story—calls for different styles and forms. She may be asked to write a story that includes literary language and style: "once upon a time," "at last they came upon . . . ," "lo and behold." She might write a sequel to a familiar story or retell the story with a twist of her own. By the end of second grade, she may also be asked to prepare a simple report, which will help her learn the basics of such skills as note taking, organizing, paraphrasing, and summarizing. All of these skills, of course, are ones she will continue to refine and deepen throughout her school years, but second grade is where the groundwork is laid.

For many children, these research-related tasks can feel overwhelming or confusing. If your child seems to be struggling with taking notes or organizing her thoughts, it's worth spending some time walking her through the process and showing her how you might approach each task. Note taking is a unique combination of reading and writing, and it's a skill that requires the ability to distill a text

SPELL CHECK

Here is a quick inventory that will help you assess your child's spelling skills. The 20 words listed here cover a range of developing spelling skills and are uncommon enough that they are not likely to be "known words" (that is, memorized). Therefore, they should indicate how well your second-grader understands the spelling of English words.

1. pan	6. main	11. reach	16. water
2. set	7. bunk	12. plate	17. lunches
3. fog	8. champ	13. toast	18. powder
4. dip	9. slide	14. bright	19. chipped
5. robe	10. shack	15. growing	20. striking

If you want to try this at home, call out one word at a time for your child to write, using it in a sentence to make sure she understands the meaning of the word. If she's struggling, stop after the first ten words.

Now let's look at how two second-graders might do on this test. First, we have Ricky, a second-grader with age-appropriate word knowledge. Here's how he spelled the first 12 words: *pan, set, fog, dip, robe, mane, bungk, chmp, slied, shack, reech, plait.*

Note that Ricky represents almost every sound with a letter, even though he may not always choose the right one. He is accurate in spelling the first five words, which reflect the skills taught in first grade. With more difficult words, he manages to represent all sounds logically even if his spelling is not quite correct.

Now, here are those same 12 words as spelled by Tanya, a second-grader who is having trouble grasping the basic principles of spelling: *PAN, sAT, FoG, beP, rOd, mlAn, Buk, ChmAP, sLID, SHAKC, rECH, PATLE.*

Tanya's list shows that she's having some trouble matching sounds to letters. As is common for children in mid-first grade, Tanya does not always represent both consonants in beginning and ending blends, or put them in the proper order. She also tends to make mistakes in spelling short vowel sounds. In addition, the random mix of upper- and lowercase letters is a warning sign in a second-grader's writing.

Tanya's parent should consult with the teacher to figure out and remedy the causes of this difficulty. She may need a boost in motivation, more practice, clearer instruction, or more specialized help.

SOUNDS LIKE A SOUNDALIKE

Homophones are words that sound the same but have different meanings and different spellings. Here are some of the homophones second-graders are very likely to confuse and misspell.

The most difficult to keep straight are:

1. its, it's
2. there, their, they're
3. who's, whose

Here are 20 more troublemakers, in alphabetical order:

blew, blue

buy, by

cent, scent, sent

dear, deer

flour, flower

hear, here

hoarse, horse

hole, whole

hour, our

knew, new

knight, night

know, no

main, mane

meat, meet

pair, pare, pear

read, red

right, write

sea, see

son, sun

tail, tale

threw, through

to, too, two

weak, week

wear, where

wood, would

your, you're

down to its essence. You can help by showing your child how to look at the "bones" of what she's reading—to find a topic sentence, then notice how other sentences offer supporting details, and to see the larger structure that underlies the finished work. Next, show her how to take notes in a way that outlines that structure. Being able to analyze text in this way comes more easily to some children than others; the best way to help your child get started is to demonstrate the process.

WHAT YOU CAN DO AT HOME

Probably the most important thing you can do for your child this year is to help her become a more fluent reader. You may want to turn back to the section on fluency for a few suggestions, or you can just remember this simple rule: read together, as much as you can, and read a variety of books. Hearing you read, as well as practicing her own independent reading, continues to be important, so you'll want to find time each day both for your child's reading and for your own.

This is a stage when it may get harder to make time for reading together. For one thing, now that children have made the adjustment to grade school, many of them begin to take up new hobbies and activities—soccer, skating, tae kwon do. You may find yourself spending a lot more time behind the wheel of the family car or riding the bus together than collaborating in the kitchen or snuggling on the sofa. Children this age may develop intense friendships, too—for girls, at least, second grade is often the year for dressing alike and doing their hair the way their friends do. For both genders, emerging

friendships can entail a daily drama of who's in and who's out. It's easy for children at this age to drift away from the reading habit, now that the mystery of cracking the code has been solved and real life has become more complicated. (See the box "What to Do for Reluctant Readers.")

On the plus side, much of what your child may be experiencing is grist for great, or at least pretty good, literature. There are sports books, like those by Matt Christopher or Gordon Korman, for kids who like sports. There are tons of series about friendships, from the Babysitters Club on up. And for those precocious second-grade worriers, you may be amazed to discover the wealth of nonfiction resources available to your child on almost any contemporary topic. (See the box "Thirty Really Good Books for Second-Graders" at the end of this chapter.)

Your child's increasing maturity also means that you and she can connect with books together at a much deeper level. This may be a time to tackle some more challenging read-aloud books together—classics like *Sounder* or *A Little Princess*. No matter who's reading, encourage your child to talk about the book: what she likes about her favorite characters and authors, how she might have told a story differently, what surprised her in a book she just read. These kinds of conversations not only deepen your child's connection to books but also provide a simple, natural way to expand her vocabulary and strengthen her ability to reflect on what she's reading in a more sophisticated way.

Don't forget to make regular trips to the library with your child. There's no better way to expose your child to a rich variety of genres,

WHAT TO DO FOR RELUCTANT READERS

Keep trying to find books that spark your reluctant reader's interest and engagement—even if they are different from the books everyone else is reading. It is essential that your child read *a lot* if she is ever going to read well. Worrying about exactly what she's reading can come later, after the habit is set. Consider:

❖ Nonfiction books about topics that interest her: science, history, religion, animals, creepy crawlies, magic, rocks and minerals, etc.

❖ Comic books

❖ Joke and riddle books

❖ Magazines (sports, car racing, hobbies, and, yes, even *MAD*)

❖ Baseball cards or other card collections

❖ Manuals: instructions for bike assembly, hobbies, video games, etc.

❖ Biographies of sports and entertainment heroes

❖ Cookbooks and recipes

❖ Song lyrics (yes, you're allowed to decide which ones)

If your child shies away from the difficult text contained in these materials, consult her teacher for more suggestions that are appropriate to her reading level. Many reluctant readers enjoy putting on plays (see the description of Readers' Theater) or tape-recording a story using different voices.

One thing to stay away from is the habit of using tangible rewards as an incentive for academic performance. Reading experts say that rewards actually make kids less motivated, not more; they start working for the rewards instead of for the intrinsic pleasure of learning, and then the rewards inevitably lose their luster, leaving the child with no incentive to keep going. You're better off encouraging your child to see reading as its own reward.

literary traditions, and styles. As children develop their own taste and interests, librarians can be very helpful in pointing them toward appropriate books and emerging classics that you may never have heard of. In addition, many libraries offer reading clubs and other programs, which can be a wonderful way to bolster your child's interest in reading.

Second grade is also the ideal time to introduce your child to the many series books written especially for young readers. Series books hold the promise of something new in each installment, but the characters, plot, and writing style are comfortingly familiar, so your child can follow a favorite character through a series of new adventures with greater ease. There's little chance of failing, and every opportunity to become more fluent. Reminisce with your child by picking up a few Nancy Drews or Hardy Boys, or explore some of the newer series, from Arthur up to and including Harry Potter. The *Little House on the Prairie* books or Lloyd Alexander's tales of Prydain are also good bets for many second-graders. *Goosebumps,* though it annoys some parents, has real appeal for kids—especially boys.

This is also an age when children may enjoy special-interest magazines. Check the selection at your local library, or ask other parents for advice. Many magazines, such as *Sports Illustrated* and *National Geographic,* now have special editions for young readers. And don't turn up your nose at comic books (though you might want to screen them for objectionable content)—many reluctant readers find themselves drawn in by the vivid pictures and compelling story lines, and, before you know it, they're clamoring to read more.

If your child expresses an interest in joining a book club or a drama group, encourage her. The combination of social interaction and reading can enliven the printed page for many young readers, and putting on a show is a great way to work on expression and verbal skills. Again, though, you'll want to follow your child's lead. Participating in too many activities at once not only is exhausting for your child, but also cuts down on the free time that she might use for, among other things, reading!

Even in a busy schedule, though, you can find time for independent reading. Encourage your child to carry a book to soccer practice or dance class, so she can take advantage of any down time; remember to keep books in the car, by the door to grab on your way out, or even in the bathroom. Think about any bits of unoccupied time that crop up regularly—the half hour before dinner or early Sunday morning—and try to have books available for those times.

As we've mentioned, another big issue that comes up in second grade is homework. This is the year most schools start to assign homework more regularly. Second-graders benefit from homework in lots of ways. It's a chance to practice the skills they are developing and to learn to manage projects over time. Doing math problems or taking notes on reading also underscores and reinforces the material they are learning at school and helps them prepare for the following day's discussion. Suddenly, homework is real work.

Many children find this transition a real challenge. And, for parents, it can be hard to balance the desire to foster a child's ability to work independently with the need to stay

HOMEWORK: STARTING OFF RIGHT

This year, for the first time, your second-grader is likely to start having homework that requires considerable time and effort. Here's how you can help:

- ❖ Have your child work independently on routine tasks, like worksheets. These involve practicing skills she will already have learned at school.

- ❖ Make yourself available for study drills, such as practicing for a spelling test.

- ❖ Encourage your child to work through at least the initial draft of a writing assignment on her own.

- ❖ For long-term projects, help your child plan a step-by-step schedule and use it to check her progress.

- ❖ Some projects may require adult supervision for safety reasons—messy science projects (baking-soda volcano, anyone?) or projects involving Internet research.

- ❖ Feel free to ask the teacher how much help is appropriate. Different teachers have different standards.

- ❖ Make sure your child has a quiet, comfortable place to work—whether it's in her own room or at the kitchen table. Provide good lighting, a comfortable chair, and ample room to spread out her papers.

- ❖ Try to make the homework routine as consistent as possible from day to day.

If homework begins to feel like a battle, talk with your child's teacher and make sure you share the same expectations. Friction over homework may be a sign of other issues (such as eyesight or hearing problems or other obstacles to learning) that need to be addressed.

involved. There are lots of ways you can help your child develop good study habits, while sending the message that you are there to support her. (See the box "Homework: Starting Off Right.")

Finally, keep encouraging your child to write. Just as her teacher will at school, you'll want to move her gradually this year toward using correct spelling. Perhaps you could enlist her help in writing a periodic newsletter to distant family members, or start a scrapbook or photo album together. When you travel as a family, encourage everyone to keep a vacation journal. Maybe you and your child could write up a few of your favorite recipes and give them to family and friends as gifts—along with a sample of the finished product. Anything that combines a favorite activity with writing or reading is a good idea. The more your child grasps that literacy is embedded in the activities that matter to her, the more she'll want to become a fully literate person. As second grade comes to an end, you'll be amazed how close she is to that goal.

BUILDING BLOCKS: WHAT YOUR SECOND-GRADER NEEDS

Time to catch up, practice, and consolidate skills
- ❖ Lots of practice with easier texts to build fluency
- ❖ Some practice with harder texts to build vocabulary
- ❖ At least half an hour daily of silent reading alone
- ❖ Opportunities to explore many different genres and styles of texts

Direct, systematic instruction in phonics
- ❖ Advanced practice in segmenting, blending, and manipulating sounds
- ❖ Filling in details on more advanced combinations, *r*-controlled vowels, the schwa sound, and so forth
- ❖ Tackling multisyllabic words
- ❖ Playing with homophones and other tricky words
- ❖ Continued instruction and practice in structural analysis: prefixes, suffixes, compound words

Spelling, mechanics, and writing for different purposes
- ❖ Instruction and testing in correct spelling
- ❖ Introductory instruction in punctuation, proofreading, note taking, and research

Active reading
- ❖ Instruction in story grammar (the features of stories)
- ❖ Engaging with texts to construct meaning rather than just identifying the words

Habits and routines
- ❖ Reading and being read to every day
- ❖ Developing a regular time, place, and method for doing homework
- ❖ Taking regular family outings to build vocabulary and background knowledge and to connect book learning to the outside world

1 GET WILD ABOUT WILDLIFE   Help your child start a nature journal, recording her observations of the local fauna. You don't have to live in an exotic locale for this to be fascinating; even common birds and squirrels have interesting habits, and children enjoy getting to know them. Your child could put up a bird feeder and make a daily record of its clientele; perhaps she'll even want to convert her data into a graph or chart. She could put out different kinds of feed and note which one the squirrels prefer, or check each morning for tracks in the snow and record the number and variety of nocturnal visitors. Even insects, for the child who likes them, can serve as an introduction to the wonders of the natural world—and a worthy subject for your child's written observations.

2 SHOW TIME   For the child with a dramatic bent, there are lots of ways to play around with stories and books. You could encourage your child to set up her own talk show—you can be Charo. (Okay, your kid's too young to know who that is. Be Cleo instead—or ask your child which literary character she'd most like to interview.) Help her turn a favorite story into a simple script and do Readers' Theater—each player reads dramatically from a hand-held script, as in a radio drama, so there's no need to memorize. Some of the stories on the BETWEEN THE LIONS Web site (www.pbskids. org/lions) make great Readers' Theater scripts: "Little Big Mouse" can be a three-person play (lion, mouse, narrator), and "The Last Cliff Hanger" text would also make an amusing script for two or three readers. Tape-record the drama to bring along on your next car trip. Think of other genres your child might enjoy, and help her bring them to life in your living room: a talk show, a news flash, a scientific lecture from a dinosaur hunter just back from her latest expedition. Or maybe she'd like to put on a musical. Anybody got a barn?

3 BABY, IT'S YOU   Second-graders love to reminisce about their youth, and they especially enjoy seeing pictures of themselves as babies. Meanwhile, mothers everywhere feel guilty about not keeping up with their children's baby books. Make everybody happy: help your child create her own baby book. Gather up all those photos, birth announcements, and congratulatory cards, and help your child arrange them in a scrapbook. You can also take her to the library to get a copy (from microfilm, most likely) of the front page of the newspaper on the day she was born, and to research the big news stories, fashion trends, and hit songs of the day. Meanwhile, have her interview you to get the story of the day she was born, how you chose her name, who came to visit first—all the details that children love to hear. Write it all down together, and cross another item off your guilt list.

4 THE JOKE'S ON US Appeal to the second-grader's love of silly jokes with an offer to help compile all your family's favorites. Now is the time to dredge up all those elephant jokes and knock-knocks from the memory banks. Or, if memory fails, check out Lionel's pages on the BETWEEN THE LIONS Web site (www.pbskids.org/lions)—the kid's a regular Henny Younglion. You'll find more groaners in the story "There's a Fly in My Soup" or the game "There's a Fly in My Alphabet Soup." You can easily extend this idea to make it a scrapbook of all kinds of family favorites, not just jokes: favorite recipes, favorite movies, favorite TV shows, favorite places to go on vacation, favorite ways to tease a little brother, favorite memories, great moments in your family's history.

5 HOUSEHOLD EXPLORER Encourage creative storytelling and use of language with this mock-serious activity. Tell your child that the two of you are working today as archaeologists, and you've been put down in the midst of an alien civilization (your home). Your job is to examine the artifacts of this culture and determine their use. For example—and here you can hold up your keys, an eggbeater, or the TV remote—this object is believed to have some ritual significance. What might it be? Get as playful and inventive as you can in your own explanations, and encourage your child to do the same. You might want to help her write a report of your expedition once you return to base camp.

6 MYSTERY WORD Write a short story and leave out important words, using only the first letter. Have your child fill in the blanks to make a logical story—or an extremely silly one. For inspiration, check out the series of *Mad Libs* books from Price, Stern, Sloan, which organize the stories around a particular theme. For more advanced readers who've learned terms like *noun* and *adjective*, you can leave out the first letter as well and just ask for a word in the proper category—without reading the story at all until it's done. This is guaranteed to produce a ludicrous result.

7 SEARCH ME Help your child start learning to use a dictionary by playing a few games with it. You could start by having her find a word that starts with each letter of her name. Then have a race: use a stopwatch to see how long it takes her to look up the word *tangerine*. Just locating words in the dictionary is a challenge for children, and adding a little friendly competition may motivate them to get better at it. Next, she could try to think of synonyms for common words, then look up each one to discover the subtle differences among them. For *look*, she could start with *gaze, glare, study, examine, glimpse,* and *stare;* for walk, get moving with *step, stroll, stride, strut, limp, hike,* and *march.* Then you could show her how to use a thesaurus to find some more. Finally, play around a bit by finding a word that no one in the group knows. (May we recommend *quagga* or *gangue*?) Then have each person write a definition. Read all of them aloud, including the real one from the dictionary, and award points to any players who guess the right one—or fool their competitors into choosing their invention instead.

8 CATEGORIES Choose a word with five or more different letters. Write it across the top of a page, with a separate column under each letter (leave some space at the left margin). Now choose five categories (say, animals, food, colors, sports, and countries). List the categories down the left margin of the page, and draw a line across, so that you have a row for each category. Now have children fill in the grid, with a word for each category that starts with the letter at the top of the column. This game helps children strengthen their vocabulary by organizing words by topic. And, if you choose words that your child has been struggling to learn, the emphasis on each letter of the word may strengthen her spelling, too.

9 MARGANAS—ER, ANAGRAMS Help your child think of anagrams of her name or other familiar words, then take turns guessing each other's words. (If just scrambling the letters of her name doesn't yield any interesting results, try adding your hometown, your street name, your pet's name, or some other significant word until you get a winner.) You can also look at the letters that correspond to each digit of your telephone number, then see who can come up with the best word for your number. If you find a lot of anagrams you like, you could try combining them into a story. And if this kind of wordplay appeals to your child, check the Web for anagram sites and other forms of puzzles. A child who likes anagrams, for instance, will probably also enjoy cryptograms.

10 CODE READ If the cryptograms are a hit, help your child explore other forms of code making. She might enjoy learning Morse code, for example, and using it to communicate with a friend. Or show her how to do mirror writing—write backward, then hold the result up to a mirror to decode it. (Leonardo da Vinci recorded many of his inventions this way.) Invisible ink is fun at this age, too; your child can use lemon juice, which turns brown when you hold it over a lightbulb or other source of heat. (Make sure she doesn't try to use a candle!) She may also want to come up with codes of her own—making an alphabetical list of key words, for example, then using the appropriate word (or, to make it harder to crack, a synonym of the word) for each letter of the message. Playing with codes requires logical thinking and encourages your child to look for patterns in language and the structure of words.

Thirty Really Good Books for Second-Graders

Ten Favorite Series of Chapter Books

David Adler, Cam Jansen mystery series (Penguin Putnam)

Marc Brown, Arthur's Adventure series (Little, Brown)

Ann Cameron, *The Stories Julian Tells* (Alfred A. Knopf), and others

Bill Cosby, Little Bill series (Scholastic)

Patricia Reilly Giff, *Kids of the Polk Street School* (Bantam Doubleday)

Suzy Kline, Horrible Harry series (Penguin Putnam)

Mary Pope Osborne, *The Magic Tree House* (Random House)

Barbara Park, Junie B. Jones series (Random House)

Dav Pilky, Captain Underpants series (Scholastic)

Laura Ingalls Wilder, Little House series (HarperCollins Juvenile Books)

Five Read-Alouds to Build Vocabulary, Knowledge, and Comprehension

Lynne Reid Banks, *The Indian in the Cupboard* (HarperCollins)

C.S. Lewis, *The Chronicles of Narnia* (HarperCollins)

J.K. Rowling, *Harry Potter and The Sorcerer's Stone* and its sequels (Scholastic)

Shel Silverstein, *Lafcadio, the Lion Who Shot Back* (HarperCollins)

E.B. White, *The Trumpet of the Swan* (HarperCollins)

Five Children's Magazines

Cricket: The Magazine for Children (literature and art from around the world)

Ranger Rick (animals and the environment)

Science Weekly (problem solving, math, technology)

Stone Soup (stories and poems written by children)

World (*National Geographic*'s version for children)

Five Read-Togethers Featured on
BETWEEN THE LIONS

Aliki, *The Gods and Goddesses of Olympus* (HarperCollins)

Barbara Bader, *Aesop and Company* (Houghton Mifflin)

Steven Kellogg, *Pecos Bill* (William Morrow)

Jeff Moss, *Bone Poems* (Workman Publishing)

Robert Louis Stevenson, *A Child's Garden of Verses* (Simon & Schuster)

Five Read-Alouds Related to
BETWEEN THE LIONS Episodes

True Kelley, *Pablo Picasso: Breaking All the Rules* (Grosset & Dunlop "Smart About Art" series)

William Miller, *Night Golf* (Bantam Books)

Brian Selznick, *The Houdini Box* (Aladdin Paperbacks)

Seymour Simon, *Big Cats* (HarperCollins)

David Wisniewski, *Tough Cookie* (HarperCollins)

Third-Grade Milestones

By the end of third grade, you can expect to see these signs of fluent literacy. A child who is progressing smoothly through this phase:

❖ Reads grade-level books fluently, with comprehension and confidence, including chapter books and nonfiction
❖ Recognizes most words in grade-level texts and uses a variety of strategies (phonics, structural analysis, context) to figure out the pronunciation and meaning of unfamiliar words
❖ Can participate in discussions of what he reads, offering a summary and identifying the main ideas and supporting details
❖ Can compare and contrast various story elements: characters, plot, settings, and author's style
❖ Writes expressively, using descriptive adjectives and metaphors
❖ Produces reports that draw on several sources
❖ Correctly spells words he has studied and words that follow known patterns
❖ Edits and revises his own work and can offer useful suggestions on other students' work
❖ Produces a final draft in cursive writing or well-formed print

Warning Signs
You should look for help if your child:

❖ Is not reading third-grade-level books by the middle of the year
❖ Skips over or misreads multisyllabic words or frequently confuses lookalikes: *when/then, were/where, though/through/thought, tired/tried*
❖ Seems not to understand much of what he reads, which is sometimes indicated by not correcting his own mistakes as he reads aloud
❖ Continues to struggle with handwriting, spelling, or other aspects of his writing assignments
❖ Avoids reading and writing or complains often that these tasks are too hard

Remember that children follow different paths to literacy. If you are concerned about your child's progress, consult his or her teacher. You can also ask your pediatrician for advice or referrals if you have concerns about your child's hearing, speech, or other developmental issues. In addition, your school district is required by federal law to identify and assist children who need help. At your request, your school will conduct an academic, psychological, and language assessment, at no cost to you. Consult the principal's office of your school, or see Chapter 8 for more information.

Chapter 7

Fluent Literacy: Reading and Writing for Third-Graders

Third grade is both an end and a beginning. For most students, this is the end of systematic instruction in reading. By the end of the school year, they will have the basic skills of reading under their belts. And, because of that newfound competence, it's the beginning of the kind of reading they will do for the rest of their lives: fluent, skillful, automatic reading that focuses their attention not on the mechanics of the reading process but on the content of what they read. To use a distinction that you may already have heard your child's teachers make, this is the last year that instruction focuses on learning to read. From here on out, the emphasis shifts to reading to learn.

What that means for your third-grader is that his teacher will be doing as much as she can to make sure he is ready to make that leap. Your child will receive instruction in the most advanced points of the phonetic code, and will spend much of the year demonstrating his mastery of that code. He will also spend a lot of time reading, getting as much practice as possible in order to sharpen his skills and increase his fluency. As for what he's reading, you'll find that the books he chooses are becoming increasingly complex, varied, and sophisticated. He will read not only chapter books and other challenging forms of fiction but also longer books on other subjects, from math to social studies. Reading a variety of texts will help him deepen his understanding of the many different styles, structures, vocabularies, and approaches authors can use. And that understanding will prepare him for the many kinds of reading material he will encounter in the years ahead.

Because of this shift in emphasis from mastering skills to deepening understanding, you'll see that we spend only a little time in this chapter talking about phonics skills, and much more on comprehension. We'll also look at the relatively complex and sophisticated writing projects that your child will be expected to undertake this year, and we'll discuss third-grade expectations for spelling and cursive writing. In addition, we'll explore some of the issues that may already have come up at home but are even more likely to become relevant this year, from struggles over homework to strategies for continuing to encourage a reluctant reader. Finally, we'll glance ahead toward the world of reading that awaits your child in fourth grade and beyond.

As your child progresses through this exciting and challenging year, most of the reading-related time you spend together will probably involve reviewing and discussing the material he's reading. That's completely appropriate. If all is going well, your child really doesn't need much more coaching in basic reading skills. Naturally, if you have any concerns about his mastery of these skills, it's important to look for help this year, so that he'll enter fourth grade ready to dive in. But if he's sailing along, the best thing you can do is sail along with him. And read along, too! This is a wonderful year for many parents, because so many of the classic books you enjoyed as a child are now accessible to your own child. You can read them to him or just hand them over, depending on his skills and temperament; either way, you're in for a rare pleasure when your child gets to know a character you've loved for decades. It's like discovering you have a friend in common, and it's a wonderful opportunity to share in the joy that reading can bring.

PHONEMIC AWARENESS: AT'S-THAY IMPLE-SAY!

Most third-graders have acquired the ability to hear the distinct sounds that make up words. Some children, however, will still need coaching here. If your child seems to have trouble breaking words into their sounds, distinguishing between sounds, or playing with them, check out some of the phonemic-awareness activities in earlier chapters to give him some extra help. And if his problems with these tasks seem severe, don't hesitate to look for guidance from his school or seek a formal assessment.

For some third-graders, a task like separating consonant blends—hearing, for example, that *stretch* starts with the distinct sounds of *s, t,* and *r*—can be difficult. Other children become real linguistic gymnasts at this age. If you've got one in your house, brace yourself for endless conversations in Pig Latin or Ubbi Dubbi. (As you may *emember-ray*, Pig Latin involves taking the first sound of a word and putting it at the end with a long /a/ sound, while Ubbi Dubbi inserts /ub/ in every syllable, *lubbike thubbis.*) In addition to being a great way to annoy parents on long car rides, secret languages are a sign of advanced phonemic awareness—so try to console yourself with that as you drive. As the ability to manipulate phonemes comes more easily, it enables children to improve steadily in spelling and decoding unfamiliar words.

Many children this age love tongue twisters, too. If you're tired of "She sells seashells by the sea shore," "Rugged rubber baby buggy bumpers," or "Unique New York," check out the BETWEEN THE LIONS Web site (www.pbskids.org/lions) for some of Lionel's favorites.

PHONICS: THE FINISHING TOUCHES

Third-graders typically receive instruction in some of the remaining fine points of the phonetic code. These may include:

- ❖ Vowels with variant or exceptional pronunciations, as in *head* and *heard* or in *touch, pouch, should,* and *shoulder; ey* in *key* and *obey; ai* in *said* and *plaid*
- ❖ Uncommon vowel combinations with silent consonants: *ough, augh, aigh, eigh*

- ❖ Consonants with variant or exceptional pronunciations, as in *though* and *tough, party* and *partial, face* and *facial,* or *use* and *usual*
- ❖ Uncommon consonant combinations: *ps* and *ch* (in *psychology*), *sc* (*science*), *mb* (*lamb*), *pn* (*pneumonia*), *st* (*whistle*)
- ❖ A review and expanded exploration of homophones, or words that sound alike but have different meanings, with particular attention to such common pitfalls as *its/it's, you're/your,* and *there/they're/their*
- ❖ The spelling patterns *-ance* vs. *-ence* and *-able* vs. *-ible*
- ❖ The ways in which some word parts change their pronunciation when a suffix is added, as in *sign* becoming *signal* or *magic* transforming itself into *magical* or *magician*

Most of a third-grader's time, however, is spent practicing what he already knows, rather than mastering new material. Third-graders can still use plenty of practice in recognizing phonetic patterns quickly and smoothly, and they may get this practice both by reading and by doing worksheets or other skill-based exercises.

While direct instruction in phonics is unlikely to take place beyond third grade, there are still some areas of knowledge to be encountered and mastered in later years, such as the syllabication of very long words or certain spelling rules that are based on derivation, rather than more obvious criteria. Alert students will pick up and integrate most of these. For others who are less attuned, a more direct, explicit approach may still be needed. For instance, most children will benefit from a good, systematic spelling program taught by a savvy teacher. (See the box "Eight Spelling Rules.")

EIGHT SPELLING RULES

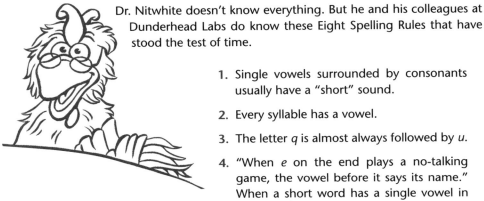

Dr. Nitwhite doesn't know everything. But he and his colleagues at Dunderhead Labs do know these Eight Spelling Rules that have stood the test of time.

1. Single vowels surrounded by consonants usually have a "short" sound.

2. Every syllable has a vowel.

3. The letter *q* is almost always followed by *u*.

4. "When *e* on the end plays a no-talking game, the vowel before it says its name." When a short word has a single vowel in the middle and an *e* at the end, the first vowel is usually "long," and the *e* is silent.

5. "When two vowels go walking, the first one does the talking"—in vowel combinations like *ai, oa, ee,* and *ea,* you hear the sound of the first letter, not the second.

6. The letters *c* and *g* have their "soft" sounds when they are followed by *i, e,* or *y.* Examples: *city, ice, fancy; ginger, age, gym.*

7. Endings have several rules of their own. For one-syllable *CVC* words like *tap,* you double the consonant before an ending that starts with a vowel. (Change *tap* to *tapped* or *tapping,* for example.) For silent *e,* drop the *e* before the ending (e.g., *tape, taped, taping*). And in common nouns change *y* to *i* (*baby, babies*), unless it's preceded by a vowel, as in *monkeys.*

8. "*I* before *e,* except after *c,* or when sounded like *a,* as in *neighbor* and *weigh.*" And here's a sentence to help you remember some other exceptions: *Neither leisurely foreigner seized* the *weird heights.*

SEVENTY-FIVE SPELLING DEMONS

Here are 75 words that trip up young spellers. You can help your child master these tricksters.

again	heard	straight
already	hour	sure
although	knew	surprise
always	know	their
any	learn	there
because	many	they
been	maybe	though
beautiful	minute	thought
birthday	neighbor	through
bought	neither	touch
build	none	trouble
busy	often	very
buy	once	view
children	only	wear
coming	other	were
could	people	where
does	piece	which
either	really	woman
enough	receive	women
every	remember	would
fourth	right	write
friend	said	wrong
great	school	young
guess	something	your
haven't	special	you're

Third-graders will also continue their study of structural analysis, or how to break down long words into smaller chunks of meaning (known as morphemes). A typical program will both review and expand your child's knowledge in these areas:

❖ Prefixes and suffixes and their meanings, including *dis-, im-, post-, pre-, sub-, super-,* and *trans-; -able, -ible, -ous, -ion, -tion, -sion, -ment, -ty, -ic,* and *-al*
❖ The contractions *-'ll, -n't, -'d,* and *-'re,* along with the other contractions your child has already learned
❖ Syllable patterns, or the ways to break multisyllabic words into their meaningful parts
❖ Rules for joining syllables together and adding endings, such as dropping a silent *e* or doubling some consonants

In addition, some programs—especially those designed for struggling readers—go into detail about the six different types of syllables in English. They are (1) "closed," or those that end with a consonant and have a short vowel sound; (2) "open," or those that end in a vowel and have a long vowel sound; (3) "r-controlled," which contain a vowel plus *r* and have unique vowel sounds of their own; (4) "vowel team," or syllables that contain a combination of vowels; (5) "silent *e*," which has, you guessed it, silent *e* after a vowel and a consonant; and (6) "C-*le*," or a consonant followed by *le.* Some teachers find that this level of detail can help students develop a deeper sense of the structure of words and, therefore, a more comprehensive understanding of how they are spelled; others feel that providing this much information about syllable types confuses more than it clarifies. In either case, however, your child should get plenty of practice in breaking words down into their individual syllables, studying their structure, and putting them back together again.

FLUENCY: SMOOTH OPERATORS

Fluency, as we've mentioned before, is the ability to read with speed and accuracy, so that the mind is free to focus on the meaning of the text rather than on the surface details of its spelling and pronunciation. It isn't simply a matter of how fast a child reads. The point is to make word recognition so automatic that he is free to think about what he's reading, compare it with other things he's read, consider how it relates to his own ideas, and remember all this after he puts the book down. These are complex cognitive tasks that a third-grader simply can't handle if he's still struggling with the basics of identifying words and connecting them into meaningful phrases. And they're tasks that will become absolutely essential as he moves into fourth grade, with its new and challenging emphasis on reading to learn.

Reading that is too slow not only indicates a lack of fluency but also contributes to it: If the gap between one word and the next grows too great, the reader can't hold them together in his mind to make sense of them. In general, a reading rate of less than 60 words per minute is considered to be too slow to permit full comprehension. A good goal for students at the end of third grade is to read 110 words per minute correctly. (For first-graders, the goal might be to read 40 words per minute accurately by spring; for second-graders, the target is 60 words.) To assess your child properly, be sure he is reading text at his own grade level.

To improve your child's fluency, offer him plenty of opportunities to read, listen as he reads aloud, and encourage him to try repeated readings in order to increase his accuracy and expressiveness. Make sure that your child gets plenty of time to read at home, and check with your child's teacher to see if his schedule at school makes room for reading on his own.

Chapter books and particularly series novels continue to be great for enhancing fluency. As we've noted about series books before, because the characters, structure, and style carry over from one chapter or novel to the next, your child doesn't have to master a whole new world with the beginning of each chapter but can instead stay within a familiar environment and start speeding right along with the story. The pleasure and reassurance of familiarity is one reason that many children grow attached to a series of books or a favorite author. They not only enter a book they already know they are likely to enjoy, but they also can spend more energy deepening their comprehension with each new version of a familiar formula.

Meanwhile, because fluency depends in part on familiarity with the subject, your child will be well prepared for the shift to reading to learn in the years ahead if, starting now, he branches out from storybooks to age-appropriate biographies, science texts, news reports, and other examples drawing from a whole range of nonfiction genres. Knowledge is cumulative: the more you know, the easier it is to learn more. So you can give your child a real advantage in the years of study to come by helping him lay the groundwork in a wide range of fields this year. Bear in mind, though, that nonfiction poses new challenges in vocabulary and structure, and it can be difficult for an early reader to gain momentum as he reads along. You may want to lend a hand with these challenging texts by taking turns reading them aloud with your child. Or you could try reading several pages aloud, then listening as your child reads the same pages back to you.

VOCABULARY:
MY, WHAT BIG WORDS YOU HAVE!

Third-graders can read texts with fairly advanced vocabulary, and many are good at figuring out the meaning of new words. In part, this is because of the work they do in structural analysis, which helps them look for meaning in the parts of words and then to use those partial meanings to attempt a definition. But it also comes from the increasing complexity of their cognitive abilities: as his brain matures, a third-grader is able to hold different thoughts in his head at once. That ability is key for deducing the meaning of a new word from its context: the child can think at the same time about the context that makes sense to him and the word that doesn't, and use what he knows to extrapolate what he doesn't.

Because of this new cognitive sophistication, your child may find it easier this year to use a dictionary effectively. Up until now, it was just too confusing and overwhelming to try to make sense of one, but now he can understand what a dictionary is for and how to use it. He will also be learning more this year about synonyms and antonyms, so now a thesaurus becomes a useful tool.

Many schools, either this year or the next, will introduce more formal, systematic vocabulary instruction than your child has seen

---

Third-graders may find the Word Helper feature on the BETWEEN THE LIONS Web site useful (www.pbskids.org/lions). As they read the stories on the Web site, they can click on underlined words to get illustrations, simple definitions, and sentences that use the word in context. In many instances, the target word is also translated into Spanish.

---

before. He may be given lists of words to learn or may participate in other exercises that are specifically designed to build vocabulary, such as building lists of synonyms or antonyms or studying literature with a particular focus on a book's specialized vocabulary. The most effective programs offer direct instruction not only in structural analysis, which we've already discussed, but also in contextual analysis. This means teaching children how to use clues embedded in the text to infer the meaning of an unfamiliar word. These clues might involve restatements of the unknown word, synonyms, antonyms, and compare/contrast statements. You may notice some of these helpful phrases when you encounter esoteric, or highly specialized, words in your own reading.

In addition, your child's teacher will probably help students explore words with multiple meanings, as well as the subtle shades of

meaning within groups of closely related words. Think, for example, of the different connotations of *looked, glared, stared*, and *gazed*. Children vary in their sensitivity to nuances of meaning, but the more different kinds of books a child reads, the more he will develop a grasp of these subtleties.

In fact, this year marks a turning point in the way children acquire new vocabulary. Until now, children have learned most of their new words from conversation. Now, for the first time, they will acquire more new words from reading than from speech. Because they can read more quickly and smoothly and can figure out the meaning of new words in context, third-graders can start to zoom through new areas of study, acquiring a wide and deep range of new vocabulary as they go. That's why it's especially important to make sure your child has access to as great a variety of books as possible this year. The library is always a wonderful place for young readers, but it's an especially important resource now. Make sure you visit regularly, and make sure your child knows how to get around the library to discover all the different kinds of books available on the shelves.

Of course, this growing ability to learn words from books doesn't mean that conversation stops being important. As you continue to talk with your child about all kinds of things, you may be delighted to find what sophisticated conversations he is now capable of handling. If you want to give him extra practice in extending his vocabulary, you may find it especially helpful to explore an unfamiliar subject together. If you're both learning something new about bats or poetry, knitting or sports cars, you'll naturally use a whole new specialized vocabulary in your conversations. These shared interests can also provide inspiration for books to read together, and in particular for books that you can read to him. That's something, by the way, that you should continue to do, because even though his skills are more advanced than before, you can still read on a more sophisticated level and so can continue to bring more advanced knowledge, vocabulary, and structure into his reading world. It's worth noting, too, that the most memorable way to learn vocabulary is still through hands-on experience, and so those trips and hobbies and collections of shells, stamps, bugs, or whatever can be a very worthwhile investment.

Vocabulary is more than just an end in itself. There's plenty of evidence that large vocabularies and skilled reading go hand in hand. To take just one example: skilled third-grade readers have about 12,000 words in their working vocabulary, while less skilled third-graders know only half that number. And consider the high correlation between vocabulary and comprehension: your achievement in one area accounts for 75 percent of your achievement in the other. The two reinforce each other, because knowing more words aids comprehension, and being able to comprehend a text enables you to learn the new words you encounter in it.

COMPREHENSION: THE FINAL PIECE OF THE PUZZLE

As the process of reading becomes increasingly automatic for your child, he will have more and more mental resources available for the point of all this work: comprehension. When he's reading simple texts, he will be able to understand them without giving the process much conscious thought; as his skill and fluency increases he will find more and more texts opening themselves to him without mystery or confusion. When he confronts challenging material, however, he will need to have a powerful array of tools at his disposal. His teacher this year will spend much of her time helping him to practice the skills he has already learned and teaching him some more sophisticated strategies as well. These strategies will increasingly focus on comprehension of the text as a whole, rather than the narrower "word attack" strategies that he has probably mastered by now. Now, he will be encouraged to monitor his own understanding of what he reads and to figure out what to do whenever something doesn't make sense: reread, identify unfamiliar words or confusing phrases, ask questions.

The teacher may start by encouraging your child to preview a text before he begins to read it, making informed guesses as to what kind of information it contains, what genre of writing it falls into, and how it connects with what he already knows. She may demonstrate what's often called the K-W-L technique, in which a reader asks himself three questions. Before beginning to read, he asks, "What do I already *Know* about this subject?" and "What do I *Want* to know?" After reading, he asks, "What have I *Learned*?"

This kind of self-examination, although it will probably become less formal and more unconscious as your child becomes more proficient, helps a reader link what he's reading to his own experience and background knowledge. These links help him to fix the new material more completely in his mind. For the same reason, your child will often be encouraged to make connections between the texts he reads and his own life. The more he connects books to real things and real ideas, the more he will be motivated to learn and the more easily he will retain new information. This kind of deep involvement in a text is entertaining and exciting, as you already know if your child has fallen deeply into a book he's reading, but it also serves a vital educational purpose. If a child lives inside a book, the book will live inside the child.

If they didn't already do so in second grade, third-graders often begin to study "story grammar," or the principles of constructing a narrative, with an opening setup, an event that sets the story in motion, a line of tension and conflict that rises toward a dramatic climax, and a resolution of themes and actions at the end. Some teachers find that third-graders become more alert to story structure when they create "story maps": outlines of the main events and their effects that help students summarize and retell the story. Your child's teacher will continue to encourage him to visualize the details of a story, as well as the descriptive passages of a nonfiction text.

Two other challenges worth noting, as your child reads more advanced novels and texts, occur at the sentence level. First, the syntax, or sentence structure, of written language is quite different from that of speech. Speakers tend to use *and*, *so, like,* or *but* as a link between parallel clauses. Writers, in contrast, often use more complex clauses and link them with more subtle connective words: *although, regardless, despite, moreover,* and the like. See if your child understands these more literary words and can grasp the longer, sometimes convoluted sentences they permit. Compare, for example, these two ways of expressing a similar thought: "It was hot, and I wanted to go to the beach. But it rained, so I didn't" and "Although I wanted to go to the beach because it was hot, the rain prevented me."

The second common stumbling block for third-graders involves pronoun referents, or the words that pronouns stand in for. Writers and editors of texts for early readers are usually careful to avoid the potentially confusing use of *his, it, their,* and other pronouns unless the meaning is very clear. But as your child tackles more grown-up kinds of writing, he will need to make the adjustment.

Nonfiction is particularly important this year, as children start making the transition to the faster pace and higher expectations of learning in the fourth grade. Next year, they will be expected to use textbooks, magazine articles, and encyclopedias to do research and write reports, so their learning this year must lay the foundation for that more advanced work. This year, your child will probably be asked to start producing simple reports using two or three sources, synthesizing information in his own words. He will need to know how to use a glossary, an index, and a table of contents, and he will also become more adept at reading such specialized elements as headlines, captions, charts, and diagrams. He will be expected to know how to sort through the details of a passage and recognize the main idea, to identify the topic sentence in a paragraph, and to note how the other sentences relate to the topic. This poses a challenge for many students.

He also may focus this year on the distinctions between different kinds of writing and their appropriate structures and styles. He may even begin to analyze and identify the underlying structure of text that is written to convey information. Most nonfiction paragraphs are written in one of four ways: as a description (say, what sharks look like), as a sequence (in chronological order, as in the life cycle of a shark), by comparison and contrast (how sharks differ from whales), or as a case of cause and effect (how sharks are adapted to their environment). He may be introduced to "graphic organizers," diagrams that will help him visualize how a text is organized and remember the information it contains. Being able to imagine, or even sketch, this kind of picture of a text's structure can help him understand it better and more quickly. (See the box "Picture This.")

You can reinforce what your child learns at school by helping him to look for the central ideas of a text, to find topic sentences and supporting details in each section, and to take note of the relevant information he finds in each source. Naturally, he'll be applying these techniques to relatively simple texts, but the principles of analysis and research are the same ones that will carry him through all the years of his school career and beyond. It's great to help him get started now. (See the box "The Art of Research.") You can also show him how to paraphrase, turning direct quotations from text into his own words. Just as if you were discussing a story, ask him to tell you about the passage he's reading, to explain—in simple terms—what that means, and how that adds to his understanding about a topic.

One excellent study technique, known as SQ3R, was described in a book called *Effec-*tive Study* (F. P. Robinson) in 1946 and is still taught frequently in schools today. The students follow a sequence of five steps. First, they *survey* the assigned material to get an overview. Then they make a list of *questions,* based on their impressions. They *read* the material, keeping their questions in mind, stopping periodically to think aloud (*recite*) about what they have read so far and whether it answers their questions. Finally, they *review* the material, summarizing the content in their own words and making notes of any other important information. You may want to help your children try this technique at home.

In addition to skills, good school programs take motivation into account as well. Some of the best ways to motivate a child are to let him choose a topic and to encourage him to work with others. Your child's teacher will probably invite him to find topics that interest him, to come up with questions he's curious about, to join other students in exploring these topics, and to present what he has learned—perhaps as an oral report, poster display, or project. You can support your child's enthusiasm by offering rides to the library, prompting him with questions, or acting as the audience as he rehearses his presentation. Be constructive in your criticisms, pointing out not just flaws but strengths, and offer plenty of encouragement along with your suggestions.

WRITING: CURSIVE, CURVEBALLS, AND COMPLEXITY

Both in mechanics and in the more abstract skills of composition, the teacher's expecta-

PICTURE THIS

There are four basic ways that informational text is organized, and certain words offer cues as to which pattern the writer is using. You can help a young reader use these cues to categorize and then visualize the structure of the text, making it easier to follow.

Descriptive
If you drew a diagram to represent this information, it might look like a sunburst: the sun is the subject, and the rays are all separate pieces of information that relate to it. Cues include: *for example, such as, for instance, includes, characteristics are.*

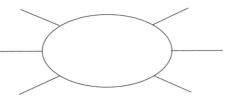

Sequential/Chronological Order
The writer is taking you through a process or a story step by step. Cues include: *first, second, finally, next, before, after, then, now, on* (date).

Comparison and Contrast
Visualize interlocking circles. Cues include: *similarly, by contrast, same, different, however, but, instead, although, on the other hand, more than, less than, other.*

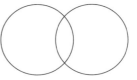

Cause and Effect
Picture this information as a tree: the trunk is the cause and the branches are the effects. Cues include: *because, as a result, therefore, since, reasons why, if . . . then, nevertheless, thus.*

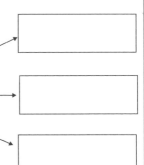

tions increase considerably from second grade to third. Let's look at each area in turn.

This is generally the year when children learn to write in cursive script. There is some question about how intensive this instruction needs to be. The trend in recent years has been to provide an introduction to letter formation and some practice in workbooks or on paper, and then to allow students to do written work in either cursive or manuscript printing. The problem with this is that cursive writing requires more practice than most students are likely to get. Although, in the long run, cursive is quicker than printing, the first attempts can be slow and painstaking. Given the choice, many children discontinue the cursive effort well before they get to see any of its benefits.

To compound the problem, children in many schools are never taught to form their printed letters properly, so your child may have invented his own "creative" way of forming letters. This original style, however, may not hold up in legibility or efficiency as children start to write faster and for longer periods of time. Third grade may be the moment for your child to focus on improving the legibility and efficiency of his writing (or printing), in preparation for the note taking and essay writing that are bound to greet him in fourth grade and beyond. In the chapter on second grade, we discussed this goal and described the alternative style of print called D'Nealian. Whether he prefers to use manuscript, D'Nealian, or cursive is less important than how masterful and fluent he becomes.

In fact, the concept of fluency is as relevant to handwriting as it is to reading, and it's in third grade that your child should be working hard to achieve fluent, effortless writing. If he needs to think about how a letter is written, or if teachers and classmates find themselves puzzling over his written work, it is important to take time now to address the issue. Being able to write legibly and fluently is connected to both spelling and composition skills, because a child who is struggling just to form letters correctly will be distracted both from the word he is trying to spell and from the deeper purpose of writing, which is to express thought. Beyond that, for better or worse, your child's performance in future years will be judged to some extent on the quality of his handwriting. Whether the performance is on an official essay (a component of most state assessments) or in thank-you notes to relatives, people will get an impression of his level of competence from the handwriting and spelling they see. (By the way, handwriting has a genetic component, so you may not need to look very far to find out where your child's handwriting came from!)

If your child is struggling with writing, ask his teacher for advice. It may be that all he needs is a lot of practice and a strong desire to improve. Persistent, intractable difficulties with holding a pencil or forming letters call for consultation with a specialist; don't hesitate to ask the school for help if you think your child needs it. Most school systems have occupational therapists on hand to advise and coach struggling writers. They may have just the right apparatus or routine for addressing the difficulty.

Since handwriting and spelling require the same motor processes, it's not surprising that children with poor handwriting are often poor spellers as well—and, unfortunately, that their difficulties with these skills also lead to difficulties in the more abstract processes of composition. Children who are struggling with the curveballs that English spelling can throw at them need lots of practice—one study found that at-risk second-graders needed 24 practice tests, over two months, to spell specific words correctly and consistently—and this year is the best time to zero in on spelling. Your child will benefit from a systematic spelling program that organizes words by spelling pattern and encourages lots of practice. Ideally, he will also be reviewing (and be expected to master) those high-frequency words that "glue" most sentences together. (See the Chapter 5 box "One Hundred Greatest Hits: The Most Common Words in English" and, earlier in this chapter, "Seventy-Five Spelling Demons.") There will never be a better time to encourage your child to become a proficient speller.

This year your child will probably be expected to produce multiple drafts of his work, with increasing attention to proofreading, grammar, and spelling as he creates a finished piece. (Invented spelling, by the way, is now being left behind; he will be expected this year to spell correctly all the time.) He may be asked to produce final drafts on a computer, so it is not too early to help him learn how to type by touch. Several good typing programs for children are available. Children often enjoy learning this new skill, which can feel repetitive and tedious to an older student, because it makes them feel very grown up. Even if your child becomes a proficient typist, however, he should continue to write his earlier drafts by hand, because composition on the screen can hold unexpected pitfalls for the beginning writer. (See the box "Is the Pen Mightier Than the Mouse?")

Whether on the screen or on paper, the content of the writing your child produces this year will be increasingly sophisticated and complex. He will be expected to know how to summarize a nonfiction text, to discuss what he has learned from it, and to compare one text with another. In addition, he will be encouraged to develop his descriptive skills as a writer, depicting scenes and events in vivid detail, organizing his ideas, and expressing them gracefully.

Many children need help with organizing their compositions and coming up with ideas. If your child is stuck, you can try getting him started with questions like "What else can you think of? Can you say more about that? What's an example of that?" You can also encourage him to organize his thoughts by writing an outline or making a "graphic organizer," a quick drawing or diagram that sketches out the relationships between ideas. All of these compositional skills will become critical as he moves up toward middle school, so it's important that your child start developing them now. (See the box "Editing: Four Simple Steps.")

Writing is also important because it reinforces and deepens the knowledge children acquire through reading. By writing summaries and analyses of what they read, children gain a firmer grasp of the material. You can provide real help to your child as his most devoted reader and editor.

WHAT YOU CAN DO AT HOME

Because your child has now mastered the basics of reading, there's also a whole world of

THE ART OF RESEARCH

Your third-grader will probably be asked to complete several research projects, using textbooks and other nonfiction sources. This is a new task for your child, and at first he may feel overwhelmed or confused by it. You can help by showing him some simple techniques and helping him plan his work.

❖ Sit down with him and look over some books he will use. Show him how to use the index and table of contents to find the information he needs. Subheads within each chapter can be useful too.

❖ If he needs to use an atlas, show him how to find the map he needs and how to use it. In the same way, guide him through any charts, graphs, or tables he comes across.

❖ Use stickies to mark useful references.

❖ Help your child develop his Web skills, crafting search criteria that are neither too narrow nor too broad and evaluating sites for reliability. Remind him that cutting and pasting from the Web is not the same as creating original work.

❖ Create a "favorites" file to bookmark useful sites.

❖ As your child reads, help him organize what he learns by looking for the topic sentence of each paragraph. It usually states the main idea of the paragraph. Encourage him to underline the main idea of each paragraph or to summarize it in the margin.

IS THE PEN MIGHTIER THAN THE MOUSE?

Now that computers are widely available, you might think that children could stop writing by hand and just start typing their work from an earlier age. But there are several reasons to encourage your child to keep writing, even while he's learning to type.

For one thing, handwriting will always be a necessary skill. In class and on tests he'll need to write quickly and with ease. The more practice he gets now, the more legible and efficient his handwriting will be. Handwriting also improves your child's fine motor development and hand-eye coordination.

On a deeper level, there are real differences between how children compose when they're using pencils and how they write at the keyboard. Because the computer makes it so easy to move sentences around and to express thoughts rapidly, it can encourage children to produce a rush of disconnected thoughts. For a skilled writer, the power to edit and reorganize quickly is a wonderful time-saver, but it can make it almost too easy for young writers to shuffle their ideas around. That may be fine as a brainstorming technique, but not for producing a coherent, finished piece.

There's another problem with producing work on-screen: The neatly typed words and appealingly formatted layout can make work look "finished" long before it is. It's hard to remember that a printed document is still a rough draft.

All this is not to say that your child shouldn't use a computer. Its speed can make it a liberating medium for brainstorming or other forms of playing around with ideas in an unstructured way. The spell checker is also a wonderful feature for children.

Nonetheless, it is worth encouraging your child to start out the old-fashioned way, alone at a desk, with a pencil in his hand and a blank sheet of paper waiting for him. Creation *should* be messy, and crossed-out words and restructured sentences remind us of that important fact.

EDITING: FOUR SIMPLE STEPS

Here's a simple process for helping your child develop self-editing skills.

1. When he sits down to revise his earlier draft, encourage him to read the whole work through once without making any changes. This is a chance to get a feel for the overall shape of the piece.
   ❖ Does it have a beginning, middle, and end?
   ❖ Does it flow smoothly?
   ❖ Does one section take up more than its share of space?
   ❖ Help him make notes about any restructuring he needs to do.

2. Next, have him go through the piece, sentence by sentence, with a pencil in his hand. He may want to use a different color for editing. On this pass, have him think sentence by sentence.
   ❖ Is each one clear and grammatically correct?
   ❖ Do the sentences follow each other logically?
   ❖ Does any thought need to move to another sentence, or is the general flow right?

3. Now he should get down to the word-by-word level.
   ❖ Is everything spelled correctly?
   ❖ Are any words missing or doubled?
   ❖ How's the punctuation?
   ❖ Are there any other details to clean up?

4. Finally, once he has attended to all the fine points, he should create a new, clean version, then read through it once more.

Following these steps on every draft of a project will help your child learn to shift his focus from the big picture to the details, and to pay attention to each in a productive way.

activities you can explore together to deepen his comprehension, motivation, and enjoyment. There are also new challenges, particularly if your child is not an eager reader, and so we'll also discuss ways of encouraging a reluctant reader to drop everything and read.

"Drop Everything and Read" is, in fact, the name of one method for doing just that. The idea is to set aside some time each day—maybe half an hour after school or before bedtime—when everyone in the household puts aside other activities and obligations and settles in with a good book. This means you, too: it's important for your child to see that you read on your own, not just with him. So feel free to pick up a book you enjoy and dive in. Some families find that reading the same book, even if they're reading separate copies, increases everyone's interest in it. Think of it as a home-based book club—and why not schedule a discussion once everyone has read the current selection? Family members can take turns selecting the books. Common themes might include books that are set in your region or that draw on your ethnic heritage, for example, or that illuminate an interest you all share.

You can also use a family project as a jumping-off point for reading together. Maybe you're trying to decide where to take a vacation next summer. Brainstorm a few possibilities together, then encourage your child to do some research on each option. You can help him find resources on the Web, take him to the library to check out the reference section, read the travel section of the newspaper together, or help him write letters to a local Chamber of Commerce or tourist bureau asking for brochures and suggestions. Once he's gathered

some information, ask him to write a brief summary of all the choices and make the case for the destination he likes best. You could use similar research techniques for figuring out how to build a treehouse in the backyard, comparing several brands of the new electronic gizmo he wants, or learning more about a local museum or national park before planning a visit.

If your child is still struggling with the mechanics and fluency of reading and writing, contact his teacher to share your observations and concerns. The teacher may recommend a tutor or supplementary program to help your child refine and practice his skills. If the skills are solid, though, it may just be that he needs some extra practice. If your child is still eager for your help, you may be able to suggest some ideas for building fluency. For more fluent writing, propose a Handwriting Derby, in which your child practices letter formation or sentence writing for ten minutes every night. Find a simple text passage for him to copy, or have him rewrite "The quick brown fox jumps over the lazy dog" until it's fast and beautiful. Set a timer for one minute, and see how many legible, well-formed words he can write in that time. Keep track of the total, and have him try again after resting a bit. Some children enjoy graphing the results of such repeated trials and celebrating signs of progress.

If this practice technique is a hit, try it with reading aloud as well, and see if your child can boost his reading speed and accuracy with ten minutes of practice every day for two weeks. If his spelling needs improvement, it sometimes helps to create a personal notebook of Words to Watch, a box of index cards to practice and master, or a list (or word wall) of "spelling demons" to study. If you can manage to promote an emphasis on fun—and working together for the sake of progress—you may be able to help your child here as you did in the preschool years. Try asking, "How can I help you learn these words? What games can we play that will be fun for both of us?"

If your child already enjoys reading and writing, he might like to try some other projects. Maybe he'd enjoy publishing a family newsletter for far-flung relatives or rounding up the neighborhood doings in a local "newspaper" for his friends. How about a scrapbook or family record that you develop together? He could put on a play or produce a video—nothing fancy, just a few props, simple costumes, and a compliant sibling or two. He could interview elderly relatives and write a report on the conversation, or he could ask them to write stories about their childhood and then read them to you over dinner. He may also want to do some writing for his eyes only: journals and diaries often appeal to children at this age, and they're one more way of getting your child excited about ink on the page.

The goal is to show that literacy is connected to life. Even a child who thinks he doesn't like to read may change his mind once he realizes how much he can learn from reading about something that matters to him. Find as many ways as you can to connect your child's interests to reading. Sports biographies or books on tactics, science projects and math puzzles, magic, nature guides, mysteries, video-game tips—whatever your child wants to know more about is what you should be encouraging him to read. And if fiction is what gets him going, don't worry if it's not Great Literature. Just as many adult gourmets started life on a diet of macaroni and cheese, so many avid learners begin their academic careers with the Babysitters Club. What's important now is to help your child acquire a taste for learning through reading—the fine points of what he learns can come later, once you've gotten him hooked.

You can also use your child's interests in other media to help develop his appetite for reading. If he has a favorite television program, point out the writer's name in the credits and talk about how every show has a script. Encourage him to think about how a script is brought to life on-screen. His beloved video game, too, was written by someone—and what that someone wrote was not just the computer code that makes the thing run, but the character development and story lines that make it worth playing. How does writing for a game differ from writing for a movie? Maybe he'd like to try writing a game that's based on his favorite film. He's into music? Read the lyrics together and talk about their structure and style. If he's watching a football game, encourage him to listen to the announcers and think about whether some of their jokes and comments were written in advance; point out how much information on the players and the game is conveyed by text on the screen.

The Web, too, often engages children who don't think of themselves as readers. You can remind him as he surfs that these pages didn't just spring out of the ether; someone wrote them. This is also a good opportunity to point out that Web sites are not infallible sources of knowledge but rather a wildly variable collection, made by imperfect humans, of resources both excellent and ridiculous. Encourage your child to think about the author of each site and what his motivations might be; show him the kinds of criteria you use to evaluate a site's reliability. Is it sponsored by a commercial interest? Does it offer documentation for its claims or just put them out there? Does it link to other apparently reliable sites? Children need to learn, with Web sites as with other forms of text, that the fact that something is set in type is not proof that it is true. With your gentle prodding, they can start to make their own wise judgments about content and bias.

In all of these attempts to make connections between your child and the texts that surround him, you're focused on a larger goal: to help your child become an active participant in constructing his own knowledge, rather than a passive recipient of information. An active reader engages deeply with the text, analyzing its structure and studying what it is trying to convey. He learns by questioning what he reads, challenging its assumptions and unconscious biases, comparing what it says about the world with what he knows and believes to be true. An active reader is utterly involved, using the text to test his own assumptions and to deepen, correct, and extend his knowledge of the world. He is constantly thinking as he reads, both about the words in front of him and about the thoughts they provoke. He is fully aware, alive, and engaged. With your help, that is the kind of reader your child can become.

AFTERWORD: READING FOR FOURTH-GRADERS—AND FOR LIFE

With the end of third grade, for students who are progressing on track, comes the end of spe-cialized instruction in reading. But that doesn't mean that your child will stop learning about reading. On the contrary, his learning will become more complex, sophisticated, and self-directed, as he starts to use this powerful tool to learn everything else he will acquire throughout his years of school. Up until now, he has been laying the groundwork, developing as firm a grasp as possible of the skills and strategies he will need. Now, he's ready to go to work.

As he moves ahead, his ability to construct his own system of knowledge from what he reads will become increasingly important. Each bit of knowledge he acquires serves as scaffolding for the next bit to come; that's why his teachers in the early grades have spent so much time helping him develop a firm base of understanding and skill, so that the tower of knowledge he's starting to construct will rest on a solid foundation. Now, he will start to move from studying skills to using those skills to study specific subjects. Instead of reading just to read, he will be reading to learn—about everything from algebra to astrophysics, social studies to the history of ancient Greece. With the tools you have helped him acquire and refine, he will be able to unlock all the wisdom of the world.

Of course, many academic challenges may still lie ahead. One well-known phenomenon, in fact, may be just around the corner: the dreaded Fourth-Grade Slump. Many children who perform successfully during the primary grades suddenly seem to fall apart in fourth grade: their test scores and grades slip, their confidence erodes, their teachers worry. Of course, there may be many underlying causes for the slump, and in fact fourth grade holds some particular challenges. Fourth-graders face new demands in a variety of subject areas, each with an increasingly specialized and complex vocabulary that, coupled with the more complex syntax of textbooks at this level, can stump a struggling reader. At the same time, children often face more frequent and intense testing this year; adults' expectations of them rise, just as adult support often falls off. Small wonder that the "achievement gap" starts to widen in fourth grade: students who can keep up with the new demands find themselves soaring, while those who are falling behind too often get mired in a deeper and deeper hole.

So what do you do if you fear your child is slumping? Experts urge teachers to focus on three essential factors: fluency, vocabulary, and background knowledge. Are children reading quickly and accurately enough to understand the sudden explosion of material they need to tackle? If they are fluent enough, do they have the vocabulary and background knowledge to make sense of what they read? How comfortable are they in tackling the syntax and structure of textbooks? There are ways to assess each of these factors, and recent efforts to include more informative tests in schools for purposes of "accountability" have this goal in mind.

During the later elementary years, your child's school is likely to administer more tests for the purpose of assessing each student's various strengths and weaknesses. If any one of the five components of reading (phonemic awareness, phonics, fluency, vocabulary, or comprehension) seems weak, it's likely to limit achievement. You will want to ask questions about your child's performance on these tests and inquire about activities you can do at home to address any weaknesses and expand

on his strengths. You may want to review the suggestions in earlier chapters for building skills in any area where your child's performance is a concern.

Beyond the elementary years, your child will continue to face the challenges of advancing as a strategic reader—a reader who engages actively with what he reads and uses it to help construct his own system of knowledge, thoughts, and beliefs. While it is very common to see teachers devoted to moving students through the first four stages of reading, with instructional programs designed to do just that, students in the more advanced stages have not traditionally had such targeted support. Recently, however, educators have started to focus on giving content-area teachers more training in how they can help their students refine their reading skills. If he's lucky, your child may find himself in a secondary school that is committed to teaching him specialized reading strategies in every content area, from history to math. (See the box "Start Making Sense: Strategies for Comprehension.")

The writing your child will be expected to do will also change in the years ahead—and many schools place more emphasis on testing what he can write than on giving him direct instruction in how to do it. By the time he reaches high school, your child will be expected to have done a lot of imaginative writing, such as stories, poems, and scripts; personal writing in the form of letters or journal entries; and expository pieces like reports and summaries. A new challenge, essay writing, will force him to focus on organization and structure as well as on clarity, grammar, and spelling. Older students will also need to

START MAKING SENSE: STRATEGIES FOR COMPREHENSION

You can help your child improve his comprehension by encouraging him to use these strategies and by demonstrating them yourself.

1. A good reader "activates relevant prior knowledge" before, during, and after reading text. In other words, he connects what's new here with what he already knows.

2. He sorts out the important ideas and themes from the less important details.

3. He asks questions about what he is reading as he goes along.

4. He creates vivid pictures in his mind to illustrate what he is reading.

5. He uses his knowledge to make inferences and draw conclusions.

6. He tries to retell or summarize what he has read, pulling together the most important information and leaving out the details.

7. He stops reading when something doesn't make sense and tries a fix-up tactic:
   ❖ He makes sure that he understands all the words correctly.
   ❖ He backs up and rereads a passage to see if he's missed something.
   ❖ He gets help with unfamiliar words or concepts if necessary.

practice and refine their note-taking skills as they read textbooks or listen to lectures in class. Some of these challenges will be new, but most of them will build on the foundation you have helped establish in the early years. And your job as your child's number one literacy coach may not yet be over. If you're lucky, he will continue to thrive on your assistance and encouragement for years to come.

As your child moves ahead into this exciting new universe with its complex demands, you can continue to think of ways to turn practice sessions into games and challenges. Perhaps you can assist him with organization, by helping to set up a study area that's a serene haven for undistracted work. You might offer to help organize his notebooks so that assignments and due dates are easy to find. And, more generally, you can reinforce good study habits as they develop, and let him know how proud you are of his achievements. You can applaud as his abilities become more refined, his grasp of complex material more sure.

As you help your child at each stage to engage with the texts he reads, he will find it easier to grasp and interpret them. As you encourage him to express himself in writing, he will grow increasingly able to reflect on what he learns and to share it with others. As you help him learn how to learn, he will become an active, reflective, strategic learner, using words to understand the world. He will join the company of educated men and women, and he will have the skills to travel among them wherever he wants to go. And all this is possible because you, from his earliest days on the planet, have helped him learn how to read.

BUILDING BLOCKS: WHAT YOUR THIRD-GRADER NEEDS

Preparation for the leap from "learning to read" to "reading to learn"
- ❖ Lots of time reading more complex books in a variety of subjects and genres, to build vocabulary and background knowledge
- ❖ Reading together and talking about books every day
- ❖ Becoming an active reader
- ❖ Plenty of reading practice to ensure fluency
- ❖ Support for motivation, organization, and good study habits

Completion of phonics instruction
- ❖ Wrapping up loose ends like *pn* and other unusual combinations
- ❖ Instruction and practice in advanced word-attack skills
- ❖ Pig Latin, tongue twisters, and other playful language games

Writing, spelling, and composition
- ❖ Instruction and practice in cursive writing
- ❖ Systematic instruction and testing in spelling, and lots of practice
- ❖ Instruction in using a dictionary and a thesaurus
- ❖ Instruction in editing and revising one's own work

Research and organization
- ❖ Instruction in evaluating the reliability of sources and using multiple sources
- ❖ Instruction in note taking, outlining ideas, and other research skills
- ❖ Writing reports with two or three sources

1 ROOTS AND BRANCHES   Help your child create a family tree that includes his siblings, cousins, aunts and uncles, parents, grandparents, great-grandparents—as far back as you want or are able to go. Share the stories of your family with your child and encourage him to write them down. Help him go deeper into family history by interviewing his relatives—grandparents are often particularly flattered to be asked— reading old letters, or researching on the Internet. You can also help him research your family's country of origin and the story of how you came to be in this country, either by talking with relatives or by looking on the Web. If you have a lot of old family pictures, have your child track down the names of Aunt Gisela's boyfriend or the third cousin from the left at the Labor Day picnic and write captions to add to his scrapbook.

2 OUR WEEK IN REVIEW   Once a week, have everyone in the family gather together and contribute to a family journal. Each person gets to make an entry: the best or worst thing that happened during the week, the funniest thing someone said, the happiest moment, the silliest song—whatever captures the flavor of your family's life together. Date the entries, and encourage everyone to add an illustration or other embellishment—a ticket stub, maybe, or a note from a teacher. Make this a Sunday or Friday night ritual, and you'll have something wonderful to pull out when the grandchildren are learning to read.

3 THE STREET WHERE YOU LIVE   Help your child write a guide to your neighborhood or a local history. He could conduct research at the library, interview the neighbors—especially those who have lived there a long time—study current maps and compare them to earlier ones, and survey local businesses to compile a guide to available services. If there's a restaurant nearby, have him write a review; if there's a favorite store, have him describe the things he likes about it. Is your park named for someone? Help him find out who it is and why.

4 INSIDE INFORMATION   Brainstorm together to come up with a family trivia game. Have each member contribute five questions to get you started, then add one a week. Who named the cats Tiger and Lily? What is Daddy's favorite color? What was Grandma's favorite activity as a child, and where did she do it? Having everyone contribute should ensure that no one knows the answer to every question—but everyone knows some.

5 PET PROJECT   Have your child research the pedigree and breed history of the family pet. He could contact the kennel club or other breeders' association, interview your veterinarian, or visit the library to get the scoop. He can also consult a book to find out the ideal diet, exercise routine, and habitat for your animals—then draw up a chart to share his knowledge with the rest of the family. And, if you don't have a pet but your child is begging for one, have him research the kind of animal he'd like to have. No chance of a pet in your future, for allergies or other reasons? He can still make a case for a dragon or a unicorn—surely there's a dragon-breeders' association on the Web.

6 VCR ABCS   Most electronic gadgets are so easy to program, a child could do it—but somehow it seems as if only a child can do it. Tap into that valuable storehouse of knowledge by having your child write a clear, concise guide to programming the VCR. Heck, he may even be able to teach you how to set the clock. Or encourage him to write a manual for his own favorite gadget, toy, or game. Maybe he'd like to give you a set of instructions on exactly what to wear, do, and say when his friends are around. Writing any kind of instructions demonstrates the need for clarity and precision in communication, and it encourages logical thinking and accurate expression.

7 HOUSE WITH A VIEW   Encourage your child to conduct a family poll. Give him a clipboard and a pen, and suggest a few topics to get him started. Political events are the obvious choice, but he could also conduct a more personalized survey. What's everyone's favorite dinner? Where should we go on vacation? Chocolate or banana pudding for dessert? Which movie should we see this weekend? What's your favorite television show? Once everyone has weighed in, the young pollster can tally the results—and maybe even plot them on a chart. At least, that's what 66 percent of one sampled family would do.

8 CURLICUE U   If your child enjoys writing in cursive script—or, on the other hand, if he could use a little extra practice to get into the flow of it—encourage him to become the family calligrapher. Provide an assortment of interesting pens and papers, and invite him to write out birthday poems, address invitations and greeting cards, or decorate a menu card for the family dinner. Children often enjoy making place cards, too—and it feels more like play than a handwriting drill.

9 PUZZLEMEISTER   If your child enjoys word games, show him how to construct a few simple ones of his own. He could make a list of thematically related words, then work them into a simple crossword or, even more easily, a find-a-word puzzle. (For the find-a-word, give him graph paper and have him write one of his words on every other line, with one letter per square, then write a few vertically or diagonally as well; fill in the remaining squares with randomly chosen letters.) He might like to make jumbles, scrambling the letters of his word for someone to untangle. And, if this appeals, he can go on to create the rest of the funny pages: a quotation of the day, a silly horoscope, even a comic strip or two, featuring a familiar character like Cliff Hanger or Chicken Jane or your own pet Super Mutt.

10 WORD WATCH   Every day—at breakfast, perhaps—pick a family Word of the Day. It could be a silly word, one that's relevant to the season or an impending holiday, a fancy word heard on TV, or any other word that appeals to someone. (If siblings bicker over the choice, you could put each one in charge of a specific day.) Write the word in large, clear print and post it in a prominent spot. Throughout the day, each person tries to work the word into as many conversations as possible; you could even have a contest at dinner to see who can use it correctly the most times. At the end of the week, you could use the words for a family game of charades or Hangman—or include the best ones in your family journal.

Thirty Really Good Books for Third-Graders

Five Favorite Chapter Books
Judy Blume, *Tales of a Fourth Grade Nothing* (Dell Yearling Books)

Deborah and James Howe, *Bunnicula* (Simon & Schuster)

Barbara Park, *Skinnybones* (Random House)

Daniel Manus Pinkwater, *The Hoboken Chicken Emergency* (Simon & Schuster)

E. B. White, *Charlotte's Web* (HarperCollins)

Five Popular Series
Matt Christopher, *Catch That Pass!* (Little, Brown), and others

Paula Danziger, Amber Brown series (Scholastic Paperbacks)

John Scieszka, *The Time Warp Trio* (Penguin Putnam)

Donald Sobol, Encyclopedia Brown series (Bantam Skylark)

Gertrude Chandler Warner, Boxcar Children series (Albert Whitman)

Ten Great Read-Alouds
Natalie Babbitt, *Tuck Everlasting* (Farrar, Straus, & Giroux)

Andrew Clements, *Frindle* (Simon & Schuster)

Louise Fitzhugh, *Harriet the Spy* (Random House)

Paul Fleischman, *Seedfolks* (HarperCollins)

Virginia Hamilton, *The House of Dies Drear* (Pocket Books)

E. L. Konigsberg, *Jennifer, Hecate, Macbeth, William McKinley, and Me, Elizabeth* (Bantam Doubleday)

Madeleine L'Engle, *A Wrinkle in Time* (Bantam Doubleday)

Lois Lowry, *The Giver* (Bantam Doubleday)

Scott O'Dell, *Island of the Blue Dolphins* (Bantam Doubleday Dell)

Mildred Taylor, *Roll of Thunder, Hear My Cry* (Viking Penguin)

Five Nonfiction Winners
Alma Flor Ada, *My Name Is Maria Isabel* (Simon & Schuster)

Peter Golenback, *Teammates* (Harcourt)

Stewart and Polly Ann Graff, *Helen Keller* (Bantam Doubleday)

Deborah Hopkinson, *Band of Angels* (Simon & Schuster)

Christopher Maynard, *Days of the Knights* (Dorling Kindersley Readers)

Five Favorite Storybooks Related to BETWEEN THE LIONS Episodes
Byrd Baylor, *Everybody Needs a Rock* (Simon & Schuster)

Lewis Carroll, *Through the Looking Glass* (Putnam)—you'll want to read *Alice in Wonderland* first, of course

Lucille Clifton, *Three Wishes* (Dell)

Rudyard Kipling, "How the Camel Got His Hump," in *Just So Stories* (Penguin Putnam)

Michael Pellowski, *Joke and Riddle Bonanza* (Sterling Publications)

Chapter 8

If Your Child Is Struggling

In the grade-by-grade chapters of this book, we've looked in detail at the progression from the first days of learning language through the completion of formal reading instruction. For many children, the process of learning to read flows along this path in a more or less smooth and uneventful way. But sometimes, although a child seems to be working hard and the adults in his life are doing everything they can think of to help, something's just not right. Maybe a preschooler is really having trouble understanding what you say to him. Maybe a kindergartner just can't tell whether two words rhyme. Or a first-grader knows some letters but can't link them into words, a second-grader can read simple words but freezes when he hits longer ones, or a third-grader can sound out words but doesn't seem to put them together to make sense of what he's reading. Some of these children—about 5 percent of the population—may have a learning disability, while many others have less severe difficulties but still have trouble learning. For any child who is struggling to read, books aren't a pleasure; they're a bother and a worry. And, for the parents of these struggling children, their struggles can be worrisome, too.

If you're one of these parents, this chapter is for you. Here we'll give you an overview of some of the causes of reading difficulties; we'll talk about signs of trouble to be particularly alert for and what to do if you think your child may have a problem. We'll also take a look at the kinds of remedial programs that are likely to be most helpful and why, the services that children are entitled to under federal law and how you can get access to them, the most effective strategies for working with your child's teachers in addressing his needs, and the most helpful ways to talk with your child and support him in his efforts to read.

On BETWEEN THE LIONS, Lionel's friend Gus, the rabbit, is a champion jumper—and a struggling reader. Like many children in his situation, Gus is embarrassed about his difficulties. But—again like many children with learning difficulties—he also has some real strengths that compensate for his weaknesses. He can use these strengths to help him find his own ways to learn. Reading may never come easily to Gus, but he can and will learn to read. And your child will, too.

The first thing you need to know is that, no matter how old your child is or what particular struggles he's having, there are many things you can do to help. As we've said before, virtually all children, even those with severe learning disabilities, will learn to read—*if* they receive appropriate instruction. As your child's parent, you can help to turn that "if" into a "when," and to see the smile of accomplishment on your child's face when he says, "I can read!"

The next thing to know is that, if you're worried, you shouldn't wait to start looking for assistance. Specialists are increasingly emphatic about the importance of early intervention, so whenever you have lingering concerns about your child's ability to learn—even if he hasn't yet started school—you shouldn't hesitate to ask for help. It's not uncommon to wait—a recent study found that 44 percent of parents who suspect a learning problem wait a year before looking for help—but there's no reason not to act on your instincts. In particular, seek advice if your young child is very slow to learn to speak, seems not to understand what people say to him, or starts learning to talk and then slows down or regresses to an earlier stage. If your child does have a learning disability, the earliest possible identification and intervention will be of great help to him. And if he doesn't have a disability but just needs a little extra help and encouragement, you'll be able to relax and stop worrying now instead of later. Either way, the sooner you figure out what's going on, the better.

On the other hand, if your child is already in third grade or beyond, it's still not too late to get help. He may require more intensive tutoring in order to come up to speed, and he'll likely need extra help and support to get and stay current in other subjects while he's working on his reading. But a sensitive, committed tutor, in partnership with a dedicated and loving parent, can do a lot to help the older child make real progress in reading. Early intervention is a wonderful thing, but it's never too late to make a difference.

No matter how old your child is, a talk with his doctor is a good place to start. The pediatrician can help you determine if your concerns are well founded and may be able to refer you to a specialist. Your local elementary school is another good resource. Even before your child enters school, your local school district is required by federal law to identify and assist children who are at risk of learning disabilities. Many parents don't realize that even babies are covered by this law, but they are. If you are worried about your preschooler's language development, your local elementary school can help you arrange an assessment at no cost to you. For school-age children, of course, the school is probably the first place to turn for advice. We'll walk through the process of seeking and using your local public school's help later in this chapter.

Several national organizations and state groups also provide information and support to parents; see the lists in the Resources chapter. In addition, there's a terrific, easy-to-use screening tool for four-year-olds that can help you determine whether your child's prereading skills are on track. It's called "Get Ready to Read!" and it's available through the Web site of the National Center for Learning Disabilities, www.LD.org. While you can't make a formal identification on your own, doing this simple screening with your child can help you decide if you need to look for professional advice.

DIFFERENCES, DIFFICULTIES, AND DISABILITIES

Part of the challenge for the parents of a struggling reader is that different people may use different terms to describe the same problem, or the same term to label two very different conditions. You may hear people talk about "learning differences," "learning difficulties," and "learning disabilities," and all of these terms can overlap and intertwine in various ways, depending on who's speaking. One reason for the overlap is that learning difficulties fall along a continuum. There isn't really a single, magic point at which one child has a "disability" and the next one does not; school systems or assessment tests may label one child and not the other, but their abilities may differ only slightly in degree and not at all in kind.

The labels can have very concrete effects, however, when it comes to how your child is treated and what help is available to him. A "difficulty" may sound less daunting or severe, and that can help morale; on the other hand, a formal classification of "learning disability" has a specific meaning in federal law, and it entitles a child to receive special services and accommodations that a "learning difficulty" does not. The important thing for you as a parent to remember is that, if your child is struggling, there may be specific reasons for his troubles, and there are many tools available to you—including a number of publicly funded support programs, underpinned by federal law—that you can use to help him.

For the purposes of this chapter, we use the term *difficulty* as a broad umbrella for the whole range of struggles that a child can have as he learns to read. We limit *learning disabil-*

ity to mean one of the specific conditions that are defined by the federal law on disabilities, which we discuss in greater detail in the section called "What's the Big IDEA?" In practical terms, aside from the implications for access to services, it's more important to know your child's specific strengths and weaknesses in a range of reading-related skills than to spend a lot of time wondering if he has a "difficulty" rather than a "disability."

So, just what is a learning disability? It's a neurological condition, an unusual pattern in the "wiring" or functioning of the brain, that causes difficulty in processing information. Learning disabilities (often referred to simply as "LD") have nothing to do with intelligence. In fact, people with learning disabilities have at least average intelligence—it's partly the gap between what they should be able to do and what they can actually do in a particular area that leads specialists to conclude that they have a learning disability. Beyond that, many people with learning disabilities are exceptionally bright, and some of the world's most successful people, from Winston Churchill to Whoopi Goldberg, have been identified as having a learning disability. By definition, learning disabilities are also not caused by emotional disorders, social or cultural conditions, or such physical disabilities as blindness and deafness.

There may be a genetic component to some disorders such as dyslexia, as they clearly run in families. But when it comes to helping a child learn, it doesn't matter what the cause is. The important point is that differences in how the brain works do exist, and they can cause difficulties until the child finds ways to work around them. Many people with learning disabilities have gone on to lead very successful lives. Often they have found ways to develop and cultivate some specific talents and traits that help them work around their areas of difficulty. (See the box "The Turtle's Gift.")

Disabilities can affect many different areas of development and learning. Some become apparent in early childhood, while others do not show up until a child has been in school for a year or two. Developmental speech and language disorders are often, though not always, identified before a child enters school. If your child was late in learning to speak, seems to use less complex language than other children his age, or often seems to have trouble following spoken directions or answering questions, you might want to have him evaluated for a developmental speech or language disorder.

Learning disabilities can affect many other areas besides language and reading. Some children, for example, have an impaired ability to coordinate visual perception and fine motor skills; others have difficulty understanding and working with numbers. Because this is a book about reading, we will look at one disability in greater detail: dyslexia. Dyslexia, which manifests itself as a specific set of difficulties in reading, is also the most common learning disability. (See the box "What Are the Odds?") More than 80 percent of all people who are identified as having a learning disability are found to have dyslexia. And as many as 17 percent of American schoolchildren will have some degree of difficulty in learning to read.

DYSLEXIA 101

Whole books have been written about dyslexia—and, if you need more detailed

THE TURTLE'S GIFT

The headmaster of a Hawaiian school for children with dyslexia likens his students to giant sea turtles. Put them on land and they're awkward and slow; it's painful to watch them flop and scrape across the sand. But as soon as they get to the water, they take off with grace and speed.

Within the constraints of the classroom, children with dyslexia can feel like those beached turtles. But once they're out of school and in the swim, they often glide joyfully along. As CEOs or computer programmers or filmmakers or engineers, they are likely to be the people who can multitask the best or come up with creative, outside-the-box solutions. And the most successful "turtles," researchers have found, consistently share several important traits:

❖ **Self-awareness,** including knowledge and acceptance of their strengths and weaknesses

❖ **Proactivity,** or active engagement in the world, particularly with other people, and a sense of control over and responsibility for their own actions and results

❖ **Perseverance**—the willingness to practice doggedly and never give up, despite criticism or hard times

❖ **Goal setting,** with progress along a step-by-step plan to achieve what they want

❖ **Effective support systems** and knowing when to reach out for help from teachers, family members, and friends

❖ **Emotional stability,** which includes good coping skills, communication strategies, and other ways of dealing with adversity

WHAT ARE THE ODDS?

Learning disabilities—particularly dyslexia—are more common than you might think. Consider these statistics:

- More than one out of every six children—17.5 percent—will have a problem learning to read sometime in the first three years of school.

- More than 2.8 million school-age children now receive special-education services as students with LD. That's about 5 percent of all children in public school, and it's just over half of all children who receive special education. These figures don't include children in private and religious schools, which often offer few or no special-education services.

- Of people who are identified as having learning disabilities, about 85 percent have difficulties with reading.

information, you should probably turn to those books, some of which are listed in the Resources chapter. But because it is so common, and because it can have profound effects on achievement if not identified and dealt with as soon as possible, it's important for all parents to know the basics of what dyslexia is, what it may look like in your child, and what to do if you suspect a problem.

Dyslexia is a disorder in language processing that results from differences in the structures and functions of the brain. People with dyslexia have trouble reading, not because they don't see the letters on the page or see them "backward"—a common myth about dyslexia—but because they have trouble with

"phonological processing." In other words, their brains do not link visual input to speech sounds in the normal way. Sophisticated brain imaging techniques show that, when dyslexic people read, the pattern of brain activity is different from that of unimpaired readers.

Can the dyslexic brain be trained to connect letters with speech sounds? Yes, but it can take a great deal of intensive, repetitive work in order to help the person with dyslexia to develop abilities that seem to come naturally to other people: the ability to segment words into sounds, to blend sounds together into words, and to match letters to their sounds. There are ways to work around the difficulty, though. A highly structured, "multisensory" approach apparently stimulates several areas of the brain to help with phonological processing, compensating for and perhaps even overcoming this weakness.

Dyslexia can also cause difficulties with other forms of language processing, so that a person with dyslexia may struggle with writing as well as reading, and may also have difficulty in understanding what he hears or expressing himself in speech. He may also struggle with concepts that involve sequencing information, such as telling time or learning the days of the week or the months of the year. Interestingly, many people with dyslexia are unusually gifted in other areas, particularly those involving visual and spatial integration. They may be particularly successful in such fields as art, architecture, graphics and design, electronics, mechanics and engineering, music, dance, and sports. Dyslexia is not a behavioral, psychological, motivational, or social problem. It's a difference in how the brain learns.

Dyslexia varies in severity and symptoms from person to person, and most people will not have all of the possible symptoms. Nevertheless, it's useful to know the most common signs. You may want to be particularly watchful if there's a family history of dyslexia. (See the box "Signs of Dyslexia.") Note that the total picture is more important than the presence or absence of a single sign; any lasting concern you have is reason enough to seek further testing. Although dyslexia is not a disease and there is no cure for it, early intervention can help a child find the most successful strategies for coping with his disability and getting up to speed. It will also help him to keep up in other areas of study, which will become particularly important in third grade and beyond, as students learn more and more from reading rather than listening. Addressing your child's difficulties before third grade and helping him develop good learning strategies will avert frustration and failure down the road.

Because the root of dyslexia seems to be a difficulty in processing language, it's especially important that children who have this disability get detailed, carefully organized, logically sequenced instruction in how the English language works, and especially in the relationship between letters and sounds. The most successful programs break the challenge of reading into small steps and then encourage the student to "overlearn" each step until it is automatic. In addition, people with dyslexia often learn most effectively when several senses are engaged, so it's useful to have a multisensory approach to learning—one that uses the student's hearing, speaking, and touch, as well as sight, to convey information.

Multisensory programs usually include the so-called "VAKT" learning modes: visual, auditory, kinesthetic (moving the body), and tactile (using touch). For example, students may be urged to write giant letters in the air with their arms, to use sign language to help remember the letters, or to tap their fingers as they say the sounds in words. You'll find more information about selecting programs later in this chapter.

BETWEEN THE LIONS supports struggling readers by providing visual cues to both written and spoken language. Many vowels are color-coded to highlight their presence; animated letters call attention to words that start or end the same. This multisensory approach works well with children who have language-processing disorders and/or hearing difficulties.

SIGNS OF DYSLEXIA

Dyslexia is a complex condition, and most people who have it will not display all of the possible behaviors associated with it. But the persistent appearance of several signs calls for further evaluation. The International Dyslexia Association lists these common signs:

- ❖ Lack of awareness of the sounds in words, the order of sounds, rhymes, or the order of syllables

- ❖ Difficulty in decoding single words

- ❖ Difficulty in spelling

- ❖ Poor sequencing of numbers or of letters in words when reading or writing; for example, reading *b* as *d, sing* as *sign, left* as *felt, soiled* as *solid*, or *12* as *21*

- ❖ Problems with reading comprehension

- ❖ Difficulty expressing thoughts in writing

- ❖ Delays in learning to speak or understand spoken language

- ❖ Difficulty in interpreting spoken language or expressing thoughts in speech

- ❖ Confusion about directions in space or time: right and left, up and down, early and late, yesterday and tomorrow

- ❖ Confusion about right- or left-handedness

- ❖ Difficulty in handwriting

- ❖ Difficulty in mathematics, especially in sequencing, direction, and learning the language of math

What about ADD/ADHD?

Another condition that has received a lot of attention in recent years is Attention-Deficit/Hyperactivity Disorder, or ADHD. (ADD, or Attention Deficit Disorder, is an older term for the same syndrome.) ADHD is not a learning disability but rather a neurological condition that is believed to be caused by a specific chemical imbalance in the brain. It affects how the brain responds to stimuli and processes information. It can also interfere with learning, and in many people the outward signs of

LD and ADHD can look the same. And, because as many as 30 percent of people with learning disabilities also have ADHD, parents who suspect a learning disability may want to look out for signs of ADHD.

These signs fall into three broad categories: hyperactivity, impulsivity, and inattention. Hyperactivity, as you probably know, means that a child can't seem to sit still, runs or climbs at inappropriate times, fidgets and wiggles more than a typical child his age, and in general seems to have a motor that's always running—and often at high speed. Impulsivity is closely related to hyperactivity and means that a child can't control his impulse to do something: he may repeatedly dart away though he knows he shouldn't, may blurt out his thoughts rather than waiting his turn to speak, or may appear reckless or wild in his play. Inattention means that a child often seems to have trouble focusing on a task, to avoid or lose interest in tasks that require sustained effort, to be easily distracted by other stimuli when trying to focus, or not to listen when people speak to him. People with ADHD may have only one set of these symptoms or a combination; hyperactivity and impulsivity generally appear together, whereas inattention frequently, but not always, occurs alone.

ADHD is more commonly recognized in boys than in girls, but that may be because boys tend to act out more than girls in quiet settings like the classroom. If a girl seems very dreamy or distracted, or if she's a real tomboy who never seems to stop climbing and settle down, consider whether she could have ADHD. For both girls and boys, stimulants such as Ritalin (as well as a number of other medications) often seem to calm the symp-toms of ADHD, but the use of these powerful drugs, especially on very young children, warrants extremely careful consideration. They also require monitoring by an experienced physician. Other therapies to consider include behavior modification and educational intervention, methods with a proven track record of helping a child learn how to respond to his environment in more appropriate ways.

If you notice some of the symptoms of ADHD in your child, ask his child-care provider, teacher, or pediatrician for advice. These professionals have a sense of what is normal for your child's age and stage of development—most two-year-olds, for example, can seem "hyper" to a tired adult!—and can help you decide whether to seek further testing. Your pediatrician is a good source of referrals if you want them, as are local organizations for parents and professionals. There are also many books and other sources of information for the parents of a child with ADHD. Check the Resources chapter for more guidance.

WORRIED? HERE'S WHAT TO DO

If anything you have read here or observed in your child makes you wonder if he has a problem, there are several things you can do to get help. If your child has not yet started school, you may want to begin by speaking with his pediatrician. Describe in detail the symptoms and behaviors that concern you, and don't be afraid to ask for more information or seek a second opinion if the doctor just says, "He'll grow out of it." He may, but it's reasonable to ask for a general timetable of development, milestones to watch out for, and a sense of what factors would make the doctor change her attitude from "let's wait and see" to "let's find out more."

Weigh the doctor's advice against your own gut feelings, then try to find a reasonable balance in your level of concern, somewhere near the usual parental midpoint between fretting and nonchalance. And, if you continue to be concerned over several months, don't wait for the problem to go away on its own. Bear in mind that not all pediatricians have expertise in all areas, so, for example, you may want to ask your doctor for a referral to a speech and language therapist. You can also call the principal's office of your local elementary school, even before your child starts school. Ask for a screening, and be prepared, again, to list your concerns as specifically as possible.

If your child has already started school, the first step is to speak with his teacher about your concerns. She may reassure you, but if you continue to worry that your child has a problem that isn't being addressed, you should next consider asking for a screening by the school's speech and language pathologist or reading specialist, depending on whether your concerns focus mainly on your child's reading skills or on his use of language in general. Your pediatrician may also be able to offer a useful perspective—particularly on speech and language development.

Some parents hesitate to put their children through the screening process at school, for fear that a child will be "labeled." But most parents who have worked hard to find help for their struggling learners find that it's useful to engage the school in the process of determining whether there's a problem, what

it is, and how to address it. If your child does have a disability, his teachers are probably already aware that he's having a hard time, whether or not he receives a "label." Having a clearly defined, comprehensive assessment of his strengths and weaknesses will be more useful to them in figuring out how best to teach him than simply thinking that he's "slow" or "difficult." And note that we mentioned strengths as well as weaknesses: you may find that assessment reveals abilities in your child that you took for granted, abilities that may help him adjust, catch up, and feel good about himself. Both you and his teachers can help him celebrate and build on these strengths, but first you have to know what they are.

Time to Test

If you request an evaluation, the school must provide one, at no cost to you. You must make that request in writing; the formal discovery process cannot begin without your explicit written consent as the parent or legal guardian. Once the school agrees to screen your child, he will probably take a whole array of tests to determine the nature of his difficulties. (See the box "Testing, Testing, 1-2-3.") Be sure to ask the purpose of any test and what the results will tell about your child.

You have the right to "informed consent," meaning that you can ask for a fuller explanation of any of your child's tests that don't make sense to you—and keep asking until you understand. You also have the right to have your child tested in his preferred language.

And, of course, you have the right to know what the assessments reveal about your child's strengths and weaknesses. You also have the

TESTING, TESTING, 1-2-3

There are many different tests to help parents and educators determine whether a child has a learning disability. In addition to formal testing, your child's school will probably also use what are known as informal assessments.

Informal assessment can take place while your child is playing or interacting with other children; a trained observer can use these informal settings to assess your child's social skills, language development, and ability to understand the words and actions of others. An examiner may ask your child questions and have him do informal, unscored tasks; the specialist may also interview you to gain insight into patterns of behavior and your child's development over time.

As for testing, or *formal assessment*, there's a huge range of tools available to educators today. There are two broad categories of tests.

First, there are *standardized* or *"norm-referenced" tests,* which measure a child's performance against a norm, a standard derived by comparing the test results of a large number of children. The tests that many states have recently implemented to measure school performance and set standards for promotion and graduation are standardized tests.

The second type of formal assessments includes so-called *"criterion-based tests."* These measure a child's mastery of a subject against a list of criteria or expected answers. In-class spelling tests and multiplication quizzes, for example, are criterion-based tests.

For the purposes of assessing reading ability, two kinds of tests are of greatest relevance: *tests of language and communication development* (because reading grows out of spoken language development), and, of course, *tests of reading skills.* A third category, *tests of cognition* (many are popularly known as IQ tests), can also be important, since many educators have used the relationship of potential to actual achievement as a primary benchmark of learning difficulties.

Different tests are used at different ages, and different examiners may use different tests to measure the same general areas of development or skills. You should ask the examiner to explain the purpose and design of any test your child receives if you don't understand it.

right to refuse any test for any reason—for example, if you think it's too invasive or inappropriate for your child—but make sure you understand the consequences of withholding consent, and be sure that your child isn't denied access to all the services he needs if there aren't test results to document the need.

Don't be surprised if your child's tests include a general test of his intelligence. Some parents want to limit the assessments to the particular skills that concern them—in this case, reading—but a general intelligence test is often necessary to determine whether your child's cognitive potential is a factor in his problems with learning. A gap between potential and achievement is currently the benchmark for determining whether someone actually has a "learning disability" under the law. (Note, however, that this and many other provisions may change when the federal law is reauthorized, as happens periodically in Congress.) You may want to ask which tests are being used, as some older but still commonly used tests have been challenged for ethnic and class bias. (For more information, you can go to the www.LD.org Web site.)

All the information you get about the tests your child receives will help you determine whether these tests adequately cover the areas you're most concerned about. If you think something's missing, ask for more testing in that area. If you notice that your child is struggling with rhymes, for example, you should make sure that he is screened for phonemic awareness; if he has trouble naming the objects he sees in a picture, you should ask for a test of his naming ability. (Difficulties with the rapid naming of objects, such as shapes or alphabet letters, have been identified as a possible pre-

dictor of reading disability.) To make sure that the examiner chooses the most useful tests for your child, provide as much information as you can on what you have observed about your child's language development, reading abilities, and learning style. These kinds of observations are often the key to determining exactly what's getting in a student's way.

Whenever your child is tested, you should bear in mind that these assessments are indicators, not final judgments—useful tools, not lifelong labels. They are more helpful when seen as part of a larger picture of the whole child than when viewed in isolation. That said, they can be a valuable measure of what a child can do, what he has already learned, and what is not yet making sense to him. And they're essential for determining what kind of help your struggling child needs.

Not "Disabled," but Still Not Thriving

What if screening does not identify your child as having a learning disability, but you still feel that he needs more help than he's getting in school? While this is good news, it can be a tricky situation for parents, because schools will not provide special-education services for children who do not have an identified disability. Still, there are many ways to help your child.

For starters, you may want to consider other factors that can affect a child's ability to learn. Depression, poor nutrition (including radical dieting to lose weight), sleep disorders or poor sleep habits, poor study habits (including trying to study in a very cluttered or noisy room), even something as simple as eyestrain—all can make it hard for a child to learn well, and all require immediate attention. Consider whether any of these might be affecting your child, and ask a doctor, teacher, or counselor for help. If none of these seems to be a problem, set up a time to talk with your child's teacher about your concerns, ask for her perspective and suggestions, and see if you can work together to find effective strategies for helping your child learn. Schools often have reading teachers, student teachers, community volunteers, and peer tutors who may be able to help your child, and your school may offer other programs as well. The school's special-education teachers may also be able to offer you some useful advice and, perhaps, recommendations of programs and services outside the school to pursue at your own expense. You could also consult a reading specialist or seek more information from a nearby university or a local organization that serves people with learning disabilities.

It will be especially important for you to cultivate a good relationship with your child's teacher and to make sure that you and the teacher can both communicate clearly about your concerns. You may also want to look at the advice on talking with teachers in Chapter 1 of this book, as well as the tips for communicating with teachers and administrators in the box "A Meeting of the Minds" later in this chapter. As your child moves through the grades, you might try asking parents you trust to identify specific teachers who are especially patient and successful in teaching children with learning difficulties. You may also want to meet with the school principal or director of special education to ask that your child be placed with a teacher who is particularly skilled at helping struggling readers.

If your child continues to have serious problems, you may want to ask for more test-ing. Be as specific as possible about the areas that concern you, so the school can conduct tests specifically directed at these areas. In addition to the free assessments provided by public schools, private testing is an option. If you remain convinced that your child has a specific problem that has not been identified by the school, or if you would rather seek an independent opinion before sharing your concerns with the school, you may choose to have him evaluated outside the school system. Independent testing can be expensive, but persistent difficulties might warrant considering this option. And, whether or not you choose to invest in outside testing, you may want to provide some extra tutoring or remedial instruction for your child.

Getting Help Elsewhere: Tutors and Reading Programs

If your child seems to be persistently struggling and yet does not qualify for special services from his school, you may want to hire a private tutor or enroll him in a remedial program outside school. The available options may range from a college student who will simply spend some time listening to your child read, to a retired teacher who could offer some supplemental instruction, to a comprehensive program of remediation and skill building. So you'll want to think about just how much help you're looking for, how much you can afford to pay for it, and what kind of program or tutor is likely to meet your child's needs.

If your child has been tested for reading difficulties, the test results should include a recommendation of the kind of approach that would be most likely to help him. You can ask the person who administered the test to offer some advice on what kind of program to look for. Your child's teacher, too, may be able to point you in the right direction. For many children, a structured program to build phonemic awareness seems to help, so you might start there. There are tutors trained in phonics and many structured programs that offer a sequential plan of phonics instruction. You may also want to look specifically for a tutor or program that uses a multisensory approach, engaging your child's touch and hearing as well as his sight, as this is helpful for many struggling readers. (See the box "Getting with a Program" for more suggestions on choosing a program and information on a few specific ones.)

As for getting referrals to specific tutors or programs, one of the best avenues is to ask other parents. If you're lucky enough to know someone whose child has been successfully tutored, that's a great place to start. Ask the parent whether her child found the tutoring useful, what was particularly helpful about it, and whether she'd recommend this program for your child. Failing that kind of personal recommendation, you could contact a national organization that provides information on tutors. Three good ones to start with are the National Center for Learning Disabilities, the International Dyslexia Association, and Learning Disabilities of America; the contact information for all three is listed in the Resources chapter. Check their Web sites or call their national toll-free numbers and ask about getting information on tutors in your state.

Once you've found a few possibilities, try to interview several tutors or program directors. Ask the basic questions—what they charge, how frequently they recommend meeting with your child, what their qualifications are—as well as more in-depth questions: what approach do they use, and what do they think might work for your child? You should also ask how they coordinate their work with a child's teacher and how often you can expect to meet with them, without your child present, to discuss his progress. As you ask these questions, try to get a feel for whether this person seems like someone who would "click" with your child. The rapport between tutor and student can make a huge difference in individual instruction, so if you just don't think this person, however competent, would fit well with your child, keep looking.

Keep looking, too, if anyone promises you a quick fix or a "cure" for your child's reading problems. Be especially leery of any program that touts expensive gimmicks, high-tech gadgetry, or obvious snake-oil remedies like special vitamins for reading. Difficulty in reading is not a disease, and it cannot be cured.

Once you've found a tutor or program that seems appropriate, work together with the tutor or program director to set goals for your child—for example, are you concentrating on remediation, help with homework, or simple reading practice? Decide how you will measure your child's progress. You should also set a schedule together; it's generally better to schedule more frequent lessons over a shorter period, rather than the same number over a longer time, because your child will see results more quickly. Having at least two sessions a week is ideal.

Give your child a month or so to settle in before attempting to evaluate whether the tutoring is working. You should look for improvement in your child's reading ability, of

GETTING WITH A PROGRAM

The programs that seem to be most helpful for struggling young readers present a systematic, explicit, sequential explanation of the connections between letters and sounds. Their step-by-step procedures include direct instruction and repeated practice to ensure that students master individual skills.

The most well-known of these programs are based on a sequence developed decades ago and categorized as an Orton-Gillingham (O-G) approach. O-G–trained teachers spend many hours learning the program under strict supervision. Although other home-based instructional programs are available, we believe that students with language-processing disabilities need to receive systematic, direct, sequential instruction from a trained instructor.

Below is a list of some programs whose effectiveness with these students is well demonstrated:

Alphabetic Phonics: This classroom adaptation of O-G with books and workbooks is designed for individuals or small groups at the elementary or secondary level.

Project Read: This program adds engaging cues (puppets and gestures) to help younger students; it also includes a text comprehension and memory component called *Language Circle.*

Slingerland Multisensory Approach: This classroom O-G adaptation places extra emphasis on phoneme blending and handwriting.

The Spalding Method: Also known as "The Writing Road to Reading," the program begins with writing; letter formation and spelling receive a heavy emphasis.

Wilson Reading System: This program targets students in middle school and above who have not yet mastered sounds, spelling patterns, and syllable types. A new component for younger students is called *Fundations.*

Language!: This program for students "several years behind grade level" covers 18 areas of reading and language comprehension. All are introduced by direct instruction and reinforced by repeated practice.

LiPS: Lindamood-Bell's *Lindamood Phoneme Sequencing* program, also known as *Auditory Discrimination in Depth,* emphasizes speech sounds and mouth movements before introducing letter-sound relationships. *Visualizing and Verbalizing* is a complementary component for studying syntax and composition.

course, but you should also keep an eye out for more subtle signs. Does he seem eager to work with the tutor, or is he increasingly whiny and hesitant about going? Does he seem enthusiastic after his reading sessions, or does he not want to talk about them? Part of the point of getting assistance outside school is to help your child learn that reading can be enjoyable, so if this extra help is just seeming like more drudgery to him, you may want to reevaluate it.

You may wonder whether your child's teacher will feel defensive on hearing that he's getting outside help, and this may make you reluctant to mention it. Don't be. If your child has been struggling in a teacher's class, she will most likely be pleased to know that you are aware of the problem and are working, like her, to address it. Your best bet is to explain, in a friendly and nonaccusing way, that you feel your child needs some extra help and that you have found some. It's best if the tutor and the teacher each knows what the other is doing, as some approaches can give conflicting information and confuse the student. Ideally, you, your child's teacher, and your child's tutor are all working toward the same goal—helping your child learn to read—and so the more you share information and work together, the better off your child will be.

IF YOUR CHILD HAS A LEARNING DISABILITY

What if testing does indicate that your child has a learning disability? There's a lot for you to learn, and there are many things you can do. But the first thing to do is really quite simple: take a deep breath. Seeing test results in black and white can be unsettling, and you need to give yourself a chance to let the information sink in. You may also want to spend some time sorting out your own feelings and concerns before you feel ready to focus on helping your child. Once you have acknowledged that this isn't the outcome you were hoping for, it becomes possible to approach the problem in a more positive way.

For one thing, it can be a relief to know that there's a reason for your child's struggles, that it's not because he isn't trying or hasn't gotten enough help. He has a problem, and now you know what it is. You have some specific information about your child's strengths and weaknesses as a learner, and that will help you and his teachers figure out the best ways to help him learn. Fortunately, we know a lot more about learning disabilities than people did when today's parents were growing up, so there's a lot more help available. If you approach your child's difficulties with a realistic but hopeful attitude, you will find many ways to help him learn.

Many parents find it useful to learn as much as they can about their child's specific disability and to talk with other families who have faced similar problems. For both these purposes, parents' groups can be of real help. You'll find more information about support groups, along with books and Web sites, in the Resources chapter. You'll also find it useful to talk with your child's teacher, both to keep her informed and to ask her advice. If your child is older and has more than one teacher, it's particularly important to remember that learning disabilities can affect learning in all areas. Particularly if a child has a reading-related disability, such as dyslexia, he will have to deal with it in every subject that requires reading—and, let's face it, that's every subject. Your child's teachers may have useful suggestions for helping him learn their subjects in spite of the challenges he'll encounter.

Finally, if your child is formally found to have a learning disability, this classification gives him certain legal rights to special services and accommodations, at no cost to you. In fact, the rights conferred by the label of "learning disability" are often an important factor in deciding whether to have a child screened and how to label his difficulties once they're identified, so you will probably want to familiarize yourself with the federal law that covers education for students with learning disabilities: the Individuals with Disabilities Education Act.

What's the Big IDEA?

The Individuals with Disabilities Education Act is commonly referred to as IDEA—and that's one of the easier acronyms to remember in the alphabet soup that any parent of a child with special needs soon finds herself swimming in. IDEA requires your local school district to provide a free, appropriate public education, or FAPE, for all children, and to do so in the least restrictive environment, or LRE, that is possible for each child. This broad mandate is what will govern many decisions about your child's schooling, so here's a shorthand version to file in your memory bank: FAPE in LRE, thanks to IDEA.

What this means in practical terms is that, if you formally request (in writing) that your child be evaluated for a learning disability, your local school must provide an evaluation, at no cost to you. If you disagree with the findings of that assessment, you can have your child undergo an independent evaluation. If

these findings shed new light on your child's eligibility for classification, the school district pays for this second screening. If your child is found (through either publicly or privately funded screening) to have a learning disability, he will be eligible for an array of remedial services and accommodations.

In its more specific sections, IDEA spells out the 13 categories of disability that it covers, including learning disabilities. As for ADHD, some schools provide services under this law, while others consider that it falls under a different federal statute known as Section 504. In any case, the result is the same: each student who is found to have a disability is entitled to receive, at no cost to his family, the specialized services he needs in order to learn. (See the box "Services and Accommodations" for some common examples of what schools provide.)

It's important, in trying to get help for your child, that you be as well informed as possible about his needs and the school's available programs. This means that you should understand all his test results, and ask for explanations if you don't; it also means that you should feel free to ask what services the school provides, and then to develop a proposal for what you think would best meet your child's needs. Be clear and specific about what you think your child needs and what you would like the school to provide.

The ABCs of an IEP

In order to spell out the school's and parents' shared understanding of the student's needs and to specify the services the school will provide, each student who qualifies must have a so-called IEP, or Individualized Education Program. This means that every student with

SERVICES AND ACCOMMODATIONS

Schools can offer students with learning disabilities a range of special services and accommodations, or modifications to the usual classroom program.

Special services, sometimes called "related services," might include:

❖ remedial reading instruction

❖ speech therapy

❖ intensive handwriting instruction

❖ an aide who can help read assignments or test questions, or take notes or take dictation if writing is an issue

Accommodations may include:

❖ Changing the pace or timing of work: The student may have more time to complete a test, for example, or may be allowed to take a test over several days.

❖ Reducing the amount of work: The student may complete fewer math problems, read a shorter passage, or otherwise do less; the idea is that he can demonstrate mastery of a subject with fewer examples.

❖ Adjusting the complexity: The teacher might explain the steps of a required task or use concrete demonstrations to make it clearer.

❖ Using special devices: The student might use a computer, a tape recorder, books on tape, graphic organizers, or other tools.

❖ Assessing progress differently: The student could give an oral report, make a poster, or complete a special project to show what he has learned, instead of or in addition to taking regular tests and writing reports.

special education needs between the ages of 3 and 21 will have an IEP. (From birth to age 3, children receive an Individualized Family Service Plan, or IFSP, which functions in a more or less similar way.) This plan must be reviewed at least annually, and it is an important document that can affect your child's future, so you should make sure that you understand and agree with all of its provisions. (Note that the requirement of an annual review, along with other provisions of IDEA, is currently under discussion in Congress as part of a periodic reauthorization. It may be changed to a requirement of revising the IEP every three years.)

The IEP is a legally binding document that federal law requires public schools to develop for every student with LD. Its purpose is to describe in detail the child's specific areas of strength and weakness and to document how his disabilities affect his progress in class, as well as to spell out exactly which services the school will provide to help the student learn. The IEP also sets a long-term goal for the student—usually a goal that lies one to five years ahead—and lists short-term goals, based on the child's strengths and weaknesses; it explains how progress toward these goals will be measured. For older students, the IEP presents a "transition" plan to ensure progress through the grades and on to graduation, and beyond.

In describing how the school will educate your child, the IEP lists special services such as remedial reading instruction or speech therapy, along with any necessary accommodations, or special provisions, that your child may require—for example, receiving extra time to complete assignments, receiving both written and spoken assignments, listening to books on tape instead of reading them, or having a "scribe," a person to write down test answers, if his disability makes writing unduly difficult. The plan also specifies modifications of the academic program that may be appropriate, such as requiring a math-impaired student to complete fewer problems on homework assignments.

The IEP also lists any summer services and transportation requirements that are agreed on—for example, if the school provides some special-education programs in another location, the IEP describes how your child will get there and back—and spells out any behavior-management techniques that may be used with students who have behavioral or emotional problems. Finally, the IEP specifies the type of placement in which your child will receive help, whether in a regular classroom with supplemental services or in a special-education class.

The law requires that your local school develop your child's IEP by holding a meeting that includes you, one or more special-education teachers, a person qualified to interpret your child's test results (often a special-education teacher or a psychologist), a representative of the school system, and your child's regular classroom teacher. Depending on your child's age, he may be included in the meeting as well; this generally doesn't happen before middle school. Either you or the school's representatives can request a meeting to review and update the IEP at any time; in addition, you should feel free to meet informally with members of the IEP team as often as necessary.

The purpose of the IEP meeting is to discuss your child's strengths and weaknesses, to determine what accommodations and modifications to the regular academic program would help him learn, and to develop the written IEP. Note that everyone in this meeting is an "expert" of one kind or another. The other people there are experts on learning disabilities and on what the school can provide, but you are the expert on your child. By pooling your knowledge, you will be able to make the best fit between the system and his needs.

Every student's IEP must be reviewed annually, so you should take note of any concerns or questions throughout the year in order to bring them up at the next meeting— or sooner, if you think it's necessary. In addition, the school is required to notify you of any plans to change your child's placement or to reevaluate him (reevaluation is required at least every three years) and to keep you informed of his progress at least as often as it informs the parents of children without disabilities. The school must also obtain your informed consent before placing your child in any program; this means that you understand and agree in writing to the evaluation and program decisions for him. You do not have to consent to any proposed placement of your child, you can withdraw your consent at any time, and the school cannot place him in a special program without your consent. You can also obtain an independent evaluation if you disagree with the school's findings.

Used wisely, the process of developing and using an IEP, which includes a meeting once a year (or more often if necessary) to discuss the student's challenges and goals, can give parents, teachers, and administrators a chance to talk about your child: what he needs, what he can do easily and what he could use some help on, what progress you would like him to make

toward acquiring skills and meeting specific goals, what each of you can do to help him learn. Each year's meeting provides an occasion for measuring your child's performance over the past year, reassessing his needs and determining whether they're being met, and setting new goals for the year to come. If you approach the IEP meeting as an opportunity to share information and gain insight, you may find it a valuable tool for improving your struggling child's experience at school. (See the box "A Meeting of the Minds.")

All of this, by the way, is only the most basic introduction to the provisions of IDEA. You may want to look at the Resources chapter for other sources of information. In addition, local parents' organizations and advocacy groups may provide valuable advice and support, tailored to the particular circumstances of local law, which varies considerably from state to state—and even, sometimes, in practice from district to district. For detailed questions about your child's rights and the best way to help him, you may want to consult a local or regional office of your state's department of education. If you think you are being denied appropriate help for your child, it may be helpful to speak with a local attorney who specializes in disability law or consult a mediator or advocate in this field. Just remember, as you negotiate the sometimes confusing maze of disability assessments and regulations, that you know your child better than anyone, and that the goal is to help him find the assistance and support he needs.

Becoming an Advocate for Your Child

It's important to start out with a positive attitude, as it is most likely to help you get results for your child. Sometimes, however, you may find that despite your best efforts you're not getting the answers and support you want, and so you may need to develop some new strategies in order to advocate effectively for your child. Many parents of struggling readers find themselves developing skills and areas of expertise they never knew they had. They research the law, they educate themselves about their child's disability and ways of dealing with it, and they become expert record keepers, note takers, and negotiators. (See the box "Record Keepers' Checklist.") All of these skills may come in handy as you search for help for your child. But don't be overwhelmed by it all; you can take things one step at a time and learn new skills and information only as you need them.

Your first step, as we've said before, is to develop as good a relationship as possible with your child's teacher. Even if you disagree with her, she spends a lot of time with your child and can provide valuable insights into his situation. She can also prove to be an ally in your search for support, so do try to keep the lines of communication open. Volunteer in the school library, or be a chaperone on field trips. Arrange to talk with the teacher regularly, if possible, and generally try to get to know the teacher and help her get to know you. Be friendly, positive, and straightforward in your dealings with her, and don't go up the chain of command above her unless you feel you must. (See the box "Going Up the Ladder.")

The same rule applies in dealing with special-education teachers and with local school administrators. State your concerns and requests openly, clearly, and politely, and try to resolve any differences at the lowest possi-

ble level. In meetings, try to stay calm and positive, to make sure that you are making yourself understood, and to understand what others are saying. Remember, always, what the goal is: to get the best help for your child that you can.

Talking with Your Child

In all this talk of screening and regulations, it's easy to lose sight of the person at the center of it all: the child who needs help. As his parent, though, you're not likely to forget that he's the reason for all this hard work, and you'll want to know how to talk with him about the challenges that lie ahead. You'll also want to find the most effective ways of supporting him as he learns and of reinforcing the work of his teachers and other professionals to help him succeed.

In part, how much information you share with your child will depend on his age and level of understanding. And, no matter what his age, it can sometimes be hard to figure out the right words to use when you're explaining to your child that he has a learning disability. It may help you to realize that your child already knows more about his troubles than you might think. He may not be able to put it into words, but he knows that reading is not as easy as he would like it to be and not as easy as it is for his peers. It can be a huge weight off his shoulders to learn that a disability, not a lack of effort, is causing his troubles. Rather than shocking him, your calm statement that he has a learning disability may come as a relief.

This is the first step in what specialists call demystifying your child's difficulties for him. By giving your child specific words for the problems he has been having, you make it

A MEETING OF THE MINDS

Here's how to prepare for the meetings to set up or review your child's Individualized Education Program, or IEP.

1. Ask the school to make sure that the meeting is scheduled at a time that is convenient for everyone involved. By law, the meeting must include you, your child's regular classroom teacher, one or more special-education teachers, a person qualified to interpret test results (who may be the special-education teacher or another expert), a representative of the school administration, and, depending on how old he is, your child. You have the right to know ahead of time who will attend the meeting and to bring along a specialist in your child's condition, a trained advocate, a translator, or a friend who can take notes and offer support.

2. A week or so before the meeting, review your records and notes about your child and make sure you have everything you need. Make a list of specific goals for your child in the coming year. Talk with your child, too, about how he thinks he's doing and what he'd like to accomplish.

3. If this is a follow-up meeting, review the current IEP and note how your child has progressed, whether the goals need to be updated, and how his needs may have changed. It can be helpful to speak briefly with his teacher before the meeting, to compare notes on how your child is doing. Prepare a brief summary of his progress this year, which will be used in next year's IEP.

4. Ask if the school is preparing a draft IEP in advance of the meeting; if so, request an advance copy and make notes on it before you go.

5. For the meeting, make sure to bring the file with your child's records and other information, along with your list of goals and challenges and the summary you prepared. After reviewing the current situation, you and the other participants will work together to come up with goals for the next year and agree on how to measure your child's progress. You will also discuss what special services and accommodations the school will provide.

Some Do's and Don'ts

❖ Try to maintain a positive tone and to be an effective listener.

❖ To make sure you understand what others are saying, you might rephrase their words: "What I'm hearing is . . ." "So what you're suggesting we do is . . ."

❖ If you dislike a proposal, try to frame your objections in impersonal and friendly terms: "I think a better approach might be . . ." or "I don't think that will work because . . ." instead of "You're not giving him what he needs" or "That's never going to work."

❖ Try to speak calmly and clearly; being assertive will help your child, but being aggressive will not.

❖ You do not have to finish the plan in one sitting, so don't feel pressed for time or refrain from asking questions out of fear that it will take too long.

❖ Feel free to take detailed notes and to ask for time to review them before agreeing to anything. Don't feel pressured to decide anything right away; take time to consult with others.

❖ Always make sure that you understand and agree with all the provisions of your child's IEP before signing off on it. If you believe the school should provide a service that is not included, say so.

The school is responsible for creating and maintaining the IEP, but you are responsible for participating to ensure that it is a useful, workable tool for helping your child get what he needs.

GOING UP THE LADDER

If, despite all your best efforts, you feel that you are not getting the response you need from your child's school, there are other avenues you can pursue. This is where it will be particularly helpful to have good records, so make sure your files are in order. Make sure, too, that you are clear about what you think your child needs and why you feel the school has not met his needs and should do so, and be certain that you have done everything you can to try to resolve the issue locally.

If you're ready to take another step, you might start by calling your state education department's *special-education coordinator*. The state may be able to clarify legal issues or provide your school district with funds for technical support or staff training that could solve your problem. You can also request an *administrative review* or resolution conference within your school district, if you believe your child is entitled to a service that the school refuses to provide. And you can contact your school district if you think the problems your child is having may violate his civil rights under *antidiscrimination laws*, which entitle him to any reasonable accommodations he needs in order to receive equal access to a free, appropriate public education.

Still not satisfied? If you think your concerns involve a violation of state or federal special-education law or regulations, you can *file a complaint* with your state department of education. IDEA requires every state to adopt a written procedure for handling complaints about systems or individual cases. You may also request *impartial mediation* to help you and the school reach an agreement; ask the school's special-education director, the district superintendent, or the district supervisor of special-education services to participate.

Finally, if all else fails, you can request a *due process hearing,* which is a legally binding proceeding that takes place before a due process officer—and, if either side cares to pursue the matter beyond that stage, could be appealed in *state or federal court*. This is a last resort, because it will almost by definition result in an adversarial relationship between you and the school. With luck, persistence, and the careful application of good negotiating techniques, however, you can almost surely avoid having to go that far.

RECORD KEEPERS' CHECKLIST

Here's a checklist of the information you should keep in a file. Take the file to every IEP meeting; at home, keep it easily accessible so you can consult it frequently, keep it up to date, and add to it whenever you have a phone conversation or teacher conference about your child.

_____ Test results and the examiner's interpretations of them

_____ A copy of your child's Individualized Education Program, with annual updates

_____ Report cards and other assessments from your child's teachers

_____ Relevant medical records

_____ Notes (with names and dates) on all conversations with teachers, administrators, special-education staff members, psychologists, and so on

_____ Samples of your child's work—both school assignments and writing or drawing he does at home

_____ Your own observations and questions about your child's progress

_____ Notes (with dates) on your child's comments about his progress

_____ Contact information for anyone involved in your child's learning

_____ A copy of your local school district's special-education policy; the school is required to provide one to you

possible for him to put these problems in their proper perspective, to see them as only one part of a larger picture. "It's hard for you to make the connection between letters and sounds" or "Your brain has trouble breaking down words and paying attention to the sounds in them" is more accurate and less painful than what he may have been thinking, such as "I'm stupid" or "I'll never learn how to read." By being as specific and focused as you can about the nature of his trouble, you will help him to concentrate on what the problem is, what he will need to work harder on, and why he struggles sometimes with things that seem easy to his friends.

It may sometimes be challenging, of course, to find age-appropriate ways to explain his disability. Keep your explanations as simple as possible—one sentence at a time, and one thought per sentence—and try to use precise, concrete language whenever possible: "brain" instead of "mind," "eyes" instead of "visual processing," "words on the page" instead of "printed text," and so forth. The specialists you consult may have useful suggestions about what to say to your child, as may other parents in similar situations. Just don't feel you have to explain everything all at once, don't tell your child more than he seems to want to know, and don't be surprised if you have to repeat your explanations many times, in different ways, before he fully absorbs the information.

Because learning disabilities can often affect a child's sense of his own worth, it's important to reinforce for your child all the things that he can do well—and to remind him that you love him simply for who he is, and not for what he can or can't do. All children

need to find activities in which they feel competent, but this is especially important for children with learning disabilities. (See the box "Lights, Camera, Activities" for some good ones to try.) Helping your child develop a realistic but positive sense of his own strengths and weaknesses, and showing him how to use his strengths to work around his weaknesses, will help to give him the sense of competence and mastery that is the basis of all true self-esteem. You can also work with him to develop reasonable goals for himself and to reinforce his sense that, with hard work and persistence, he will be able to achieve them.

When it comes to helping him learn, it's useful to remember that you're a parent, not a teacher or a tutor. Your child may resist formal drilling from you even more than he would in a classroom, and you may have greater success with more casual or playful activities. (See the box "Winning Strategies" for some techniques that may make learning easier.) Many of the activities in this book could prove useful for you; look especially for the ones that help to build phonemic awareness and fluency. And make an effort to find literacy-related activities elsewhere—on TV, on the Web, and in other publications—that you and your child can enjoy together.

One of the most important ways to help your child as he works on improving his independent reading is to keep reading to him every day, and to encourage him to read to you. In particular, you should read to him in different subject areas so he doesn't fall behind. One of the greatest difficulties for children who struggle with reading is that their problems in this area begin to affect their learning in every subject, especially

LIGHTS, CAMERA, ACTIVITIES

For children who struggle in the classroom, outside activities are especially important. Not only can they give children a chance to explore their abilities and build their confidence in a less regimented and pressured setting, but also they often make use of the particular gifts and aptitudes that seem to accompany many learning disabilities.

For example, people with learning disabilities in reading often seem particularly drawn to fields that make use of *spatial perception, holistic processing,* and *creativity,* such as graphic design, filmmaking and animation in movies and video, engineering, architecture, software development, construction, acting and other performance arts, and product development. Visual art, music, cooking, and photography are other areas that often appeal as well.

Many *sports and other physical activities* are also wonderful outlets for a child who feels stifled and pressured in class all day. Team sports can sometimes be too pressured for children with learning disabilities, but don't discourage your child if it's something he loves. On the other hand, if he hasn't picked a sport, you might gently steer him toward a less winner-take-all sport or a more individually focused activity. To consider:

- ❖ Swimming and diving
- ❖ Skateboarding and snowboarding
- ❖ Hiking
- ❖ Running
- ❖ Skating
- ❖ Yoga and martial arts
- ❖ Dance
- ❖ Cycling
- ❖ Skiing
- ❖ Rock climbing

In any activity your child chooses, encourage him to focus on improving his own skills and having fun, rather than worrying about how other people are evaluating his performance or whether he's winning every game.

WINNING STRATEGIES

People with learning disabilities need help in learning how to learn. Here are some tips to help your child become a more strategic and confident learner.

- ❖ **Make information automatic:** Encourage your child to "overlearn" information. For example, have him practice spelling words by copying a word, then tracing over it with his pencil, then writing the word again while looking at it, then writing it without looking at it—saying the letters aloud each time. Repeat this process with the same word until spelling becomes automatic.

- ❖ **Break learning into discrete steps:** When your child is trying to master a new skill, help him think about each step. Instead of just saying, "Sound it out," remind him to look at each letter of a word, make its sound, say the sounds rapidly in sequence, and then try to hear what the word is.

- ❖ **Isolate the weakness:** Pinpoint his difficulty as precisely as possible. If he has trouble with handwriting, is it because of coordination difficulties, confusion about how letters are formed, or other factors?

- ❖ **Organize tasks and set deadlines:** Help your child keep from getting overwhelmed by showing him how to take a large project one step at a time. Encourage him to keep a calendar for tracking his assignments.

- ❖ **Find a peer tutor or mentor:** If your child has a friend who learns easily, encourage them to study together.

- ❖ **Model explicit strategies:** When you're showing your child how to learn, think about your own mental processes and describe them as clearly as you can.

- ❖ **Think out loud:** Help your child get in the habit of talking himself through a mental process or task.

- ❖ **Use strengths to support weaknesses:** Every child has things he does well, which can offset the areas that are hard for him. Help your child identify his strengths and think of ways he can use them to build up his weaker skills.

once they get past third grade. If your child can't read and understand his history book or the language of math problems, you need to read these texts to him or find someone else who can. This may sound like too much parental involvement, but it's essential if your child is to keep up with the pace of learning that's expected from fourth grade on. If you can help your child stay current with his peers by building his vocabulary and comprehension in specialized subjects, you'll be minimizing the negative effects of his reading troubles and giving him an important foundation for later years. And make sure to read to him for pure pleasure, too. Making sense of text may always be harder for him than it is for other people, but by introducing him to the delights of reading, you will be encouraging him to think of it as more than an onerous task. If you can get your child to fall in love with a book, even as you encourage and support him in his struggles to crack the code, you'll have given him the key to a lifetime of learning and joy.

Part III

Having a few simple items on hand makes it easy to come up with spontaneous activities that enhance language and literacy for children at any age. Here are ten ideas to get you started. They're all suggestions that you can use from preschool through third grade and beyond. Start simply, then build your collections as your child's interests and needs dictate.

1 WORLD IN A BOX   Collect a few cardboard boxes or small plastic storage containers—no bigger than a shoe box, so your child can take it out and put it away himself—and fill each one with an assortment of simple props connected to a particular setting for dramatic play. Put menus, order pads, and recipes in the "restaurant" box; a chart on a clipboard, a labeled box of bandages, and a "prescription pad" in the "doctor's office"; ticket stubs, programs, and an autograph album in the "theater" box. Add dress-up items for more fun—an apron, a toy stethoscope. You can make your own props (keep it simple so children have room to imagine), and it's also great to use real items—a takeout menu from your family's favorite spot, or ticket stubs from a play you saw together. Some other possible worlds to put in a box: airplane, spaceship, subway, library, office, science lab, art gallery.

2 CAST OF CHARACTERS   Round up a few puppets or stuffed animals to play a variety of roles in acted-out stories, plays, and imaginative games. Encourage your child to use the puppets to talk with each other, tell stories, conduct interviews—anything that extends the use of language. You can make simple finger puppets by cutting the fingers off old gloves (fleece works best). Glue on felt features, yarn hair, or googly eyes from the craft store. Or make a puppet family by gluing a couple of eyes and a yarn mouth to each finger of a whole glove. You can also make a stick puppet of a favorite character from a book—just make a color photocopy, paste it onto cardboard, and attach a Popsicle stick as a handle. Or do the same thing with the image of a BETWEEN THE LIONS character you download from the Web site, www.pbskids.org/lions. Why not have Theo handle the bedtime reading tonight?

3 MAGICAL MAPS   Collect maps, atlases, and globes, or help your child make her own. She could draw a simple map of her room, for example, or plot the path from your home to the park. And buy maps of anything from your town to the solar system—then help your child learn how to read them and connect them to the world they represent. If you're planning a family trip, show your child how to use maps for a more efficient and rewarding journey; on family outings, show her how to use the subway route map or the museum's floor plan—and encourage her to draw and annotate a map of where you went when you get back home. Maps and globes also make wonderful "story starters"—spin the globe, then spin a tale set in the spot where your finger happens to land. Or look for unusual or amusing place names on a map and play games with them:

make up limericks or rhymes (or try "A, My Name Is Alice, and I Live in Albuquerque"), invent a local legend, or make a list of places that start with Z.

4 WHAT'S COOKING Build a collection of your child's favorite recipes. Several good books for young cooks are available, but you can also look for simple, clear recipes in newspapers and magazines or write down a few family favorites in language your child can understand. Older children might enjoy developing and writing a recipe of their own—and a child of any age will have fun making up silly recipes for butterfly soup or paintbrush pie. You can help your child make a scrapbook or folder to hold his collection—a looseleaf binder with clear sheet protectors is great for holding an assortment of oddly shaped clippings and cards—then encourage him to pick a recipe and prepare it with you. Cooking together is a great opportunity to practice reading skills and to connect text to various senses: read "cinnamon" and then smell it, spell "chocolate" and take a taste, read "knead" and then feel how the dough yields under your hands. And there's no better way to demonstrate what reading can help you do than to eat the delicious results.

5 PICTURE THIS Give your child an inexpensive photo album or scrapbook, then encourage him to collect his mementos in it. You can help him write simple labels for each picture or item, or help him type the captions on a computer and then print them out on labels. This is a particularly rewarding activity if it's focused around a specific event: a family vacation, say, or a visit from a distant relative. Or help your child make a scrapbook of his favorite characters from books, movies, or television, with his own drawings, tracings, downloaded images, or other memorabilia. The BETWEEN THE LIONS Web site (www.pbskids.org/lions) has lots of downloadable materials about the Lions—and even some "Pawlaroids" that might give your child some rip-roaring ideas.

6 YOU'VE GOT GAME Many time-tested board games and card games help reinforce reading and spelling skills—and just the act of playing together encourages conversation, joking, and playful language. If money is tight, look for games at yard sales or bargain stores, or encourage relatives to give them instead of the latest electronic gadget. Some classics to try: Boggle, Scrabble, Password, Monopoly, Pictionary, and Trivial Pursuit. For card games, try "go fish" to reinforce your young child's number-recognition and matching skills.

7 WRITE ON Create a "writing center" when your child first shows an interest in scribbling, and add to it as she grows. It can be as simple as a box full of different kinds of pens, pencils, and markers, with assorted papers to use them on: old stationery, wrapping paper, shopping bags, the return envelopes from junk mail, and of course all the beautiful papers, from origami to handmade wrappings, you'd like to buy. Glitter, stencils, stamps, stickers, glue sticks, and gold stars add to the fun. Your child can use these for all kinds of writing; she can make name banners, signs, and labels for her room or for yours. As she gets older, you can expand the writing center to include a "publishing house," with more paper, a hole punch, ribbons or string, brads or other fasteners, and other supplies for making her own books. Books can be simple—a few folded sheets of construction paper, stapled together down the fold—or more complex, with glue or stitching to hold the pages together and heavier paper or cardboard to serve as a cover. Your help with the computer or a trip to the copy shop can take her publishing efforts to the next level.

8 CAPTAIN'S LOG   Encourage your child to keep a log or chart of the books he reads. Some children just like to make a simple list, perhaps with a one-to-four-star rating of each entry; others will enjoy writing elaborate reviews or descriptions. He could make a poster of his favorites, with drawings and summaries. He could also keep separate lists for different kinds of books: stories, poems, natural history. And creating a similar log for his favorite television series is an excellent way to link watching and reading.

9 LAB SUPPLIES   Combine literacy with early science education by collecting a few tools for your budding scientist or nature explorer. A magnifying glass, simple binoculars, notebook, and pencil will get her started on looking at the world around her and recording her observations—of birds, trees, the plants on the windowsill or the bugs in the yard. You could also encourage a "word-watching expedition," using the field glasses to explore signs, posters, billboards, and other print in the environment around her.

10 HAVE A LITTLE LIST   Help your child get in the habit of making lists and using writing in other everyday ways. You could get notepads personalized with his name or buy him a simple spiral-bound notebook to use. Then encourage your child to make all kinds of lists: things to do, birthday presents he wants, his favorite songs or books or movies, his relatives' birthdays, his friends' addresses and phone numbers, his wishes and dreams, his favorite words or sayings—or a list of all the kinds of lists he can think of!

Resources

In this section, we've gathered some of our favorite reading-related books and Web sites. This is by no means an exhaustive list, but it will get you started if you're hungry for more information and ideas. And, as we've mentioned before, the BETWEEN THE LIONS Web site (www.pbskids.org/lions) contains a lot of valuable resources for parents as well as children. You'll also find book lists and links to many terrific reading-related sites there.

GENERAL INFORMATION

Beginning to Read: Thinking and Learning About Print, by Marilyn Jager Adams (MIT Press, 1990), is sometimes necessarily technical and dense, but it's the best comprehensive survey of recent research and theory about how we read, and it's enlivened with wit and sharp insight.

Emergent Literacy: Writing and Reading, edited by William H. Teale and Elizabeth Sulzby (Ablex Publishing, 1986), contains a variety of perspectives on the early stages of becoming a reader.

Phonics from A to Z, by Wiley Blevins (Scholastic Professional Books, 1998), is a practical guide to phonics instruction, written by one of Jeanne S. Chall's former students. It includes word lists, book lists, and activities for developing phonemic awareness.

Read to Me: Raising Kids Who Love to Read, by Bernice Cullinan (Scholastic Trade, 1992), presents a longtime educator's passionate argument for "junk" reading—getting kids to read without worrying about what they're reading—and clear, helpful advice on how to raise a reader.

Stages of Reading Development, by Jeanne S. Chall (McGraw-Hill, 1983), presents an influential, useful model of the process of learning to read.

Starting Out Right: A Guide to Promoting Children's Reading Success, edited by M. Susan Burns, Peg Griffin, and Catherine E. Snow (National Academy Press, 1999), is a clear, accessible guide to early reading. It includes activities and a resource guide.

Straight Talk About Reading: How Parents Can Make a Difference During the Early Years, by Susan L. Hall and Louisa C. Moats (NTC Publishing Group: Contemporary Books, 1998), provides lots of practical advice, activities, and information. It's a useful, accessible overview.

Teaching and Assessing Phonics: Why, What, When, How, by Jeanne S. Chall and Helen M. Popp (Educators Publishing Service, 1996), is a concise explanation of why phonics instruction matters and how to do it.

The American Library Association (www.ala.org/parents) offers lots of useful links and information.

Celebrating Children (www.celebratingchildren.com), an excellent African American parenting Web site, offers articles exploring children's literature, education, music, and more, primarily for families with kids under ten.

Centro para el Estudio de Libros Infantiles y Juveniles en Español/Center for the Study of Books in Spanish for Children and Adolescents (www.csusm.edu/csb) is a bilingual site promoting Spanish literacy. It includes 5,500 recommended Spanish-language books and many other resources.

The Children's Literature Web Guide (www.acs.ucalgary.ca/~dkbrown) is a fantastic resource, with guidance, terrific links, and charmingly opinionated commentary from a professional librarian.

The Educational Resources Information Center (http://askeric.org) is a rich resource for parents and teachers on a whole range of education topics, not just reading. ERIC also has clearinghouses in a variety of subject areas, all with a searchable database of research papers and expert advice. The **ERIC Clearinghouse on Reading, English, and Communication** (http://eric.indiana.edu) is a great place to start if you're looking for information on the latest findings from academic research.

Fairrosa Cyber Library (www.fairrosa.info) is another, equally charming and slightly quirkier site maintained by a librarian. It features links to many authors' sites, as well as to a number of children's classics and e-books available on-line.

Family Education Network (www.familyeducation.com) contains a lot of good information for parents on many topics, including reading, and it hosts the "Get Ready to Read!" screening tool (www.getreadytoread.org) developed by the National Center for Learning Disabilities.

Federal Resources for Educational Excellence (www.ed.gov/free) is a set of links to publicly funded resources in various subject areas, including reading. Check the site's index (www.ed.gov/index.jsp) for other information from the U.S. Department of Education, including a link to the on-line edition of "Preventing Reading Difficulties in Young Children."

The National Institute for Literacy (www.nifl.gov) features several searchable databases, including the one found at www.literacydirectory.org, a searchable directory of literacy and remedial programs nationwide. You'll also find a link to the Partnership for Reading here.

The Office Bedtime Story (www.the-office.com/bedtime-story) might be fun to check out some night. Here you'll find an illustrated story you can read from the computer—perfect for business travelers with a laptop and Net access.

PBS Kids (www.pbskids.org) is the Lions' neighborhood—and our neighbors have lots of wonderful activities, stories, and resources for parents and children, too.

PBS Online (www.pbs.org) includes pages for all Public Broadcasting Service programming, many of which contain useful resources for teachers and parents—especially as your child grows.

Reading Rockets (www.readingrockets.org) is a wonderful on-line resource for parents, with a wealth of articles, activities, and reliable links to other good literacy-related sites.

FINDING BOOKS FOR CHILDREN

To find appropriate books for your child, look at the age-by-age lists that appear at the end of each chapter. Also, many of the Web sites we've just mentioned include annotated book lists and recommendations. You might also want to check out the **Children's Picture Book Database** (www.lib.muohio.edu/pictbks), which is searchable by keywords, or try one of the guidebooks we list here. Often, though, the best way to find a book for your child is to consult your local librarian, combining your knowledge of your child's interests with her expertise and experience in pairing children and books.

99 Ways to Get Your Kids to Love Reading: And 100 Books They'll Love, by Mary Leonhardt (Crown, 1997), is less overwhelming than some of the larger guides and offers some parent-friendly, workable tips for incorporating reading into busy lives.

100 Books for Girls to Grow On, by Shireen Dodson (HarperPerennial Library, 1998), includes discussion questions and suggestions for ways to connect the books to life, using field trips and other activities.

Babies Need Books: Sharing the Joy of Books with Children from Birth to Six, by Dorothy Butler (Heinemann, 1998), discusses the importance of reading to even the youngest children and suggests books by age level, with summaries.

Black Books Galore! Guide to Great African American Children's Books, by Donna Rand, Toni Trent Parker, and Sheila Foster (John Wiley and Sons, 1998) provides an annotated list of 500 titles, including valuable information on any language issues or stereotyping. Other books from the same series focus on books for boys and books for girls.

Choosing Books for Children: A Commonsense Guide, by Betsy Gould Hearne (University of Illinois Press, 1999), is just what it says, and more: a wonderfully sensible, warm companion in the process of finding books your child will love.

Great Books for Boys: More Than 600 Books for Boys 2 to 14, by Kathleen Odean (Ballantine Books, 1998), spotlights books with themes, characters, or content that is likely to appeal particularly to boys.

The New York Times Parent's Guide to the Best Books for Children, by Eden Ross Lipson (Three Rivers Press, 2000), is full of titles for all ages. Its most useful feature is the variety of indexes that allow you to look for books in a particular subject area, to organize your search by age level, or to find favorite authors or illustrators.

The Read-Aloud Handbook, by Jim Trelease (Penguin, 2001), the regularly updated best-seller, offers the author's passionate argument for reading aloud and includes a "Treasury of Read-Alouds"—hundreds of recommended books, annotated by age and grade level.

LITERACY GAMES AND ACTIVITIES

Montessori Read and Write: A Parent's Guide to Learning for Children, by Lynne Lawrence (Three Rivers Press, 1998), draws on the theories and practices of Maria Montessori to provide an interesting perspective on children's learning and some stimulating activities.

Phonemic Awareness in Young Children: A Classroom Curriculum, by Marilyn Jager Adams, Barbara R. Foorman, Ingvar Lundberg, and Terri Beeler (Paul H. Brookes Publishing, 1998), is a collection of engaging and effective games to play with language sounds, boosting phonemic awareness in children from preschool through first grade.

Ready, Set, Read and Write: 60 Playful Activities for You and Your Child to Share, by Marlene Barron (Wiley, 1995), another Montessori-based book, is particularly strong in activities that grow naturally out of everyday life.

HELPING CHILDREN WITH LEARNING DISABILITIES

Multisensory Teaching of Basic Language Skills, by Judith R. Birsh (Paul H. Brookes Publishing, 1999), is a useful explanation of why multisensory programs are especially helpful to struggling readers and how the most effective ones work.

Supporting Struggling Readers and Writers: Strategies for Classroom Intervention 3–6, by Dorothy S. Strickland, Kathy Ganske, and Joanne K. Monroe (Stenhouse Publishers, 2002), provides a different perspective, emphasizing comprehension strategies.

Teaching and Assessing Phonics: Why, What, When, How, by Jeanne S. Chall and Helen M. Popp (Educators Publishing Service, 1996), is particularly valuable for parents of struggling readers.

All Kinds of Minds (www.allkindsofminds.org) presents Dr. Mel Levine's sensitive and thoughtful approach to individuals with learning disabilities.

International Dyslexia Association (www.interdys.org) contains a wealth of information on dyslexia and Orton-Gillingham remedial programs.

LD Online (www.ldonline.com) includes lots of articles on just about every imaginable topic related to learning disabilities, well organized and easily searched.

National Center for Learning Disabilities (www.LD.org) is an invaluable resource for parents, educators, and students, full of information and links. It includes a link to the "Get Ready to Read!" screening tool.

Reading for the Blind and Dyslexic (www.rfbd. org) is a terrific resource for people with learning disabilities. The site offers information on obtaining recorded books, with lists of titles.

Schwab Learning (www.schwablearning.org) is full of wonderful resources for people with learning disabilities.

The William Ennis Cosby Foundation (www. hellofriend.org) is truly a friendly, welcoming site for people with learning disabilities.

Remedial programs all have their own sites, including www.language-usa.net, www.lindamoodbell. com, www.ortonacademy.org, www.interdys.org, www.projectread.com, www.slingerland.org, and www.spalding.org.

BOOKS WE USED

In addition to the books we recommend, we found these useful in researching this book. Many of them may be more academic or specialized than you're looking for, but we thought you'd like to know about them anyway.

Donald R. Bear, Marcia Invernizzi, Shane Templeton, and Francine Johnston, *Words Their Way: Word Study for Phonics, Vocabulary, and Spelling Instruction* (Upper Saddle River, NJ: Prentice-Hall, 1996).

Sara Brody, ed., *Teaching Reading: Language, Letters & Thought* (Milford, NH: LARC Publishing, 2001).

Jeanne S. Chall, *The Academic Achievement Challenge: What Really Works in the Classroom* (New York: Guilford Press, 2000).

Jeanne S. Chall, Vicki A. Jacobs, and Luke E. Baldwin, *The Reading Crisis: Why Poor Children Fall Behind* (Cambridge: Harvard University Press, 1990).

Marie M. Clay, *An Observation Survey of Early Literacy Achievement* (Portsmouth, NH: Heinemann, 1993).

———, *Becoming Literate: The Construction of Inner Control* (Portsmouth, NH: Heinemann, 1997).

Commission on Reading, *Becoming a Nation of Readers: The Report of the Commission on Reading* (Washington, DC: Center for the Study of Reading, 1985).

Committee on the Prevention of Reading Difficulties in Young Children, *Preventing Reading Difficulties in Young Children* (Washington, DC: National Academy Press, 1998).

David K. Dickinson and Patton O. Tabors, *Beginning Literacy with Language* (Baltimore, MD: Paul H. Brookes Publishing, 2001).

Alan E. Farstrup and S. Jay Samuels, eds., *What Research Has to Say About Reading Instruction, Third Edition* (Newark, DC: International Reading Association, 2002).

Rudolf Flesch, *Why Johnny Can't Read* (New York: HarperPerennial, reissued 1986).

Caleb Gattegno, *Words in Color* (New York: Educational Solutions, 1978).

Betty Hart and Todd R. Risley, *Meaningful Differences in the Everyday Experiences of Young American Children* (Baltimore, MD: Paul H. Brookes Publishing, 1995).

Don Holdaway, *The Foundations of Literacy* (Sydney, Australia: Scholastic, 1979).

Ellin Oliver Keene and Susan Zimmermann, *Mosaic of Thought: Teaching Comprehension in a Reader's Workshop* (Portsmouth, NH: Heinemann, 1997).

National Reading Panel, *Teaching Children to Read: Report of the National Reading Panel* (Washington, DC: National Institutes of Child Health and Human Development, 2000).

Susan B. Neuman and Kathleen A. Roskos, eds., *Children Achieving: Best Practices in Early Literacy* (Newark, DE: International Reading Association, 1998).

Susan Neuman, Carol Copple, and Sue Bredekamp, *Learning to Read and Write: Developmentally Appropriate Practices for Young Children* (Washington, DC: National Association for the Education of Young Children, 2000).

Linda K. Rath, "BETWEEN THE LIONS: Using Television to Promote Literacy," *Book Links* (March 2000), pp. 41–45.

———, "Get Wild about Reading: Using BETWEEN THE LIONS to Support Early Literacy," *Young Children,* Vol. 57, No. 2 (2002), pp. 80–87.

Dorothy S. Strickland, *Teaching Phonics Today: A Primer for Educators* (Newark, DE: International Reading Association, 1998).

WEB SITES FOR CHILDREN

The Web is full of kid-friendly sites, some of which you'll find links for at the BETWEEN THE LIONS Web site (www.pbskids.org/lions). If your child goes searching on his own, encourage him to use one of the search engines designed especially for children, which will help to ensure that he visits only appropriate sites. You may want to surf with him until you're confident that he can find his way around safely on his own. Meanwhile, here are a few good places to visit.

Africa Online (www.africaonline.com) is the Lion family's favorite site, with lots of information and activities to help children learn more about Africa.

Ask Jeeves for Kids (www.ajkids.com) is a wonderful search engine for children. It also includes a dictionary, a thesaurus, games, and other resources.

Children's Television Workshop (www.ctw.org) includes lots of activities for preschoolers and kindergartners, tied to *Sesame Street* and CTW's other wonderful programs for children.

Enchanted Learning (www.enchantedlearning.com) is a very kid-friendly, easy-to-use online encyclopedia. It has lots of great information and activities about rain forests, dinosaurs, and much more.

Fablevision (www.fablevision.com) has lots of wonderful stuff, including interactive stories.

Headbone (www.headbone.com) may be best for slightly older kids, with a multitude of well-designed, challenging games.

KidSites.com (www.kidsites.com) has some terrific links to games, stories, and lively learning.

KidSites.org (www.kidsites.org) also has links to some wonderful games and informative sites.

Mamamedia (www.mamamedia.com) has tons of games and activities in a very stimulating format.

Mrs. Alphabet (www.mrsalphabet.com) offers lots of lively, educational games.

Poetry for Kids (www.poetry4kids.com) has plenty of silly poems and how-to instructions to help young poets write their own.

Yahooligans (www.yahooligans.com), like Yahoo, features directories of Web sites by category. It also has a dictionary and many other reference tools.

Glossary

This glossary includes the specialized terms we use in this book, as well as some terms that we don't use but that you may come across in other books about reading. Note that here, as throughout the book, we use slashes around a letter to represent the letter's sound—for example, /s/ means "the sound *sss*"—and italics to signify letters as letters and words as words: "the letter *f,*" "the word *sleep.*" If a word appears in bold type, you'll find a definition for it here.

ADHD (Attention-Deficit/Hyperactivity Disorder): A neurological condition marked by difficulties with paying attention, staying still, and controlling impulses. This is the term adopted in the most recent diagnostic manual of the American Psychiatric Association; **Attention Deficit Disorder (ADD)** is an older term for the same condition, which is not classified as a learning dis-

ability but can nevertheless interfere with learning to read. See Chapter 8 for more information.

Alliteration: The repetition of the beginning sound, or **onset**, of words, as in "Peter Piper picked a peck of pickled peppers." Like **rhyme**, alliteration focuses attention on the individual sounds of words, which helps to build **phonemic awareness**.

Alphabetic principle: The idea that the letters we use in print represent the sounds we use in speech. English is an alphabetic language, in contrast to an ideographic language like Chinese, which uses characters to represent whole ideas, or a pictographic language like Egyptian hieroglyphics, which used pictures to represent words. A child learning to read an alphabetic language, English included, must understand this principle in order to put letters together into words—and, therefore, to read.

Attention Deficit Disorder (ADD): An older term for **Attention-Deficit/Hyperactivity Disorder (ADHD).**

Ball-and-stick: The classic way of teaching children to form printed lowercase letters, named for the combinations of circles and straight lines that make up most letters. See **manuscript** and **D'Nealian.**

Basal reader: A comprehensive set of published materials used to teach reading—phonics, vocabulary, and comprehension—to a whole class. The set usually includes student texts, a teacher's guide, and individual workbooks. These programs have been widely used over the years. Recently, however, many teachers now combine **phonics** instruction as needed with high-quality children's literature.

Base: The essential part of a word that carries its central meaning—also known as the "root." In *information, form* is the base, while *in* is a **prefix** and *ation* is a **suffix.** By studying these meaningful word parts, or **morphemes,** students learn to use **structural analysis** as a **word attack** strategy.

Blend: A sequence of two or more **consonants** in which each letter retains its own sound, as in *str* or *mp*. Compare with **digraph.**

Blending: Combining individual sounds to make words: "Say *sss . . . uh . . . nnn*. Now say the word: *sun*" is a simple blending exercise. Compare with **segmenting.**

Bouncing: Repeating a speech sound several times in quick succession, to make it more obvious. We bounce sounds like /b/ and /d/ that we can't **stretch.** The sounds that can't be stretched and must be bounced are *b*, hard *c* (as in *cat*), *d*, *g* (as in *go*), *h*, *j*, *k*, *p*, *q*, *t*, *w*, *x*, *y* (as in *yes*), and *ch* (as in either *chop* or *chorus*).

Choral reading: A technique of reading aloud with one or more other people, slowly and in unison, that can help children become more fluent by matching their pace and intonation to a mature reader's.

Chunking: Reading text a few words at a time, rather than word by word. Chunking helps the reader connect individual words into meaningful phrases, improving **fluency**, and is something the mature reader does without thinking about it.

C-le syllable: A **syllable** consisting of a **consonant** followed by *le*, as in the *-ble* of *able* or the *-tle* of *little*. One of six **syllable types.**

Closed syllable: A **syllable** that ends with a **consonant**, giving it a **short vowel** sound. One of six **syllable types.**

Code-based approach: Reading instruction that emphasizes teaching **phonics** and other aspects of **decoding** text, rather than emphasizing meaning or focusing on high-quality literature. Compare with a **meaning-based,** or **whole language,** approach. Experts now recommend a **combined** (or **combination**) **approach** that spotlights both skills and meaning.

Combined approach: Reading instruction that teaches skills, including **phonics,** along with a focus on meaningful texts. It's an attempt to combine the strongest features of both **code-based** and **meaning-based,** or **whole language,** programs.

Compound words: Words formed by combining two smaller words: *starfish, cowboy*. Breaking compounds into their parts helps children deconstruct long words and develop an understanding of word structure.

Comprehension: The understanding of written text—both word by word and as a whole—that is the ultimate goal of reading and, therefore, of reading instruction. In fact, it's one of the **five key areas** of reading instruction. (There's also "oral comprehension," or the understanding of spoken language, but when we use "comprehension" alone, we generally mean reading comprehension.)

Concept of word: The understanding that the language we speak is formed of individual words. Though it seems obvious to adults, it is not always clear from listening to speech; some children don't understand that *Wansaponnatyme*, for example, is actually a series of discrete words: *Once upon a time*.

Concepts of print: The basic facts about how text and books work—for example, that we read English from left to right and that we read books from front to back. Understanding of these concepts grows out of being read to and having other experiences with books and text that lead to **print awareness**.

Consonant: A speech sound made by completely or partially blocking the passage of air, or the letter representing such a sound. In English, the consonants are *b, c, d, f, g, h, j, k, l, m, n, p, q, r, s, t, v, w, x, z*, and sometimes *y*. In addition, some consonant sounds are represented by **digraphs**, as in *ch*. Compare with **vowel**.

Context clues: Information gleaned from surrounding words or passages, from accompanying illustrations, or from the reader's understanding of the book as a whole that helps the reader decode or understand an unfamiliar word. Using context clues is a valuable **word attack** strategy.

Controlled vocabulary: A limited number of words, usually **sight words** or ones with **phonetic** spellings, used in some beginners' books to make

reading easier and provide practice in skills as they're taught.

Cursive: Handwriting that joins the letters together with smooth, flowing strokes, usually taught in third grade. Compare with **manuscript** and **D'Nealian**.

CVC and *CVCe* words: Consonant-vowel-consonant *(CVC)* words, such as *sit*, and consonant-vowel-consonant-silent *e* words, such as *site*, are two basic patterns of English spelling. They're often among the first words a child learns to read, as their pronunciations are among the most predictable of English words.

Decoding: Matching speech sounds to printed letters in order to identify written words. For example, being able to put the letters *v, a*, and *t* together to form *vat* and to pronounce the resulting word as "vat" is a decoding task. Note that it's a separate skill from understanding the meaning of the word. In fact, simply **sounding out** words without understanding them is sometimes negatively characterized as "word calling."

Digraph: A combination of two letters that together represent just one sound. **Consonant digraphs** include *th* and *ch*; contrast them with **blends**, which include two or more consonants but retain the separate sounds of each. **Vowel digraphs** include *oo* and *ea*, in contrast to **diphthongs**, such as *ow*, which are a combination of two speech sounds.

Diphthong: A combination vowel sound that glides from one sound to the next, as in *cow* (/ah/ and /w/) or *oil* (/aw/ and /yih/). Compare with **digraph**.

D'Nealian: A method of handwriting that is smoother and more flowing than traditional **ball-and-stick** printing but not as fully connected as

cursive writing. Instruction in D'Nealian can help children who struggle with **manuscript** printing, and some children move naturally into a D'Nealian-like script on their own.

Dysgraphia: A learning disability that causes difficulties in producing written text. It is often, but not always, linked to **dyslexia**.

Dyslexia: A learning disability, centered in the language-processing areas of the brain, that causes difficulties in reading. **Structured, sequential, multisensory instruction** in **phonics** and other basic skills can help to compensate for some of these difficulties in **phonological** processing. See Chapter 8 for more information.

Emergent literacy: The stage of development, from birth to about age six, when children are developing **print awareness**, knowledge of the **alphabetic principle**, and other elements of understanding about print, but are not yet capable of reading on their own.

Experimental literacy: Another term for **emergent literacy**, and the one we use in this book because it emphasizes the playful, curious nature of children's explorations of print at this stage.

Explicit instruction: Teaching that directly states, explains, and demonstrates a principle or fact, rather than indirectly alluding to it or expecting students to infer it from their own explorations and thinking. Explicit instruction in **phonics** has been proven more effective than assuming that students will acquire phonics knowledge by looking at words and noting patterns in the way they are spelled.

FAPE: An acronym for "free, appropriate public education," which is guaranteed to all students under the federal law known as **IDEA**. See Chapter 8.

Five key areas: The essential aspects of reading instruction, as laid out by the Partnership for Reading: **phonemic awareness, phonics, fluency, vocabulary**, and **comprehension**. Children need to develop strong skills in each of these areas in order to become successful readers.

Fluency: The ability to read in a smooth, flowing, connected way. Reading fluently makes it possible to link words together into meaningful phrases, and it's one of the **five key areas** of reading instruction.

"Glued to print": Jeanne Chall's phrase for the reading style of beginning readers, in which so much of the reader's attention is devoted to **decoding** a text, word by word, that little is left over for gaining **fluency** of expression or **comprehension** of meaning. Most students get "unglued" by the end of second grade.

Glue words: Another term for **sight words**, particularly for the small, common words like *and* and *of* that "glue" sentences together. Also known as "function words."

Grapheme: Any of the letters or combinations of letters that can represent a given **phoneme**, or speech sound. *A, ai, ay, ea, ey* and *eigh* are all graphemes for the long *a* sound.

Graphic organizer: A visual representation of the structure of an idea or a text that can help students learn more effectively. Flow charts, "trees" depicting main and subsidiary ideas, and "starbursts" connecting main ideas to related ones are all graphic organizers. See the box "Picture This" in Chapter 7.

Homophone, homonym: A word with the same pronunciation as another but a different spelling and meaning, as in *where* and *wear*.

Hyperactivity: The inability to remain still for long or to adapt to a quiet environment. Other behaviors often accompany this "overactive motor," including impulsiveness, distractibility, inability to concentrate, and aggressiveness. This group of behaviors is often a sign of **Attention-Deficit/Hyperactivity Disorder.**

IDEA: The Individuals with Disabilities Education Act, which is the federal law that covers education for people with learning disabilities. It guarantees a free, appropriate public education in the least restrictive environment possible, or **FAPE** in **LRE,** for all children. See Chapter 8 for details.

IEP: Individualized Education Program, the document that describes a child's learning disability in detail and spells out the special services and accommodations the school will provide in order to meet his needs. See Chapter 8 for information.

Invented spelling: The mostly phonetic spelling that young children use as they begin to write; it is often incorrect but usually follows a clear internal logic that demonstrates understanding of the principles of English **orthography.** It has been found to encourage freer written expression and not to cause spelling difficulties later; children are gradually encouraged to move from invented spelling to conventional spelling by about the end of second grade.

K-W-L: A comprehension-building technique that encourages readers to ask, before reading a book, "What do I *Know* about this topic? What do I *Want* to know?" and to ask after reading, "What have I *Learned*?" It is easier to remember and build on new information that is anchored in previous knowledge in this way.

LD: Shorthand for **learning disability.**

Learning disability: A neurological condition that causes difficulties in processing information. People with **LD** have at least average intelligence and are often very bright. LD can take many forms and, though it cannot be cured, can be worked around and compensated for. See Chapter 8.

Letter-sound correspondence: The relationship between letters and the sounds they represent. Understanding that this connection exists and learning the details of its patterns (**phonics**) is fundamental to learning to read.

Lexile scale: A way of measuring the difficulty of a text. See **reading level**.

Literacy: The ability to use text to make meaning—both by reading the texts that others have written and by writing texts yourself. Reading and writing are two sides of the literacy coin, and neither is complete without the other.

Long vowel: A vowel that occurs in an accented syllable and often "says its name"—for example, the *a* in *relate*, the *o* in *no*, or the double *e* in *sleep*. Long vowel sounds can be represented in several different ways, by single letters or by digraphs, and appear in these **syllable types:** open, vowel team, and silent *e*. Linguists, by the way, call them "tense" vowels.

"Long word freakout": A common condition in young readers when they confront a multisyllabic word and feel as if they can't read any of it. The best cure, as demonstrated by "Dr. Ruth Wordheimer," is to break the word into parts and read one part at a time, then put them together.

LRE: The "least restrictive environment" in which a student can learn successfully without disrupting other students' education; this is the mandated placement for all students under **IDEA**.

Manuscript: Printed handwriting, traditionally taught by the **ball-and-stick** method but also now sometimes done in the more flowing **D'Nealian** style. Children usually master it by second grade, then move on to **cursive** writing in third grade; lingering problems with printing, forming letters in the conventional way, or adopting a standard pencil grip can be a sign of learning difficulties.

Meaning-based: See **whole language**; contrast with **code-based**.

Morpheme: The smallest unit of meaning. It may be a **prefix**, a **suffix**, or a **base**—for example, *trans* and *form* in *transform*, or *re, form*, and *ed* in *reformed*. In **structural analysis**, students learn to look for morphemes as a way of understanding words.

Morphology: The study of word formations, particularly the word parts known as **morphemes**. This study helps to build **vocabulary** knowledge and deepen **comprehension**.

Onset: The initial sound of a word, as opposed to its **rime**. In *change, street*, and *mat*, the sounds /ch/, /str/, and /m/ are onsets.

Open syllable: A **syllable** that ends with a vowel, giving it a **long vowel** sound. One of six **syllable types**.

Orthography: Correct letter formation and standard spelling, including silent letters. In many programs today, students are encouraged to begin with **invented spelling** and move gradually into spelling orthographically. Students need to master the **alphabetic principle** first, learning to hear a word's sounds and represent them phonetically; later, they can focus on how the word

looks. As an example of the difference, *enuf* is **phonetically** correct; *enough* is orthographically correct.

"Outlaw words": Words that don't follow the rules, because they're not spelled the way they sound. See Chapter 5 for some examples of these unphonetic tricksters and some advice on helping your child rope them in.

Paired reading: A technique of reading aloud with another person to build **fluency** and **comprehension**. The readers may take turns, each read the same text in succession, or read in unison as in **choral reading**.

Phoneme: The smallest unit of sound in speech that combines with others to make a word. The word *bat* has three phonemes, /b/, /a/, and /t/; so does the word *through*: /th/, /r/, and /oo/. The ability to notice phonemes, or **phonemic awareness**, is important for success in learning to read and write.

Phonemic awareness: The ability to focus on the individual speech sounds in words and to break words into their sounds (**segmenting**), play with the sounds, and **blend** them back together again. Because paying attention to individual sounds makes it possible to learn how letters represent sounds, phonemic awareness is one of the **five key areas** of reading instruction.

Phonetic: Spelled the way it sounds. Alas, English contains many unphonetic words. They include every word in that sentence—even, alas, *alas*.

Phonics: The study and use of letter-sound relationships to help identify written words. Phonics is one of the **five key areas** of reading instruction because systematic, **explicit instruction** in phonics gives children a solid foundation for reading and spelling.

Phonological awareness: A more general grasp of the sound system of a language than **phonemic awareness**, which is an important refinement of this ability. The terms are sometimes used interchangeably, but phonological awareness refers more to an ability to notice features of words such as patterns, syllables, **rimes** (endings) and **onsets** (initial sounds).

Phonology: The study of speech sounds.

Prefix: A word part, or **morpheme**, that is affixed to the beginning of a word to alter its meaning. In *transform* and *reform, trans-* and *re-* are prefixes. Children study **prefixes** and **suffixes** to improve **comprehension.**

Print awareness: Understanding that print carries meaning and being able to distinguish print from pictures and other images. This awareness is necessary in order to grasp the **concepts of print** and is an important early step toward **literacy.**

Print-rich environment: A child's home or schoolroom that contains many books, labels, magazines, signs, and other forms of print to encourage the development of **print awareness, concepts of print,** and familiarity with reading and books. See Chapter 3 for some simple, low-cost suggestions on creating this atmosphere for your child.

Rapid naming: The ability to see a series of pictured objects (sometimes letters) and quickly identify them. Tests of this ability are common, because difficulties with rapid naming may predict difficulties in learning to read.

R-controlled syllable: A **syllable** containing a **vowel** followed by *r*, which alters the sound of the vowel. (The *a* in *car* sounds different from the *a* in *cat*, for example.) One of six **syllable types.**

Readers' Theater: A technique of reading aloud a story or script without staging, props, or cos-

tumes. This practice encourages fluent, expressive reading and deeper connection with the text. See Chapter 6 for more information on this engaging activity, also known (and searchable on the Web) as Reader's Theater, Readers' Theatre, etc.

Reading level: A measure of how difficult a book is to read. A book with the level "3.2" should be appropriate for an average reader in the second month of third grade. But different publishers use different numbering systems and even different methods of determining difficulty, from rough estimates to a formula called a "lexile scale," so levels are not always equivalent. Consult your child's teacher or a librarian for guidance. A simple way to find the "right" level is to look at a book your child can read, then try to find another that is similar in the size of type, number of words on a page, length and complexity of sentences, ratio of text to pictures, and so forth.

Reading readiness: A term that is falling into disuse as the understanding of reading development increases. Researchers now believe that **literacy** has its roots in infancy with the development of language and moves along a continuum; there is no magic point at which a child is suddenly "ready" to be taught to read. Instead, giving children a **print-rich environment** and providing instruction in the **five key areas** leads to gradual improvement and eventual mastery.

Reading Recovery: An intensive intervention program for struggling first-grade readers, developed in New Zealand by Marie M. Clay and popular in the United States since the 1980s. Its goal is to have highly trained teachers provide support in daily, half-hour one-to-one tutoring sessions, which are very organized and systematic. Good results have been documented, but the program has been criticized because it is expensive and because its positive effects do not seem to continue once students are released from the one-to-one tutorials.

Rhyme: The repetition of the ending sounds, or **rime**, of a word, as in "The rain in Spain falls mainly on the plain." Playing with rhymes builds **phonemic awareness**. It's also fun.

Rime: The ending part of a word. In *rain* and *Spain*, the long *a* and *n* sounds form the rime of *ain*, while /r/ and /sp/, respectively, are the **onset**.

Schwa: The sound, represented in dictionaries by a character that looks like an upside-down *e*, of all unaccented vowels in English. In *about, quarrel, festival, collapse,* and *rebus*, the unaccented *a, e, i, o,* and *u* have the schwa sound.

Screening: A quick assessment of a particular skill or set of skills, used as a basic means of identifying students who may need further testing and help.

Scribe: An aide who takes notes for a student in class or takes dictation from the student for studying or tests, often provided as an **accommodation** when a **learning disability** causes difficulty with writing.

Segmenting: Separating words into their individual sounds. "Say *sun*. Now say its sounds: sss, uh, nnn" is a simple segmenting exercise. Compare with blending.

Short vowel: A **vowel** sound that isn't long—for example, *a* in *cat, e* in *pet, i* in *sit, o* in *not,* and *u* in *but*. Short vowels occur in **closed syllables**, such as *CVC* **words**. Linguists call them "lax" vowels.

Sight words: Common words that are often not spelled phonetically but must be learned, so they can be recognized automatically on sight.

Silent *e* syllable: A **syllable** containing a **vowel** and a **consonant** followed by silent *e*, which affects the sound of the vowel. One of six **syllable types**.

Sounding out: Reading words by pronouncing sounds for their letters in sequence and then **blending** the sounds together. Identifying words in this way is also called **decoding**; it does not necessarily indicate an understanding of a word's meaning.

SQ3R: An acronym for a study technique: Survey, Question, Read, Recite, Review.

Story grammar: The features of a story, including its setting, characters, problems and goals, events and plot, resolution and consequences. Some teachers give explicit instruction in identifying these features, while others assume children will develop a sense of them through reading stories in a variety of genres and styles.

Stretching: Elongating a speech sound to make it more obvious. Some sounds can't be stretched (see **bouncing**), but the ones that can be include all the **vowel** sounds—for example, /ah/, /oo/, /ee/, /aw/— and the **consonant** sounds /f/, /l/, /m/, /n/, /ng/, /r/, /s/, /v/, /z/; /sh/, /zh/ (as in Asian), and soft *c* as in *cent*.

Structural analysis: The study of word parts to aid in **decoding**, build **vocabulary** knowledge, and increase **comprehension**. By becoming familiar with various **prefixes**, **suffixes**, and **bases**, students extend their ability to identify new words and figure out what they mean.

Structured, sequential, multisensory instruction: The recommended approach for helping children who are struggling to learn to read. See Chapter 8 for more information.

Suffix: A word part, or **morpheme**, that is affixed to the end of a word to alter its meaning. In *transportation* and *reflective*, -*ation* and -*ive* are suffixes. Studying these word parts permits accurate **decoding** and boosts **vocabulary** knowledge and **comprehension**.

Syllable: A part of a word that is pronounced as a unit. A syllable always contains a **vowel** sound (though not necessarily a vowel; think of the second syllable of *rhythm*). Learning to break words into syllables is important for **structural analysis,** which in turn helps students figure out unfamiliar words.

Syllable types: Six possible forms that the pronounceable unit of a word, or **syllable,** can take. Some teachers give instruction in the six types—**closed, open,** *r*-**controlled, vowel team, silent** *e*, and *C-le*—as a way of reinforcing knowledge of spelling and **decoding** patterns.

Syntax: The relationship among words in sentences; also known as grammar. Children develop a sophisticated understanding of the syntax of spoken language without formal instruction but may continue to make small and typical errors for the first few years of school.

Tracking: Following each word in a line of type with the eyes and, to help in this sometimes difficult task, with a pointing finger on or below the words.

Vocabulary: Knowledge of word meanings, in both spoken and written language. A large vocabulary makes it easier to understand what you read, both because you know the meanings of more of the words and because the known words provide clues to the unknown ones. That's why this is one of the **five key areas** of reading instruction.

Vowel: A speech sound made by letting air pass through the throat and mouth without blocking it, or the letter representing such a sound. Vowels can have a **short** or **long** sound, depending on the letters that surround them. Every **syllable,** by definition, contains a vowel sound. In English, the vowels are *a, e, i, o, u,* and sometimes *y.* But English has more than 15 vowel sounds, which can be represented by **digraphs,** as in *oa* or *ea,* or other letter combinations, such as the **diphthong** in *ow.* Compare with **consonant.**

Vowel-team syllable: A **syllable** that contains a combination of **vowels,** which affect each other's pronunciation. ("When two vowels go walking, the first one does the talking.") One of six **syllable types.**

Whole language: A term for a **meaning-based** approach to reading instruction, as opposed to a **code-based** one. Whole language instruction emphasizes immersion in literature and "integrated language arts," or writing and self-expression. **Phonics** and other skills are taught as needed, rather than in a systematic sequence. Experts now recommend a **combined approach** that emphasizes both meaning and sequential, **explicit instruction** in skills.

Word attack: The skill of using a variety of strategies—such as **sounding out,** applying **structural analysis,** or using **context clues**—to decode and grasp the meaning of an unfamiliar word. Students begin to learn simple word-attack strategies in first grade and continue to refine their skills over the next several years.

Word family: A group of words that share a **rime,** or ending. *Sun, bun,* and *rerun* are all in one family; *small, tall,* and *waterfall* are in another. Working with word families builds **phonemic awareness** and spotlights the **alphabetic principle.**

Notes

Chapter 1: What Is Reading?
The box "Reading: The Fine Print" is based on Part III of Marilyn Jager Adams, *Beginning to Read: Thinking and Learning About Print* (Cambridge: MIT Press, 1990).

The six stages of reading development appear in Jeanne S. Chall, *Stages of Reading Development* (New York: McGraw-Hill, 1983).

The five key areas of reading instruction—phonemic awareness, phonics, fluency, vocabulary, and text comprehension—were laid out by the Partnership for Reading in its 2001 report, *Put Reading First*. The Partnership for Reading (www.nifl.gov/ partnershipforreading) is a collaboration of three federal agencies: The National Institute for Literacy, The National Institute of Child Health and Human Development, and the U.S. Department of Education.

Chapter 2: The BETWEEN THE LIONS Curriculum
For more information on research about BETWEEN THE LIONS, see www.pbskids.org/lions/about/ research.html. For information on the Cornerstones Project, a teaching and research program using BETWEEN THE LIONS for deaf children, see "Reading and Deaf Children," by Mardi Loeterman, in the International Reading Association's peer-reviewed on-line journal at www.readingonline. org/articles/art=_index.asp?HREF=loeterman/ index.html.

Chapter 3: Emergent Literacy: Reading and
   Writing for Preschoolers
These books were particularly helpful in developing our discussion of emergent literacy: Marie M. Clay, *An Observation Survey of Early Literacy Achievement* (Portsmouth, NH: Heinemann, 1993); Don Holdaway, *The Foundations of Literacy* (Sydney: Scholastic, 1979); and Susan Neuman,

Carol Copple, and Sue Bredekamp, *Learning to Read and Write: Developmentally Appropriate Practices for Young Children* (Washington, DC: National Association for the Education of Young Children, 2000).

The box "Stages of Language Development" is adapted from Melissa Farrall, "Language: Structure and Acquisition," in *Teaching Reading: Language, Letters, and Thought*, ed. Sara Brody (Milford, NH: LARC Publishing, 2001), p. 37.

The box "Lowercase Letters: The Write Moves" is adapted from materials developed by the Center for Improving the Readiness of Children for Learning and Education (CIRCLE), directed by Susan H. Landry, University of Texas at Houston (2001).

Chapter 4: Experimental Literacy: Reading and Writing for Kindergartners
These books contributed particularly to our discussion of experimental literacy: Marilyn Jager Adams, Barbara R. Foorman, Ingvar Lundberg, and Terri Beeler, *Phonemic Awareness in Young Children* (Baltimore, MD: Paul H. Brookes Publishing, 1998); Donald R. Bear, Marcia Invernizzi, Shane Templeton, and Francine Johnston, *Words Their Way: Word Study for Phonics, Vocabulary, and Spelling Instruction* (Upper Saddle River, NJ: Prentice-Hall, 1996); and Caleb Gattegno, *Words in Color* (New York: Educational Solutions, 1978).

Chapter 5: Independent Literacy: Reading and Writing for First-Graders
Our outline of the order of phonics instruction and our explanation of its rationale draws on these books: Jeanne S. Chall and Helen M. Popp, *Teaching and Assessing Phonics: Why, What, When, How* (Cambridge, MA: Educators Publishing Service, 1996) and Louisa Cook Moats, *Spelling Development, Disability, and Instruction* (Timonium, MD: York Press, 1995).

The box "Long Word Freakout" is based on "Syllabication" in Jeanne S. Chall and Helen M. Popp, *Chall-Popp Phonics* (Elizabethtown, PA: Continental Press, 1990), Book B, p. T183.

The box "One Hundred Greatest Hits" is taken from the list by Edward B. Fry, Dona Lee Fountoukidis, and Jacqueline Kress Polk, "Instant Words," in *The NEW Reading Teacher's Book of Lists* (Englewood Cliffs, NJ: Prentice-Hall, 1985).

Chapter 6: Skillful Literacy: Reading and Writing for Second-Graders
For a discussion of why fluency matters, see Pamela E. Hook and Sandra D. Jones, "The Importance of Automaticity and Fluency for Efficient Reading Comprehension," *Perspectives*, Winter (2002), pp. 10–14.

The box "Spell Check" is adapted from Louisa Moats, "Spelling: A Window on Linguistic Development," in *Teaching Reading: Language, Letters and Thought*, ed. Sara Brody (Milford, NH: LARC Publishing, 2001), pp. 203–4.

Chapter 7: Fluent Literacy: Reading and Writing for Third-Graders
The discussion of fluency draws on Jan E. Hasbrouck and Gerald A. Tindal, "Read Naturally," www.readnaturally.com/rationale-fluencynorms.htm (1992); and Roland Good, DIBELS (Dynamic Indicators of Basic Early Literacy Skills), University of Oregon, http://dibels.uoregon.edu/benchmark/php (2002).

The box "The Art of Research" draws on Joan Sedita, "Study Skills," *The LD Network Exchange*, vol. 18 (2000), no. 1, pp. 4–5.

The box "Picture This" is adapted from Dorothy S. Strickland, Kathy Ganske, and Joanne K. Monroe, *Supporting Struggling Readers and Writers* (Portland, ME: Stenhouse Publishers, 2002), pp. 153–54.

The box "Seventy-five Spelling Demons" is adapted from the list by Edward B. Fry, Dona Lee Fountoukidis, and Jacqueline Kress Polk, "196 Elementary Spelling Demons," in *The NEW Reading Teacher's Book of Lists* (Englewood Cliffs, NJ: Prentice-Hall, 1985), p. 59.

The box "Start Making Sense" is adapted from Ellin O. Keene and Susan Zimmerman, *Mosaic of Thought* (Portsmouth, NH: Heinemann, 1997), "Table 2.1: Reading Comprehension Strategies," pp. 22–23.

Chapter 8: If Your Child Is Struggling

In the box "The Turtle's Gift," the metaphor of the sea turtle comes from Lou Salza, headmaster of the ASSETS School in Honolulu, in "Support at the Point of Performance," a paper presented at the Harvard Graduate School of Education's 18th Annual Learning Differences Conference on November 1, 2002. The list of helpful traits is adapted from Marshall H. Raskind, Roberta J. Goldberg, Eleanor L. Higgins, and Kenneth L. Herman, "Teaching Life Success to Students with LD: Lessons Learned from a 20-Year Study," *Intervention in School and Clinic*, vol. 37 (2002), no. 4, pp. 201–8.

The statistics in the box "What Are the Odds?" are drawn from the Web site of the National Center for Learning Disabilities, www.LD.org.

Some of the information about multisensory, structured programs in the box "Getting with a Program" comes from C.W. McIntyre and J.S. Pickering, eds., *Clinical Studies of Multisensory Structured Language Instruction* (Dallas, TX: International Multisensory Structured Language Education Council, 2001). A review of several programs and other helpful information appears in Susan L. Hall and Louisa C. Moats, *Straight Talk About Reading: How Parents Can Make a Difference During the Early Years* (Chicago: NTC Publishing Group, 1998).

In the box "Services and Accommodations," the list of accommodations is adapted from the booklet *Developing Minds: Management by Profile* (2002), produced by WGBH Boston in association with All Kinds of Minds. The box "Winning Strategies" is adapted from the same source.

Index

LINDA K. RATH is Curriculum Director for BETWEEN THE LIONS® and holds a doctorate in education from Harvard University and has been an elementary school teacher for more than twenty years.

LOUISE KENNEDY has been a reporter and editor at the *Boston Globe* since 1988 and has written for a variety of sections, including "Living/Arts" and the *Boston Globe Magazine*.